Colonial Travelers
in Latin America

Colonial Travelers
in Latin America

Compiled and Introduced by

IRVING A. LEONARD

The University of Michigan, Emeritus

Edited by

WILLIAM C. BRYANT

Oakland University

Juan de la Cuesta
Newark, Delaware

Copyright © 1972 by Alfred A. Knopf, Inc.
Copyright returned to the author
and assigned in 1986 to William C. Bryant.

Published by
  Juan de la Cuesta—Hispanic Monographs
  270 Indian Road
  Newark, Delware 19711

MANUFACTURED IN THE UNITED STATES OF AMERICA
The pH of the paper this book is printed on is 7.0.
ISBN: (hardback) 0-936388-30-7
ISBN: (softbound) 0-936388-29-3

To the Memory

of

DAVID PHELPS LEONARD

(1922-1984)

Gifted Teacher, Brilliant Lecturer, and Good Companion
of South American Travels Long Ago

Contents

Colonial Travelers
in Latin America

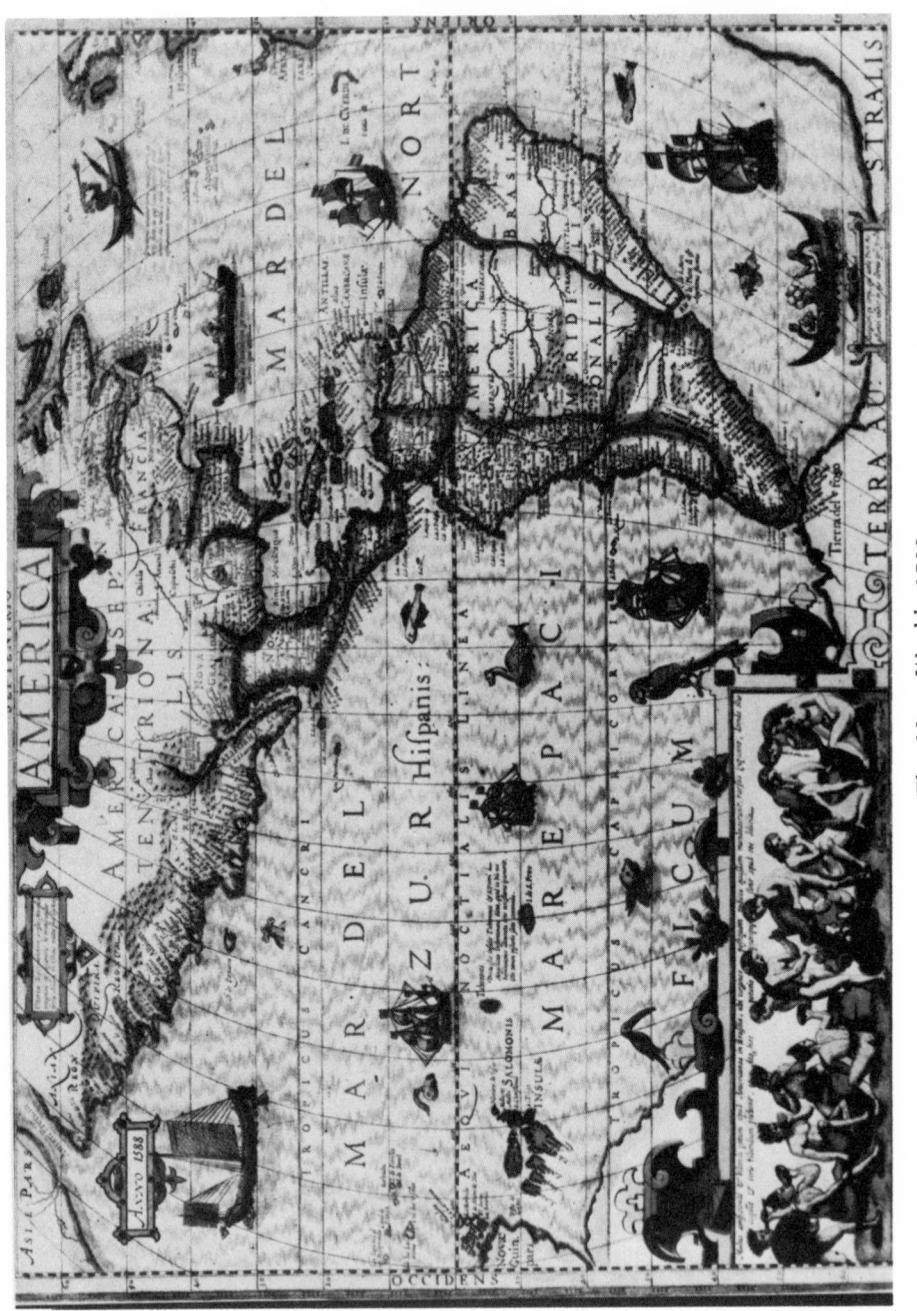

The New World, 1588.

Introduction

Travel, it is often said, is broadening. Implicit is the assumption that the experience of foreign lands assures sensitive and receptive individuals an enhanced culture and refinement. However sound in theory, this belief is essentially a modern concept and rarely influenced the travelers who ventured across the Atlantic to the New World and penetrated its strange and often forbidding interior during the three centuries of Hispanic rule. Nor did a romantic love of adventure lure them westward, for the rigors of sea voyages and overland journeys, with the constant imminence of death, required stoic courage and a fatalistic philosophy. Clearly the overriding inducements to take such grave risks were: a beguiling dream of quick wealth, a personal El Dorado, a position of power with all its perquisites, and the hope of an early return to the homeland to enjoy the rewards acquired.[1]

The representatives of Hispanic society that embarked on the annual transatlantic fleets to the Spanish Indies included merchants of all degrees, ecclesiastics of many religious orders, royal officials of varied categories, and emigrants of every social class. For them the waning fortunes of the Spanish Peninsula made the illimitable resources and submissive inhabitants of the vast New World seem a land of promise; it beckoned with the prospect of easy riches, pleasant sinecures, and a social mobility that could open the way to high office and the luxury of aristocratic pretensions. Many clergymen of Spain and Portugal, whose zeal to

[1] Hector A. Murena, "La sombra de Eldorado," in H. Ernest Lewald (ed.), *Argentina: Análisis y autoanálisis* (Buenos Aires: Sudamericana, 1969).

proselytize among the Indians had cooled, preferred the comfortable security of multiplying monasteries overseas and the privileges of ecclesiastical hierarchy. Second sons of the nobility, disinherited by a system of primogeniture, *hidalgos* with a distaste for manual labor and the artisan crafts, and energetic peasants were all united in a common desire to find a place of vantage in the swelling bureaucracy of colonial government or in the commercial prosperity of the oversea realms. The creator of Don Quixote, Miguel de Cervantes, wrote that the New World was "a refuge and haven of all the poor devils of Spain and an incomparable remedy for the few." And he himself, in 1590, then an unsuccessful playwright and an impoverished novelist, vainly begged the Council of the Indies to grant him either a royal accountancy in New Granada (modern Colombia) or in Guatemala, or the office of magistrate in the city of La Paz in present-day Bolivia. That administrative body failed to heed these requests and, perhaps fortunately for world literature, a bureaucrat scrawled on his application: "Let him look for something here." [2]

As the seventeenth century advanced and Spain sank to a third-rate power, more and more of the king's subjects from all parts of the Peninsula sought the "incomparable remedy" that Cervantes mentioned and, legally or otherwise, foreigners also slipped into the colonies. In 1604 a German-born resident of Mexico City wrote: "It happens that the majority of the people coming to these parts are fetched by poverty and necessity. As the realm has been and is, by God's mercy, rich, fertile, and abundant, those who come and wish to apply themselves industriously are able to gain an honest living by very modest effort . . ." [3] Later in the

[2] Francisco Rodríguez Marín, *El "Quijote" y Don Quijote en América* (Madrid: Librería de los Sucesores de Hernando, 1911), p. 93 fn.

[3] Francisco de la Maza, *Enrico Martínez, cosmógrafo e impresor de Nueva España* (Mexico City: Sociedad Mexicana de Geografía y Estadística, 1943), quoted in Irving A. Leonard, *Baroque Times in Old Mexico* (Ann Arbor: University of Michigan Press, 1966), p. 53.

century the colonial chronicler Father Antonio de la Calancha compared the abundance of the New World with the austerity of Spain: "Here the most commonplace person has his soup the year around while in Spain only the wealthy have it, and here the plebeian eats more in a week than the most fortunate do there in a month." [4] Such were the circumstances that inspired innumerable members of Hispanic and European society to travel across the ocean to visit or settle in colonial Latin America.

Oceanic Travel

As the Middle Ages moved toward culmination in the Renaissance discovery of the New World, travel and geographical knowledge steadily increased. Prior to this great period of expansion, however, much of the journeying for centuries was overland. In spite of improving methods of navigation, sea travel in the Western world remained largely confined to the Mediterranean and along continental coasts. Even the fifteenth-century maritime achievements of the Portuguese that flowered in the *Carreira da India* tended to skirt the African and Asiatic litorals.[5] Then it was that destiny summoned the land-minded people of Castile to initiate the great epic of transoceanic navigation, and it fell to the Castilian Crown to establish the first regular freight and passenger services across the immensities of the Atlantic and the Pacific.

Though the ships that followed in the wake of Columbus' epochal voyages usually sailed singly, roving corsairs, en-

[4] Quoted in Mariano Picón Salas, *A Cultural History of Spanish America from Conquest to Independence* (Berkeley: University of California Press, 1962; paperback ed. (1963), p. 74.

[5] See Arthur Percival Newton (ed.), *Travel and Travelers of the Middle Ages* (Freeport, N. Y.: Books for Libraries Press, Inc., 1967); Boies Penrose, *Travel and Discovery in the Renaissance, 1420–1620* (Cambridge, Mass.: Harvard University Press, 1952; paperback ed. (New York: Atheneum, 1962); J. H. Parry *The Age of Reconnaissance* (New York: Mentor Book, 1964).

couraged by rival monarchs of Europe, soon compelled Spanish authorities to organize fleets of merchantmen convoyed by armed vessels. This semi-permanent system, beginning in the mid-sixteenth century, created two separate flotillas that sailed annually. One called the *Flota* left Seville, or San Lúcar de Barrameda, at the mouth of the Guadalquivir River, each spring for the Caribbean Islands and the port of San Juan de Ulúa (Vera Cruz); the other, known as the galleons, departed later in the season from the same Spanish ports for the north coast of South America. Both fleets touched at the Canary Islands and then followed much the same course across the Atlantic until they sighted the Lesser Antilles.[6]

The customary sailing formation placed the *capitana*, or Admiral's brig, in the lead, with the merchantmen following like an orderly flock of ducks. Bringing up the rear was the *almiranta*, or vice admiral's ship, whose task was to keep stragglers from lagging too far behind. By modern standards the ships were tiny—legally their tonnage ranged from a minimum of 80 to a maximum of 550,[7] and they were invariably overloaded with manufactured goods for the colonial market.[8] It is hardly surprising that wrecks and losses of badly freighted vessels in storms were appallingly common, and the Atlantic voyage, usually lasting about forty days, was often a fearful adventure. Even more dreadful was the Pacific crossing, especially the return on the *Manila galleon,* from the Philippines to Acapulco in Mexico, which generally required about seven months at sea. Notwithstanding this ordeal, this annual freight and

[6] For a full account of the Spanish fleets, see C. H. Haring, *Trade and Navigation between Spain and the Indies in the Time of the Hapsburgs* (Cambridge, Mass.: Harvard University Press, 1918), Part II, *passim.*

[7] Parry, *op. cit.,* p. 82.

[8] José Torre Revello, "Merchandise Shipped by the Spaniards to America, 1534–1586," *Hispanic American Historical Review,* 23 (November 1943), 773–781.

passenger service continued for two and a half centuries, from 1565 to 1815.[9]

The Castilian Crown, which considered the New World dominions the patrimony of the royal family, surrounded travel on the annual fleets with the severest restrictions, and it entrusted the enforcement of these regulations to the *Casa de Contratación,* or the House of Trade, at Seville (later at Cádiz). The monarch believed his responsibility was to protect his new oversea subjects from the fearsome contamination of Lutheran heresy spreading over Europe. As piety and commerce went hand in hand, this conviction conveniently justified extreme measures to preserve the Castilian monopoly of trade and to safeguard the return of the treasure-laden ships from the Indies. To achieve these ends, the *Recopilación de Leyes de Indias,* or the *Summary of Laws Pertaining to the Indies,* contains a total of 73 royal decrees relating to passengers on the fleets, and 37 others applying specifically to foreign travelers. This legislation was promulgated mainly in the sixteenth and early seventeenth centuries. Clearly compliance with the royal will was irregular—later decrees often reiterated earlier ones, citing the kinds of violations of previous laws and describing abuses. They thus reflect many details of travel conditions.

To obtain passage in the fleets, every traveler, including the clergy, was required to procure a license corresponding to a passport, and he had to appear in person before the House of Trade to present credentials concerning his legal and marital status. When granted, the license was valid for only two years, during which time the holder was expected to sail on the first available fleet. Individuals who lacked this permit forfeited all possessions to the Crown, with one-fifth going to the person or persons reporting the violation. Only officers, sailors, and other crew members were

[9] William Lytle Schurz, *The Manila Galleon* (New York: E. P. Dutton, 1939); paperback ed. (1959), *passim.*

exempt from the obligation to have a license; if, however, they lent themselves to evasion of the law by unauthorized travelers, they, too, incurred the full penalties. Passengers had to reside in the region of the colonies indicated on their application; those en route to the Philippines through New Spain (Mexico) were not allowed to remain there; and, as far as possible, Spanish subjects living in that distant archipelago were to be denied passports to leave the islands. This decree was obviously an effort to stabilize the European population in the remote realm and thus protect Spain's precarious hold on it.

Further decrees stipulated that no person—nor his immediate relatives—considered suspect by the Inquisition could obtain authorization to sail to the Indies. Moors, Jews, and children recently converted to the Catholic faith required careful scrutiny and the express approval of the king before obtaining permission to migrate. Unmarried women could not travel alone without royal consent, but wives whose husbands had sent for them were allowed to do so; family men, even royal officials, were to be accompanied by their lawful spouses; if one marital partner died en route, the other could proceed to the designated destination.

Regulations were less strict for merchants and commercial agents, who could travel back and forth for three years without the customary license; married merchants, on the other hand, were required to carry a formal permit valid for the same period of time. The purpose of this relative leniency, of course, was to facilitate trade, but anyone who obtained this dispensation by pretending to be a merchant incurred the severest punishment. The House of Trade kept a special record book of commercial travelers.

Slaves of whatever race could travel on the fleets only by direct royal intervention, and no Negro with two years' residence in Spain or Portugal was eligible to embark for the New World; only members of the black race in transit directly from Africa, known as *bozales,* were allowed to sail.

Evasion or violation of all these regulations was common, usually with the connivance of ship officers and of the Crown's own agencies, but none, perhaps, was transgressed more often than the one covering licenses for personal servants. The ambiguous wording of these documents greatly facilitated transfer or outright sale to other persons, with the result that illegal entries were made easy. Reiterated royal decrees urged the House of Trade to take every precaution against such abuses, and officials at ports of entry in the Indies received repeated admonitions to check all credentials and prevent illicit debarkation of passengers and goods.

If these legislative decrees indicate royal distrust of travelers of national origin, the restrictions imposed upon foreigners, especially those engaged in trade, indicate stronger misgivings. Licenses and credentials of aliens were subject to close scrutiny on both sides of the ocean; if found questionable, the holder's goods were confiscated. Nationals serving as go-betweens in transactions with unauthorized foreigners—evidently a common practice—were similarly punished. Non-Spanish persons traveling legally —supposedly recognized adherents of Catholic orthodoxy— might conduct business in the ports of the Indies, but there only. It was the responsibility of colonial authorities to prevent them from going inland and from acquiring information useful to Spain's enemies. A decree of 1614 went so far as to impose the death penalty for permitting such entry of non-nationals. As the tide of Protestantism swept Europe, instructions were emphatic to clear the colonies of suspected heretics and of all foreigners except those with skills in the mechanic arts indispensable for the economic development of the New World viceroyalties. Children born of foreign parents in the Indies, however, could be naturalized.[10]

The legislation makes it clear that the royal government

[10] *Recopilación de leyes de los Reynos de las Indias,* 3 vols. (Madrid Consejo de la Hispanidad, 1943), vol. 3, book 8, sections 26 and 27.

conceived the transatlantic fleets almost exclusively as a freight service, for there were virtually no arrangements for passengers. Indeed, merchantmen lacked accommodations other than an occasional coffin-like niche in the hold. Sea travelers had no alternative to sitting or lying about on deck in whatever space they could find, where they remained exposed to the elements throughout the long voyage. Added to this neglect was the necessity to fetch their own bedding and provisions for the whole journey. A decree of 1609 is clear on this point.

> Passengers must assemble, put aboard ship, and take with them sufficient luggage, bedding, and supplies of food and water for themselves, their families, and their servants for the entire voyage. They are not permitted to make arrangements for the same with the purser or any other ship officer. It is our will that this restriction be enforced . . .[11]

And the same year another decree forbade officers of the fleets to have passengers sit at their mess tables or to release any of the crews' provisions to them.

The ship's personnel plainly fared far better in dietary matters and personal comforts than did the passengers, whom the ship owner obviously regarded as a nuisance rather than an asset. A surviving sixteenth-century document reveals that crew members enjoyed a simple but balanced fare of proteins, carbohydrates, and fats. The steward daily issued rations of 24 ounces of bread, 3.8 ounces of beans or chickpeas, supplemented on Sundays, Tuesdays, and Thursdays by 8 ounces of salt beef; on Mondays and Wednesdays, 6 ounces of cheese, and on Fridays and Saturdays, 8 ounces of salt cod varied the menu. Sometimes olives, hazelnuts, dried dates, figs, and quince marmalade gave a wider variety. Everyday each crewman received a quart of wine, a little olive oil and vinegar, while unrationed condiments

---

[11] *Ibid.*, vol. 3, book 8, section 26, statute 44.

such as cinnamon, cloves, mustard, parsley, pepper, and saffron made the fare more savory.[12]

Less clear is the nature of the passengers' larder, but another sixteenth-century document lists recommended supplies for travelers bound for the River Plate region of South America. These suggestions include: four hundred-weight of hardtack, one hogshead of flour of 28 *arrobas* (about 700 lbs.), 8 *arrobas* of wine, 2 *fanegas* (about three bushels) of beans and chickpeas, 4 *arrobas* of olive oil, 6 *arrobas* of vinegar, one of rice, two of dried fish, bacon, onions, garlic, figs, and raisins and almonds. When wind and weather permitted, passengers cooked by charcoal and wood in small hearths or stoves, but often they had to content themselves with cold and unsavory victuals for days and weeks on end. Livestock, pigs, and fowls brought aboard were consumed while they lasted. Water was doled out in small quantities daily for drinking, and about a pint for washing—a ration further reduced when calms or other causes delayed ships.[13]

Living conditions for travelers aboard vessels were unspeakable by modern standards. Sanitary facilities were utterly lacking and decks, the usual lodging places of passengers, were crowded, cluttered, and filthy beyond description. Existence onboard was an ordeal to daunt the boldest and an experience that seemingly no one could be induced to repeat. These circumstances remained essentially unchanged during the three colonial centuries, with possibly slight improvement in the eighteenth century. Yet it is clear that not only merchants, consoled by large profits, but Crown officials and clergymen endured these hardships again and again on successive voyages.

[12] Paul S. Taylor, "Spanish Seamen in the New World," *Hispanic American Historical Review*, 5 (1922), *passim*. John Masefield, in his introduction to the Everyman Library edition of *Hakluyt's Voyages*, 4 vols. (New York: Dutton, 1907) indicates the dietary of English seamen and other details of ships and shipboard life in Elizabethan times.

[13] José Torre Revello, *Crónicas de Buenos Aires* (Buenos Aires, 1942), Chap. 2, *passim*.

Father Tomás de la Torre, who crossed the Atlantic in 1544, has left probably the best description of a passenger's lot on shipboard (see selection 1); nearly thirty years later a witty royal official, Eugenio de Salazar, gave illuminating details in a shorter account. With his family he embarked from San Lúcar de Barrameda on July 7, 1573, on "Our Lady of Remedies" which, he ruefully comments "had a better name than manners" and was dubbed "the wooden horse," "the timber nag," and "the dirty bird." Once aboard they were conducted to a tiny cubicle below deck, a completely enclosed, dark, and noisome vault like a burial niche, where seasickness soon rendered the inmates helpless for three days, unable to take food or even to undress. Everywhere over the deck was a tangle of ropes, cordage, and rigging which, from outside, made the people on board "look like chickens and capons that are taken to market in woven reed hen coops," Salazar humorously declared. To drink the meager ration of water it was necessary to close one's eyes and lose one's sense of smell and taste. Men and women, young and old, clean and dirty, crowded together amid indescribable filth without privacy for even the most intimate necessities. And when the ship was becalmed, the rhythmic rise and fall of the ocean swell produced devastating effects, causing women especially to cry out in sick despair, "Ay, madre mía! Put me ashore!" When, at last, after much tribulation, they reached their destination all travelers, with rare unanimity, agreed "land for mankind, sea for the fishes!" [14]

Land Travel

While the literature of sea voyages in the adventurous colonial centuries is abundant, it is curious that narratives

[14] "Cartas de Eugenio de Salazar," *Biblioteca de autores españolas* (Madrid, 1926), vol. 62, p. 291, quoted in Irving A. Leonard, *Books of the Brave* (Cambridge, Mass.: Harvard University Press, 1949); reprinted (New York: The Gordian Press, 1964), pp. 158–159.

of land travel are comparatively rare. Francis Bacon early called attention to this fact in a brief essay "Of Travel," in which he wrote: "It is a strange thing that in sea voyages there is nothing to be seen but sky and sea, men should make diaries; but in land travel wherein so much is to be observed, for the most part they omit it." It may be speculated that the enforced immobility of shipboard life for weeks and months moved travelers to keep journals out of sheer boredom—a sedentary occupation less relished after bumping along rough trails for hours in an ox-drawn cart, or after jogging on muleback to saddle-sore exhaustion for a whole long day. Whatever the explanation, it remains true that accounts of overland journeys appear less numerous than those by sea.

Because of the topography, most travel was accomplished by muleback or, more rarely, on horseback in the vast reaches of the New World. Only rarely did waterways facilitate the travelers' progress. All too often streams were obstacles rather than means of transportation, since they required fording, ferries, or bridges. Mines high in the mountains stimulated most of the commercial activity in the interior, where rivers plunged through gorges and thundering rapids far too swift for navigation. Waterways of the level plains of the Argentine Pampas and the high plateau of Mexico, on the other hand, tended to be too shallow or sluggish for transportation. While the mightiest of all rivers, the Amazon, with its full flowing and mysterious tributaries, poured its flooding waters across a vast tropical basin to the sea, it seemed to rush from nowhere to nowhere, as Orellana learned in making his accidental descent in 1542. But floating down its thousands of miles had convinced him of the existence of El Dorados and of the realms of Amazon women rich in treasure, thus creating a legend that endured for centuries (see selection 2).

Elsewhere in Portuguese Brazil the waters of the interior flowed southward into Spanish territory, and their utility was hindered by international complications. The great eastern escarpment of Brazil was a highland barrier isolating the communities of the seaboard from the immense inland region and made coastal vessels the chief medium of communication and travel. Mountains, plains, and poor river systems largely limited transportation to rough trails, over which sturdy, wiry, and sometimes cantankerous mules were the nearly universal means of conveying goods and men throughout the Hispanic regions of the New World.

The economic development of the vast interior made necessary an army of muleteers and carters such as Spain and parts of Europe had used for centuries.[15] The discovery and exploitation of mines in Mexico and Peru in the mid-sixteenth century stimulated the cattle industry in nearby areas, notably in Argentina, especially in the eighteenth century. These prosperous economic activities required a transportation system that soon veined the enormous extent of lands with trails and dusty roads over which plodded long *recuas,* or packtrains, of heavily laden mules goaded and guided by toughened *arrieros,* or muleteers. While seasonal exchanges of wheat, wine, charcoal, coarse textiles, and hides, and the supplying of foodstuff and fuel to urban centers created much local transporting, there also developed more specialized systems of long-distance conveyance on muleback of mine products, sugar, and the like, together with imported manufactured goods from the mother country.

Regular services were instituted between Vera Cruz and Mexico City and between that viceregal capital and the flourishing mining districts to the north. Similarly, the arrival of the annual fleet at Puerto Bello[16] on the east side of the Isthmus of Panama required the transfer of silver ingots and other products of Peru's thriving economy from Panama City on the Pacific side and the subsequent return

[15] David R. Ringrose, "Carting in the Hispanic World: An Example of Divergent Development," *Hispanic American Historical Review,* 50 (February 1970), 30–51.

[16] Guillermo de Zendeguí, "Puertobelo," *Americas,* 22 (August 1970), 20–30, is an interesting description of this port, together with illustrations and maps of trade routes during the apogee of Spanish domination.

to the same port with the manufactured goods brought from Spain. This movement of freight was the major industry of the dreary, torpid community of Old Panama, a frontier between two oceans in perennial fear of pirate attacks.[17] In the early seventeenth century, thirty-three owners of packtrains with a total of 850 mules were the carriers. Two routes crossed this narrow strip of mountainous land; one was about twenty leagues over the steep Gorgona Trail, which scaled the continental divide. A later traveler reported that "some part of this road is not above two feet broad, having precipices on either side four or five hundred feet deep, so that the least slip of a mule's foot, both itself and the rider must be dashed to pieces." [18] The alternate way was by boat on the Chagres River to the head of navigation at Las Cruces, whence the remaining five leagues distance to the Pacific Ocean was covered by muleback (see selection 4).

The most extensive area of regular transport services by professional muleteers lay within the viceroyalty of Peru, which also included modern Ecuador and Bolivia. From Quito and points north long convoys of pack animals wended their laborious way almost daily over former Inca trails to Cuzco, capital of the pre-Hispanic empire, and southward to the fabulous mining city of Potosí.[19] These usually well-constructed highways had *tambos,* or inns, irregularly spaced along the route and serviced by local Indians. The most difficult highway owing to its roughness —but probably the most traveled—led from Lima, the viceregal capital near the coast, to Cuzco, high in the Andes.

[17] A valuable document concerning the isthmus in the colonial period, "Descripción de Panamá y su provincia sacada de la Relación que, por mandado del Consejo, hizo y embió aquella Audiencia" is reproduced in *Revista de los archivos nacionales* (Costa Rica), año 2, Nos. 5–6 (1938), 245–285.

[18] Quoted in Roland D. Hussey, "Spanish Colonial Trails in Panama," *Revista de Historia de América,* 6 (1939), 47–74.

[19] Gwendolin B. Cobb, "Supply and Transportation for the Potosí Mines, 1545–1640," *Hispanic American Historical Review,* 29 (1949), 24–45.

Though well maintained with cuts through passes, bridges over roaring streams, and *tambos* at short intervals, it was an exhausting climb to dizzy heights with sheer drops to swift-flowing rivers, where it was necessary to shift cases of goods from the backs of mules to the shoulders of Indian and Negro carriers and swim the animals to the opposite shore (see selection 5). Moreover, the *soroche*, or mountain sickness, often induced severe headaches and nausea. Progress of the heavily laden packtrains was rarely more than three leagues a day, and the whole journey might take 80 days,[20] though unencumbered beasts could cover the distance in a couple of weeks, allowing the rider to sleep "under a roof every night."

Like the sea-going passenger, the land traveler was obliged to bring all his provisions, though he could depend upon wayside supplies of water for himself and forage for his mounts. An experienced eighteenth-century observer offered useful hints to those who journeyed over the Lima-Cuzco road. "Take sufficient food supplies from one inn to reach the next," he counseled, and recommended that saddle-bags be stocked with "a good slab of bacon, and pepper, ground chili, tomatoes, onions, garlic, and a couple of pounds of rice . . . along with lemons and oranges to make up for the lack of vinegar . . .[21] He also urged adding chickens and parboiled meat for stews. Eggs were usually obtainable at *tambos*, but ham and sausage, however much craved, he admonished, should be eschewed because such cold foods induce a continuous thirst not readily quenched where roadside water is infrequent.

Occasionally man-carried litters bore travelers along the trails, a sight far less common than the slow, plodding packtrains. Such conveyances consisted of a bed or couch, often covered and curtained, suspended from parallel bars supported by porters. The families of viceroys and high officials

[20] Concolorcorvo, *El Lazarillo de Ciegos Caminantes desde Buenos Aires hasta Lima, 1773* (Buenos Aires: Solar, 1942), p. 13.

[21] *Ibid.*, p. 9.

sometimes journeyed to their posts of duty in this manner when travel by land was necessary or preferred. This slow and costly mode of transport was almost exclusively the privilege of the very rich or the highly placed in office. On country roads in Brazil, however, particularly in the seventeenth and eighteenth centuries, it was fairly common to see a canopied hammock suspended from a single bar, each end of which rested on the shoulder of a nearly naked Negro, his sweaty black skin glistening in the hot sunshine. Within this shaded, gently swaying couch the fortunate traveler drowsed at his ease. In one hand each bearer carried a staff terminating in a crescent-shaped fork, on both of which supports the end of the long bar were placed when a halt was made for rest.[22] When topographical conditions permitted, wheeled vehicles sometimes carried freight—and incidentally passengers. The marked advantages of this kind of conveyance over the load limitations of pack animals fostered a carting industry. Geographical and economic factors, however, largely confined wheeled transportation to areas such as the high plateau of Mexico in the early days of mining prosperity and to the broad Pampas of Argentina at a later period.[23] Clumsy *carretas*, or carts with two solid, spokeless wheels, drawn by slowly ambling oxen, hauled much of the freight from Vera Cruz to Mexico City in spite of the ascent of several thousand feet from the coast. From the viceregal capital these vehicles moved over more level terrain to the northern mining districts. These carts were called *chirriones* because of the shrill, rasping squeal of tortured axles, unlubricated save for applications of animal grease. They bumped, jolted, and jarred over rutted roads guided by stolid teamsters, who, by extension, were known as *chirrioneros*.[24]

Though cattle-raising and mule-breeding, the chief eco-

[22] Plate xxv on page 272 of Amedée François Frezier, *A Voyage to the South Sea in the Years 1712, 1713, and 1714* (London, 1717) depicts such a hammock and its two porters.

[23] Ringrose, *op. cit.*, pp. 38–44.

[24] Leonard, *Books of the Brave*, *op. cit.*, p. 181.

nomic activities of Argentina, created less wealth than the silver mines in Mexico and Andean Peru, the geographical features of the country were favorable for a lucrative carting trade. In the general region from the Río de la Plata to the western settlements of Mendoza, Tucumán, and Jujuy, freight-carrying was a prosperous business, particularly in the eighteenth century. The two wheeled *carretas* (see selection 11) toiled across the endless reaches of Argentina's northwestern plains much as the "prairie schooners" would do a century later in "winning of the West" of North America. On their long journeys, the trains of carts, slowly rumbling over the Argentina Pampas, and carrying passengers as well as freight, confronted similar hazards of hunger, thirst, and Indian attacks. To cope with these misadventures their teamsters used many of the same tactics that the leaders of emigrant wagon trains later found necessary in the wild West of the United States.

Broadly speaking, then, the modes of conveyance here indicated were the only ones available to travelers in the pre-industrial setting of colonial Latin America—modes that changed little until the nineteenth century was well advanced. The surviving travel accounts often provide graphic descriptions of the conditions and hardships encountered, and they underscore the severe difficulties of achieving economic growth in the Hispanic domains of the New World. Understandably, most individuals embarking on these hazardous excursions did so deliberately for personal gain, whether in trade or office-holding. As earlier stated, seldom did a love of adventure or a desire for an acquaintance with the secrets of nature of the strange lands animate them except, possibly, in the last colonial century.

Yet it is well to remember that solely material considerations did not propel *all* who ventured abroad in the New World. Even in the sixteenth and seventeenth centuries curiosity lured serious men of learning, who, under royal auspices, made valuable studies of what they observed and rendered impressive reports on scientific aspects of the Crown's vast patrimony. Too often, however, the Hapsburg monarchs of Spain, fearful that this knowledge might benefit European rivals and jeopardize the security of distant realms, jealously strove to keep it secret. They discouraged publication when they did not absolutely forbid it, and hence important manuscripts have lain neglected in archives and libraries until recent times. Occasionally descriptive accounts did appear in print, usually published abroad and written by foreigners (see selection 7) who, by guile, had evaded restrictions on travel; others were sometimes written by relapsed Catholics, notably the Englishman Thomas Gage, author of the well-known *A New Survey of the West Indies, 1648.*

It remained for the absolutist and reformist French Bourbons, occupying the Spanish throne after 1700, to liberalize the trade and entry policies that had prevailed so long. To a large extent it was the eighteenth-century Enlightenment, with its zeal for "useful knowledge," that altered the attitude of the new dynasty toward its oversea possessions. It opened the ports of Spanish America to freer access; it looked to a more systematic development of the resources of the interior; and it authorized and even subsidized scientific missions to make studies.[25] Portuguese authorities of the same period, however, appear to have been far less lenient with respect to allowing access to Brazil.

One of the most famous expeditions to Spanish America was that of the French scientist Charles Marie de La Condamine to the viceroyalty of Peru in 1735 to measure the arc of the meridian at the equator in what is now Ecuador. Two brilliant young Spaniards, Jorge Juan and Antonio de Ulloa, received commissions to accompany La Condamine. These two officers had nearly a decade of adventure, travel, and study in the general west coast region that resulted in

[25] German Arciniegas, *Latin America: A Cultural History,* Joan Maclean (tr.) (New York: Knopf, 1967), Chaps. 11, 12, offers useful discussions of the Enlightenment and the scientific missions in the New World.

their celebrated work, *A Voyage to South America* (1748),[26] and the later *Noticias Secretas* (Secret Information), which reported in detail the widespread corruption of colonial society and confirmed the observations of Frezier (see selection 9) and other visitors of the time. Published narratives of eighteenth-century travelers are numerous, among which the account of Louis Antoine de Bougainville, who witnessed some incidents of the Jesuit expulsion from Paraguay in 1767, has special interest (see selection 10). Exceeding all other visitors in lasting importance, however, was the great German scientist, Baron Alexander von Humboldt, who spent about five years in Spanish America at the end of the colonial period (see selection 13). His statistical surveys, acute observations, and admirably descriptive accounts of travels in South America, Mexico, and Cuba remain indispensable sources for modern scholars.

This Edition

The following readings present selections from relatively unfamiliar accounts of travel by sea and land written by Spaniards and foreigners during the three colonial centuries. They seek to represent the three hundred-year periods of that era, and they attempt to provide a wide spectrum of geographical regions of colonial Latin America, from the Marianas in the South Pacific to Mexico in Middle America, and to Brazil, Colombia, Panama, Peru, Argentina, and Venezuela in South America. Some selections also serve to describe the conditions of shipboard travel on the Atlantic and Pacific Oceans, and the hardships of land journeys over rugged mountain terrain and across undulating plains in the continental regions of Mexico, Peru, and Argentina. They also depict the means of conveyance, particularly mule packtrains, the two-

[26] Jorge Juan and Antonio de Ulloa, *A Voyage to South America*, Introduction by Irving A. Leonard (New York: Knopf, 1964) is an abridged edition.

wheeled carts, and such accommodations on the main traveled roads as there were.

With the former mystery enveloping these lands of the New World now dissipated, the modern reader, living in totally different circumstances and with a broader perspective, may well have more curiosity about the mundane details of early travel. For him, perhaps, there is also interest in the social and cultural life of those times, glimpses of which observant travelers recorded in their narratives. Journeys that were of themselves historical events retain fascination, such as Orellana's descent of the Amazon River in the days of the Spanish Conquest (see selection 2); others are eye-witness accounts of historical episodes which have a reportorial value as, for example, the few details of the Jesuit expulsion from Paraguay recorded by the world traveler Bougainville (see selection 10). Now and then, reminiscent of modern tourism, a chronicler comments on a visit to an historical site, such as Vázquez de Espinosa's mention of viewing the place of captivity of the Inca leader Atahualpa, who was executed by the Spanish conqueror, Francisco Pizarro (see selection 6) or Acarete du Biscay's description of a local pageant in Potosí (see selection 7).

The essentially cosmopolitan character of this travel literature, despite the exclusive tendencies of the Spanish and Portuguese crowns, is symbolized by the authorship of the samples here offered. A minority of four writers are Spanish; three French; two Italians; two Englishmen; one German; and one a Portuguese Jew. This array of accounts makes clear the discomforts and perils stoically endured by the hardy individuals who ventured forth to see the strange New World of deceptive promise. Long afterward a literary rambler who also journeyed to distant lands, Robert Louis Stevenson, would write an oft quoted phrase: "To travel hopefully is a better thing than to arrive." Had so gentle a philosophy of wandering come to the attention of the colonial traveler, he, recalling the ever-present fears in journeying by sea, of storms, calms, shipwrecks, pirates, scurvy, disease, thirst, hunger, nausea, and remembering the hazards of travel by land, of tedious, saddle-sore rides mule-back over precipitous trails, with tumbles of beasts—and sometimes their riders—into deep gorges or roaring mountain streams, of slow, jolting travel in oxen-drawn carts through regions of hostile Indians, that colonial traveler might well have been inclined to revise the wording of Stevenson's homily to read: "To arrive is a better thing than to travel hopefully."

A Note on the Translations

When available the text of English translations published during the colonial centuries of French and Italian travel accounts is utilized, as in selections 7, 8, 9, 10, and 13. (The German von Humboldt wrote in French.) A modern translation from the Italian is used in selection 4. With the exception of selection 2, which was partially revised, all translations of travel narratives written in Spanish were made by the editor. These include selections 1, 5, 6, and 11; in 1 and 5 the material is rendered into English for the first time: 6 and 11 are fresh versions from the original Spanish text.

I.A.L.

❧ I ❧

Sixteenth Century

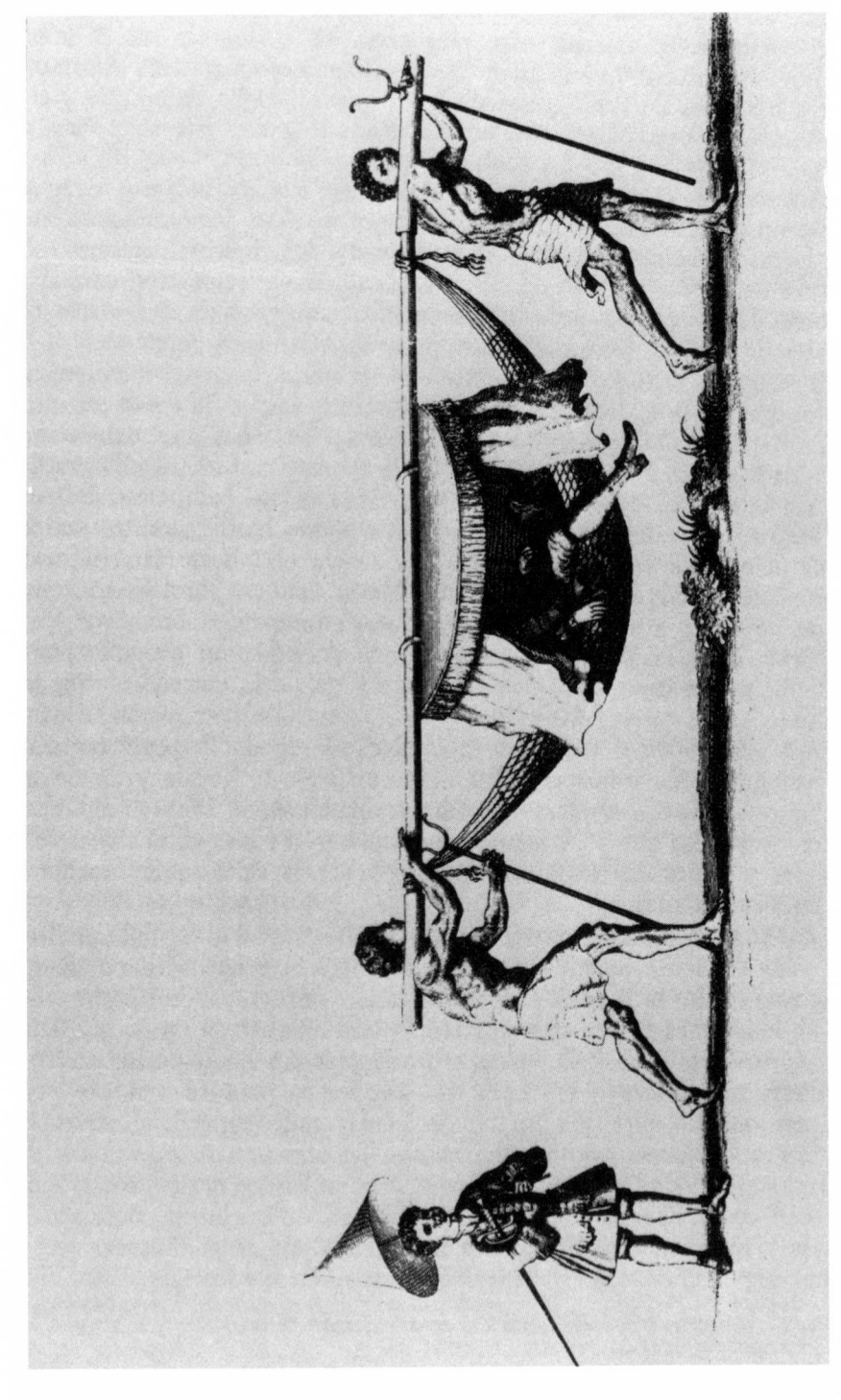

For the more fortunate traveler,
a canopied hammock was used on country roads in Brazil.

⊷§ 1 §⊷

The Atlantic Crossing of
Father Tomás de la Torre
(1544)

The best contemporary portrayal of the harsh reality of a voyage on the annual transatlantic fleets from Seville and San Lúcar de Barrameda in Spain to the sixteenth-century New World is that of the Dominican friar Tomás de la Torre. This clergyman kept a journal of an overseas journey in 1544 to Ciudad Real de Chiapas, in modern Mexico, which he made in the company of Father Bartolomé de las Casas, the controversial "Apostle of the Indians," and forty-six other members of his religious order. The wretched conditions of sea travel that he graphically describes changed but little during the three colonial centuries of Latin America.

By the grace of our Lord, on the morning of Wednesday, July 9, 1544, six months after leaving Salamanca, we hastily

---

The original narrative was incorporated in an early eighteenth-century manuscript chronicle, later published as: Fray Francisco Ximénez, *Historia de la Provincia de San Vicente de Chiapas y Guatemala de la Orden de Predicadores.* Prólogo del Lic. Antonio Villacorta C., 3 vols. (Guatemala, C. A., 1929). The text of Father de la Torre's narrative appears in I, 272–284, and is translated by the editor. The same account appears in Frans Blom, *R. P. Fray Tomás de la Torre. Desde Salamanca, España, hasta Ciudad Real de Chiapas. Diario de Viaje, 1544–1545* (Mexico City, 1944), pp. 69–93.

scrambled aboard the small boats that carried us out to the ships on which the remaining members of our order were booked for passage. For all of us, however, it was disheartening because the weather was no longer favorable for sailing, even though the fleet, consisting of twenty-seven vessels, including caravels and a galleon, was now ready to depart. Embarking all on the same ship at this time was the largest group of our order ever sent to the Indies. There were over forty-eight friars and many other secular clergy as passengers, and chief among us was the Bishop of Chiapas, the Very Reverend Bartolomé de las Casas. Having triumphed over the Council of the Indies, he came armed with royal authority to remedy the ills of the Indians and to free the slaves. Also aboard our ship was the wife of the viceroy, María de Toledo, who was returning to the island of Hispaniola; rather inopportunely, she demanded that two priests travel with her. After considerable difficulty the matter was finally adjusted by assigning to her Friar Juan de Cabrera de Córdoba from our monastery in Valladolid, and Friar Alonso de Vallisante, its vicar. Her brother, Friar Antonio de Toledo, of the same order also joined her retinue, and collectively they were made comfortable and their needs well attended to. The Father Prior of the island and city of Santo Domingo was also with our group, though not on our ship.

We came aboard joyously chanting litanies and other prayers, thus beginning our permanent exile from our country with as much gaiety as travelers customarily display at home-coming after years of hardships and wandering abroad. We did this because we anticipated pleasant rewards both on earth and in heaven for our coming trials and tribulations. Immediately, we spent the whole day broiling in the sun but, with a slight breeze, the sails were hoisted the next day because the seamen alleged that, once we were out on the high sea, we would start sailing with any kind of wind.

Every ship managed to cross the troublesome and dangerous bar at San Lúcar de Barrameda at the mouth of the Guadalquivir River except ours, which got badly stuck. The harbor pilot was blamed for this mishap, but it was not really his fault; rather, the fault lay with our own seamen who had so badly arranged the ship's ballast and had piled the cargo so high. Consequently, while the fleet sailed three leagues that day, we were left behind, grounded on the sandbar opposite the city and enduring the first of our many hardships and perils. Since our ship was visible from San Lúcar and it looked as if something was amiss, the duke sent a message from the city expressing his and the duchess' regret and stating that, if help was needed to get off the entrance bar, he would send it. Our seamen, who were touchy about their nautical skill, were furious and refused any assistance. The captain of the fleet sent back a smallboat to tell us that he would wait only a day or two inasmuch as our ship was only a merchantman picked up in the San Lúcar harbor, where we could remain. The pilot and owner of our ship, Pedro de Ibarra, went ahead to give an account of himself and to lay the blame on the harbor pilot who customarily took ships across the entrance bar.

Those two days we endured such scorching heat that I do not know how to describe it. We suffered particularly because we had just left very comfortable quarters, and because it made the ship's pitch ooze between the planking.

Since there were so many of us, the Father Vicar had arranged to have us all travel together, thinking in this way we would be a comfort to each other, help each other, and that we would thus get along with less baggage and fewer provisions. But it was a great mistake for, when only two or three clergymen are on a single ship, they are waited upon, cared for, and treated with great respect, even though they bring no supplies with them. But with all of us together, they treated us like Negroes, making most of us go below deck to sleep and tramping over us as we were seated or lay sprawled about the deck floor. And often it was not just our ecclesiastical habits that they stepped on but right on our beards and faces without the least consideration for us as holy friars. And there were a lot of other annoyances and outrages that I hardly know how to describe. The first day we chanted all the services but, because of such harassment, we sang only the *Salve* the second day, and each one recited the canonical hours whenever he could manage to do so.

The next day, Friday, July 11, we hoisted sails and dully watched the coast of our Spain disappear in the haze. A good, though faint, breeze was blowing and we soon realized that the sea was not man's natural habitat. Everyone became so deadly seasick that nothing in the world could induce us to move from the spot where we lay; only the Father Vicar and three others remained on their feet. But the latter were in no shape to be of help and only the Father Vicar was able to wait on us and push the basins and containers near us to vomit in, and if they didn't happen to be close at hand, they were useless. With us were four or five lay youths who wished to serve God in the Indies, and they waited upon us and assisted us, but soon they, in turn, succumbed and required attention. Nothing could induce us to swallow a mouthful of food, though we were faint with hunger, but we never ceased to long for a drink of water.

A more befouled hospital and one so filled with the moans of the sick can hardly be imagined. Some sufferers were cooked alive in the heat below deck, while the sun roasted others lying about the deck, where they were trod upon and trampled, and where they were so filthy that words are inadequate to describe the scene. Even though several began to recover in a few days, their improvement was too slight to enable them to nurse the others who were still completely seasick. Bishop Las Casas gave the chickens he was bringing to the sufferers since the rest of us had not brought any, and a clergyman bound for Chiapas to teach ecclesiastical studies helped the Father Vicar in the task of nursing. The severest hardship for us was to read our prayerbooks, but despite everything we recited our prayers as best we could, however tardily and badly, for we did not dare to omit them. But we only chanted the *Salve* in unison.

The night before disembarking on the island of Gomera in the Canaries, we took off our tunics and sandals and, if we could, we removed our scapularies. It was the saddest sight in the world to see us, and no one could comfort us because we were all in the same plight. At the time we left our homeland, Spain and France were engaged in a bitter war and, as a result, we sailed in constant terror of French attacks. On the afternoon of that day, those who could raise their head above the rail caught sight of sixteen sails, and that night the whole fleet was terrified fearing that they were French ships despite the fact that such opponents would have been more afraid of us. Next morning, however, not a sail was in sight and it was surmised that what we had seen was a Spanish fleet returning from the Indies.

That day we cast overboard the cabbages, lettuce, and radishes brought on the voyage in the belief that they could be eaten. By nightfall our stomachs had calmed down and we no longer vomited but, especially below deck, we endured indescribable heat. A large ship was sighted Saturday morning and, suspecting that it was a French spy, one of our vessels sailed toward it. The strange ship started to flee. Ours fired a shot, whereupon it lowered its sails. Then, recognizing that it was a Spanish bark, we allowed it to proceed on its way. When the rest of our fleet heard the shot, they thought that we had come in contact with the French enemy and that a bombardment was in progress. And when we heard the racket of getting weapons ready below deck, we were greatly alarmed, but we quickly recovered from our fear and recited a litany. Some, however, took confession from each other, while others simply made a joke of it. As soon as we knew that it was nothing to worry about, we relapsed into our usual state of torpor and dropped back into our former postures. No further disturbance followed this episode.

To help those who are unfamiliar with life at sea understand something of the hardship and suffering that it entails, especially at the outset, I shall set forth a few circumstances that are perfectly obvious to any one who has been to sea. First of all, a ship is a very narrow and stout prison from which no one can escape even if he wears no shackles or chains. In its cruelty it makes no distinction of its inmates, keeping them all equally confined. Closely crowded in cramped quarters, heat and suffocation are unbearable. The deck floor is usually one's bed and, though some passengers brought soft mats, ours were small, hard, and bad, thinly stuffed with dog hair, and our bed covering was extremely wretched goatskin blankets. Moreover, there is so much nausea and vomiting on shipboard that some passengers move about as if in a trance and are very peevish.

Some remain in this state for long periods, others for a shorter time, and still others continuously. No one has the least desire to eat and can hardly face anything sweet. The thirst that one endures is unbelievable, and it is increased by our fare of hardtack and salt beef. Water is measured out a half *azumbre* [about a liter] a day; wine is drunk by those who happen to have it. An infinite number of lice eat one alive, and clothing can not be washed because salt water shrinks it. Everywhere bad odors pervade the ship, especially below deck, and the stench becomes intolerable when the ship-pump is working. This operation varies according to whether the sailing is smooth or not, but it goes at least four or five times each day, pumping out the water that has leaked into the hold, and it smells very foul indeed. These annoyances and many other hardships are very common in shipboard life, but we feel them more keenly because they are so alien to what we are accustomed to.

In addition to the foregoing discomforts, when one feels well enough there's no place anywhere on the ship where one can study or withdraw to himself; one remains eternally seated since there is no place to stroll or move about. Everything must be done sitting down or sprawled out or, perhaps, standing up for a short while. Besides all these discomforts, death is forever before our eyes with only the

thickness of one plank sealed to another with pitch separating us from it. Seven of our group never once lifted
their heads above the rail to look at the sea since they
were seasick and miserable during the whole voyage. The
rest, however, recovered, some sooner and more completely
than others. The sea air thoroughly restored Father Domingo de Ara to health and vigor who, until he embarked,
had been in great misery.

I have already pointed out how badly our ship was
ballasted, a circumstance that kept us in great peril and
caused so much distress and suffering that I hardly know
how to express it, nor would any one unfamiliar with the
sea be able to comprehend it. Not only were we in dreadful
danger, from which God quite miraculously saved us, but
the ship was so badly laden, that is, it was empty below
and topheavy above, that it rolled from side to side, not
as it properly should, but tipped so far over that first one
side and then the other was completely under water. Sometimes the ship dipped so far under the sea that it flooded
over half the deck, and the barrels piled up there were all
afloat. Ropes were tied from one end of the ship to the
other so that one could go from the stern to the prow by
clutching them. It was impossible to cook our meals, for
the ship tilted so far over that half was under water, and
passengers lying on the deck assumed an almost perpendicular position. The effort to remedy this precarious
situation by stowing pieces of ordnance and other heavy
objects below deck was all to no avail. From the Sunday
when we embarked until the very last day, we were under
continuous threat of death. Passengers on the other ships
of the fleet prayed for us daily, and often, especially on
two days, they gave us final blessings because they felt so
sure that our ship was going down.

Archuleta, the captain-general of the fleet, sailed close
to us in his galleon twice a day to see how our ship was
faring. He even tried to tow us by ropes tied to his own
vessel, but our crew, who was haughtiness itself, refused to
allow it. No attempt was made to transfer us to other ships

because there were so many of us and the rest of the fleet was already crowded with passengers and seamen. We did not press the matter because we neither fully realized the danger, nor did we see how a transfer could be managed. The ones who really understood the situation were the pilots of the other ships; when they later inspected ours, it frightened them to think how close our escape had been, and so, after we reached land, they all congratulated us on being alive. You can imagine what shape we were in, but we had never fully appreciated our danger, nor could we be convinced that the good Lord would have let us be drowned so that people could say *ubi est Deus Coram.* The Spaniards aboard the fleet who had lived in the Indies declared that our sins and those of the Bishop Las Casas were the cause of the ills that were ruining the Indies.

Quite unexpectedly, however, God granted us the finest weather ever observed at this season of the year, and it really seemed a miracle. The atmospheric conditions astounded the seamen, who declared that God could not improve on them, while others uttered a lot of nonsense. A Franciscan aboard another ship told those who spoke ill of us that God granted this weather *because* of us, and he asserted that we gave life to the fleet, and that, even if our sails had been taken away, we would still have arrived safely. Others claimed that angels had wafted our sails, for it was not a natural breeze, and each one talked according to his feelings about us. The seamen blamed us for their own great heedlessness and complained about our provision of young pigs. That was the reason, it was said, why they threw a lot of our food supplies into the sea, broke a jar of our water, and why something disappeared everyday.

But not all of them were so disagreeable; indeed, some waited upon us and treated us with great respect. Yet there were others who, every time we recited a credo, yelled, "Friars here, friars there, and friars everywhere!" and they forced us to go below deck like a lot of Negroes and stow ourselves away to serve for what the ship so sorely needed

—ballast! We became so worn down, so totally wearied and done in by the treatment received, by our afflictions and by nausea, that I do not know how, nor shall I ever be able to describe our condition. By then we realized what a vast mistake it was to put us all on one ship, for even the merchants who accompanied their goods were careful to distribute their possessions throughout the fleet so that, if a part were lost, a part would still be saved.

With the balmy weather the fleet could make no progress and navigated its ships under foresail only. Sails were lowered entirely three quarters of each day and so, to our great annoyance, it took us twelve days for the voyage that ordinarily requires only four because of the exceptionally calm sailing conditions. Toward the end of this period, a vessel lost its rudder, thus putting it in extreme danger. The distress and anxiety of the fleet, therefore, was not solely on our account for, while it held back for the crippled ship, we raced ahead. When the fleet passed us again, it had to wait once more for the damaged vessel, and again we took the lead. And this is how we survived the hardships of our voyage.

Once when our ship had moved ahead to our great joy, we sighted land. That was the morning of July 19. Despite the fact that this event was a long anticipated one, many on board remained quite unconvinced of its reality and did not even stand up to look at the shore until the afternoon of that day. The land so happily glimpsed was an island of the Canaries called Tenerife. The latter offers a very attractive prospect owing to its hilly range, the highest I had ever seen, which tends to taper off in the shape of a pretty pine-cone. We were hugely delighted on perceiving it and gave thanks to our Lord. After consultation, the pilots of the fleet agreed not to make port because the approach was difficult and the seas were so heavy that it was useless to try to repair the rudderless ship there. As a consequence, we sailed the whole day in sight of this lovely island.

Sunday at dawn we were near Gomera, another island, that had an attractive though small harbor. As the crew had

let our ship drop far behind the fleet, it now boldly tried
to take the lead, spreading all sails. Unfortunately, the top-
sails of another vessel and ours became entangled, creating
a lot of difficulty and the loss of much rigging and gear.
Before we managed to disentangle ourselves, a third ship
from another quarter lunged toward us. By using a garnet
tackle and other means it tried to prevent a collision with
us, but the cutting of all the rigging resulting from this
mishap caused considerable damage to our ship.

Hardly were we out of that fix when a caravel moved
in from another direction and thrust its biggest lateen
yard into the crossarms of our mainsails, with the result that
a large part of them had to be cut away also. During all this
confusion there was such a din of shouting, yelling, and
cursing that we were terrified and did not know where to
betake ourselves. Finally, several smallboats put out from
the harbor to take off passengers. The Father Vicar ordered
us all ashore, a command with which we were only too happy
to comply. We were startled by the spryness and ease with
which Friar Luis and Friar Francisco de Quesada leaped
ashore, just as if they had never been ill a day in their
lives. The former had been as sick as a dog down to the
very last moment, while the latter had a pack on his back
that would have taxed the strength of a beast of burden to
carry. Well, in short, we were all eager to step ashore. . . .

During our ten days on the island we kept busy in
various matters, including stocking the ship with water and
meat and in making peace with our Lord before we embarked once again. We had reached Gomera in such dire
straits, owing to the fact that all of us had traveled together on one boat, that nothing in the world could induce
us to resume the voyage under the same conditions. We
were so mortally afraid of that ship that we felt that we
would commit suicide if they put us aboard it. We therefore begged the Father Vicar to make other arrangements
for the rest of our journey across the Atlantic. When the
seamen of our boat heard about this request they had six

smallboat-loads of stones taken aboard as ballast and got rid of several cases of merchandise. Then they demanded that the vicar should not let a single friar go elsewhere unless the vacated passage was paid for inasmuch as the ship was now in good sailing condition.

This dispute produced a great deal of noisy and angry wrangling and the captain-general was at loss which side of the controversy to take. On one hand, the pilot-owner of our ship kept harassing him while, on the other, he could fully appreciate our point of view and the dreadful peril that we had experienced. Moreover, the vicereine, María de Toledo, vowed to go back to Spain and lay a complaint before the king against the captain-general about the treatment we had received. The bishop and everyone took our side in the matter. The pilot-owner, on his part, called for an inspection of the ship and, if it was all right, we should come aboard and sail in it; if we didn't, then we should pay him our passages. This proposal created a din of shouts, demands, and yells, especially at the beginning. The vicereine offered to pay, but it seemed as if no agreement could be reached. Finally, disregarding many of our objections and difficulties and those of others, it was decided that nineteen of the friars would leave the ship. In behalf of the rest who would stay on it various measures were taken to see that it was made seaworthy, and thirteen pilots declared under oath that it was, indeed, in quite satisfactory condition. Then, however, another problem presented itself. None of the other ships was willing to take on the nineteen friars, partly because of a full load already and partly because our pilot owner retained our travel certificates to present at Santo Domingo for payment of our passages. Pilots of the other ships were, therefore, certain that they would have to transport us free of charge, so none wanted to accept us. At length, after long argument and commanded by the captain-general, they yielded and twenty-seven of us agreed to stay on our ship while nineteen others were distributed among three other vessels and a caravel. The

Father Vicar divided up our supplies of meat, water, and vinegar with the result that we had a small portion and the others a larger share. . . .

The morning of Wednesday, July 30, we set sail out of the harbor of Gomera under a favorable wind. Our ship glided along smoothly and much faster than the others; indeed, with no sails we moved more swiftly than the other ships did under full canvas. Almost at once, however, we all fell deadly seasick and not a single one could stand on his feet, not even the Vicar. In sailing away from the Canary Islands we were stricken even more severely than when we departed from Spain. This effect was largely the result of our having eaten a lot of grapes and fruit while ashore and having drunk a great deal to compensate for our past deprivation. However, with our bodies now purged from the earlier voyage, we soon recovered after vomiting up all those grapes and liquids, and inside of two or three days nearly all of us felt quite fit again. In a few cases the nausea lasted longer but was less severe than before. The ones unable to raise their heads on the previous occasion were now much better because the weather was so ideal that we could not have asked for better. Thus it was that we journeyed with great enjoyment and every member of the ship's crew waited upon us and treated us with great respect, though they did not fail to act like money-conscious seamen firmly bent on making us pay for passages as if they were transporting all of the original friars.

With the fine weather the navigators figured that we would reach the island of Santo Domingo in twenty-four days, but unfortunately some of the caravels in the fleet did not sail well even with winds astern. They gave us a lot of bother and trouble because we had to stop everyday and wait for them. During these periods of lull we began to assemble, eating together with a scriptural reading, and daily we said Mass secretly; on Sundays and holy days we sang hymns and delivered sermons to the whole ship's occupants; every evening we chanted the *Salve*. On August 6th, the day of the Father of our Order, we had a big celebration. Everyone aboard was gay, many artillery shots were fired, and our Lord granted us great joy and consolation, of which we had been deprived in not being able to say Mass and in not being at home in our monastery that day. And next day another big celebration took place because our ship was named *San Salvador*.

The occasional sight of a small bird delighted us because we took it as a sign of land. Now and then we saw clumps of vegetation floating by in the water, though it is alleged that they grow on rocks under the sea. Often ships of the fleet drew alongside of each other, permitting an exchange of greetings by their inmates. In this way we were able to see our fellow friars and learn that all were in good health. Incidents of life at sea included one man falling overboard from the admiral's ship whom they were unable to rescue; one of our casks of water had holes bored in it, but we did not allow the culprits to be punished, which leniency helped prevent the committing of other petty acts of thievery daily. It is needless to detail all these trivial happenings; those recited are enough to warn anyone who would travel by sea.

In this way we spent our days on the long voyage, sometimes shedding tears, at other times reciting the rosary, chanting psalms, and singing hymns, a group of three here, a group of six there. The neophytes strummed guitars and sang ballads, each in his own fashion, and our Lord dwelled among us with His consolation. Many friars sought out corners for prayers, others read books, and quite a few especially at night when the tumult of the day had died down, quietly wept inspired by our Lord. Then we would meditate on certain verses. When peace and well-being prevail the spirit of love wonderfully exalts the heart to God.

With regard to meals we endured much hardship, for usually there was little to eat, largely, I think, because food could only be poorly prepared. For most of us it was a morsel of bacon in the morning, a bit of cooked dried beef and some cheese at mid-day, and the same for supper. Every meal was a good deal less than a couple of eggs;

the thirst we suffered was unbelievable. We would drink a bit more than the rationed amount and, if we, who are accustomed to temperate habits, were always parched, what must it have been for the others! When the water ration was doled out to some of the neophytes, they would drink it all down at once and then went thirsty until the next day. Others kept it to sip at intervals, and some never let the bottle out of their hands. He who gave us a drink once enriched us; no one gives the poor common people anything. What exacerbated this thirst was the nature of the food, the excessive heat, and the realization that strict rationing of liquids was essential.

On St. Bernard's day, August 20th, a dead calm settled on us while waiting for the slow-sailing caravels to catch up, and for two or three days we did not stir at all. The young neophytes went diving in the water and swimming around the motionless vessels, while members of the crew fished for sharks, which we all ate. Though these denizens of the sea were reputed unfit to eat, we consumed them gladly; there was nothing bad about them except a rather strong taste as with most large fish. Since the sea was like a millpond and the ships remained absolutely still on one spot, the deck planking and the rigging grew hot in the excessive heat. Eating fish increased our thirst while, at the same time, our water ration had to be reduced because the ships stood still and made no progress at all.

Neither a breeze nor quite a dead calm because of a slight contrary wind featured the following four or five days. The pilots of the fleet took bearings and declared that we were already near land. One day their loud shouts of joy caused us to rise from the table, thinking that they had really glimpsed it, and for three days we, along with everybody else, kept asserting that we had indeed sighted it. But it proved to be nothing at all and we were very downcast. At sunset, on August 26th, the guns of the forward ship fired shots and, interpreting this volley as an effort to tell us that they had seen land, we lowered sails and did not venture to move forward that night for fear of running aground.

We slept that night in happy expectation of being at last close to land, and the next morning we were barely able to discern behind us the island named Deseada. It lay on our right hand while we found ourselves close to the island called Marigalante, the prettiest and most alluring land that we had ever seen. If I had been the first to discover that island, I would surely have thought it the Earthly Paradise because of its loveliness. These islands are below the torrid zone and so are quite warm, though not uninhabitable. Formerly they were the most densely populated in the world, but the insatiable greed and the unbelievable cruelty and tyranny of the Spaniards have made most of them desolate. We spent half a day near this island without moving an inch because of a dead calm, and so we wearied of looking at it. Deseada, like Marigalante and many other islands, is still inhabited by the former inhabitants called Caribs, who use arrows tipped with herbs of deadly poison, from which no one escapes. As these natives are bold and swift, they go stark naked and, under cover of dense underbrush, make effective use of their cruel weapons, and so they remain lords of their domains. Moved by compassion many clergymen have wished that God would send them there to save souls so irremediably lost.

With a faint afternoon breeze we floated by islands on our right; the large one is called Guadalupe, the other, Friars. The latter is covered with tiny hillocks, hence its name. It is so pretty and attractive, I think, that one is moved to be grateful to our Lord. In general, these islands are all alike, eternally green and lovely, though in sailing along their shores, that loveliness is sometimes broken by long stretches of underbrush and weeds.

That day the captain-general brought out all his flags and banners, assembled all his men, and fired many shots, which occasion was a delight to all of us. The seamen were puzzled by the circumstance that in the Gulf of Mexico, where dead calms are usual this time of the year, we should now have favorable winds, while among the islands, where breezes are ordinarily plentiful, we should experience the hardships of a motionless calm. As a result it took us much longer than expected to reach the island of Santo Domingo. Suffering from thirst, we drifted along in the excessive heat, resulting from these spells of calm. If any breeze sprang up, it was a contrary one, but our Lord tempered matters by the presence of those charming islands.

One Sunday afternoon when we were sailing along in this fashion, we went through a passageway, as the seamen called it, between two beautiful islands. One on the left was called Santa Cruz while on the right several were known as the Virgin Islands. The ships passed between and, in the middle of the channel, rose a huge, tall, and whitish rock, probably one hundred paces in circumference, placed there by the hand of Him who creates all things. At a distance it resembles a handsome ship with all sails spread. It was a joy for us to see all these things, and we gave thanks to Him who made them.

The following night and on Monday and Tuesday, another calm made us endure great thirst, heat, and weariness; we were then in sight of Puerto Rico. That Tuesday we sailed close to the ship on which Father Augustín was a passenger and learned that he and two other friars were quite ill. They asked us for wine and other refreshments and two lads swam over to fetch them. We did not, however, give them these delicacies, because two young men who were passengers on our ship, wanted to carry them over together with a reply to a letter that the first two youths had brought. The Father Vicar wished to send a large bottle of wine and a smaller one filled with raisins, almonds, and other dainties. The two young men dove overboard and swam, taking along the end of a rope. While they were swimming a little breeze came up, widely separating the two vessels with the swimmers half way between. We were sorely troubled fearing lest the two should perish, but the other ship came to their rescue by throwing some flat blocks of wood with ropes attached. Aided in this fashion the two swimmers reached their destination and tied a rope to the end of the blocks of wood they were bringing. We then pulled on the rope hauling in the blocks of wood, attached the bottles, and had them transferred safely to the other vessel. A little later the boats drifted close together again and the two lads got back who had swum from our ship and they told us about their harrowing experience.

Wednesday afternoon, September 3rd, we arrived opposite the city of San Juan de Puerto Rico and caught a glimpse of the Convent of our Order outside of the city. Here the ships and caravels destined for this port left us, together with several other vessels because so many people had died on board of them, and one was leaking badly. Consequently, the fleet was reduced to twelve ships and a caravel, some of which badly needed a supply of water. The general of the fleet, however, felt that we ought not to stop for it. . . .

After some delay we moved with the tide and presently stood off the mouth of a broad river of the city and island of Santo Domingo, or Hispaniola, as it is also known. After we had sailed into the stream and passed the fortress at the entrance, we fired a salute of many guns. Then our ship ran into great danger of being wrecked when it almost collided with a huge rock, and it would have broken up if God had not interposed His protective hand; only a mighty heave on the helm saved the ship from disaster. Almost immediately it nearly plowed into the admiral's ship, which quickly ran up a sail and so managed to veer away from us. These mishaps occurred because we were at the rear of the Fleet and our crew tried to improve its position.

On Tuesday, September 9, 1544, forty-three days after sailing from the island of Gomera in the Canaries, we stepped ashore at the city of Santo Domingo on the island of Hispaniola. Before we had set foot on dry land the Superior of our Order, Friar Antonio de León, came out to the ship. He is a very learned man and zealous in the cause of the Faith and the welfare of the Indies and their native inhabitants. We were personally acquainted with him since he had spent months at Salamanca . . . and so we were exceedingly glad to see him. When all of us were ashore, we formed a procession and marched to our monastery; en route the Bishop of Puerto Rico and many other personages came forth to meet Bishop Las Casas and the rest of us. On reaching the gateway of our Convent we sang a *Te Deum Laudamus*, whereupon the Provincial of these islands, the Prior of the Order, and the entire membership of the monastery issued forth to meet us. After offering a prayer and asking the blessing, we embraced our brother friars, delighting in seeing them. The Provincial received us with the utmost kindliness of spirit and arranged for many of his friars to give up their cells to us, while others were assigned companions, and, in this fashion, we were all lodged. The Provincial often served us at the table and the Father Superior washed our feet and fed us lavishly. Often, at the outset, he himself waited upon us at the table. The Father Provincial instructed us all to eat meat, giving us dispensation from the period of fasting then beginning because we had arrived emaciated and in dire straits from the long and arduous sea voyage. . . .

∽§ 2 §∼

Carvajal's Account of the Discovery of the Amazon (1542)

Francisco Orellana and his fifty-seven companions inadvertently traveled more than 2,000 miles down the Amazon River to its mouth in 1542. It was the first such journey by Europeans, and one of the participants, Gáspar de Carvajal (?–1587), a Dominican friar, recorded its incidents. The many months of navigation brought excitement in visits to Indian villages and in encounters with their inhabitants, some of whom were warlike women. These episodes and the longstanding legend of a tribe of female warriors, fostered by the currently popular romances of chivalry, convinced the Spaniards that they had come upon the locale of these Amazon women, and eventually the great river received this name.

Indian Villages and Customs

On Sunday after the Ascension of Our Lord we set out from this village and began to move on. We had not gone

Reprinted from Special Publication, No. 17, *The Discovery of the Amazon According to the Account of Friar Gáspar de Carvajal, and other documents,* translated by Bertram T. Lee and edited by H. C. Heaton (New York: American Geographical Society, 1934), pp. 200–207, 212–215, 218–223, by permission of the American Geographical Society. Professor Leonard has made minor revisions in the translation.

more than two leagues when we saw emptying into the
river another very powerful and wider river on the right;
so wide was it that, at the place where it emptied in, it
formed three islands, in view of which we gave it the
name of Trinity River. At this junction of the two rivers
there were numerous and very large settlements and very
pretty country and very fruitful land. All this, now, lay in
the dominion and land of Omagua, and, because the villages were so numerous and so large and because there
were so many inhabitants, the Captain did not wish to
make port, and so all that day we passed through settled
country with occasional fighting, because on the water they
attacked us so pitilessly that they made us go down mid-
river. Many times the Indians started to converse with us
and, as we did not understand them, we did not know what
they were saying to us.

At the hour of vespers we came to a village on a high
bank and, as it appeared small to us, the Captain ordered
us to capture it. Also, it looked so nice that it seemed as if
it might be a recreation spot of some overlord of the inland; and so we directed our course with a view to cap-
turing it. The Indians put up a defense for more than an
hour, but, in the end, they were beaten and we were
masters of the village, where we found great quantities
of food, of which we laid in a supply.

In this village there was a villa in which there was a
great deal of porcelain ware of various makes, both jars
and pitchers, very large, with a capacity of more than
twenty-five *arrobas,** and other small pieces such as plates
and bowls and candelabra of this porcelain of the best ever
seen in the world. That of Málaga is not its equal, because this procelain which we found is all glazed and embellished with all colors. So bright are these colors that
they astonish, and more than this, the drawings and paint-
ings on them are so accurately worked out that one wonders
how, with only natural skill, they manufacture and decorate
all these things, making them look just like Roman articles.

* One hundred gallons—*Tr.*

Here the Indians told us that, as much as there was made out of clay in this house, there was as much back in the country in gold and silver. They said that they would take us there, for it was near. In this house were two idols woven out of feathers* of divers sorts, which frightened one; they were of the stature of giants, and on their arms, stuck in the fleshy part, they had a pair of disks resembling candlestick sockets. They also had the same thing on their calves close to the knees: their ears were bored through and very large, like those of the Indians of Cuzco, and even larger. This race of people resides in the interior of the country and possesses the riches already mentioned. It is as reminders that they have the two idols there. In this village also there were gold and silver but, as our intention was merely to search for something to eat and see to it that we saved our lives and gave an account of such a great accomplishment, we did not concern ourselves with, nor were we interested in, any wealth.

Many fine roads led out from this village to the inland country. The Captain wished to find out where they went to, and for this purpose he took with him Cristóbal Maldonado and the Lieutenant and some other companions, and started to follow the roads. He had not gone half a league when the roads became more like royal highways and wider: and, when the Captain had perceived this, he decided to turn back, because he saw that it was not prudent to go on any farther. He returned to where the brigantines were, and, when he got back, the sun was now going down, and the Captain said to the companions that it would be well to depart at once from there, because it was not wise to sleep at night in a land so thickly populated. He gave orders that all embark at once, and thus it was that, with the food and all the men on board the brigantines, we began to move on when it was now night. All that night we continued to pass by numerous and large villages until the day came, when we had journeyed more than twenty

* Out of palm leaves, according to the other manuscript— *Heaton*.

leagues. In order to get away from the inhabited country our companions did nothing but row, and the farther we went, the more thickly populated and the better did we find the land, and so we continued on always at a distance from the shore so as not to furnish the Indians any occasion to attack us.

We continued our progress through this country and dominion of Omagua for more than one hundred leagues, at the end of which we began to enter another region belonging to another overlord, named Paguana, who has many quite civilized subjects. We arrived, at the beginning of the settled section of his district, at a village that must have been more than two leagues long and in which the Indians let us go into their houses without doing us any harm or damage. On the contrary, they gave presents to us out of their belongings. From this village there were many roads leading into the interior, because the overlord does not reside in a village on the river. The Indians told us to go there for, they said, he would be quite pleased with us. In this country this overlord has many sheep of the sort found in Peru, and it is very rich in silver, according to what all the Indians told us. The country is very pleasing and attractive and plentifully supplied with all kinds of food and fruit, such as pineapples and pears which, in the language of New Spain, are called "aguacates," and plums and custard apples and many other kinds of fruit and of very good quality.

We left this village and went past a very large inhabited region, for one day we passed more than twenty villages. This was on the side where we were steering our course, because we could not see the other side because the river was so wide. Thus we traveled on for two days along the right side, and afterward we crossed over and proceeded for two days more along the left side. During the time we could sight one side we could not see the other.

On the Monday after Whitsunday, in the morning, we passed in sight of, and close to, a very large and flourishing village. It had many sections, and in each section there was a landing place down on the river. At each landing place there was a great horde of Indians, and this village extended for more than two and a half leagues, to the very end of which it was still of the type just stated. Because the Indians of this village were so numerous, the Captain commanded us to pass by without doing them any harm and without attacking them. Having observed that we were passing by without doing them any harm, they got into their canoes and attacked us, but to their detriment, because the crossbows and arquebuses made them fall back to their houses, and they let us go on down the river.

This same day we seized a small village where we found food, and here we reached the end of the province of the aforementioned overlord Paguana, and entered into another province very much more warlike and one having a large population and one which forced much fighting upon us. Regarding this province, we did not learn the name of its overlord, but they are a people of medium stature, of highly developed manners and customs; their shields are made of wood and they defend their persons in a very manly fashion.

On Saturday, the eve of Holy Trinity, the Captain gave orders to make port at a village where the Indians put themselves on the defensive, but in spite of that we drove them from their homes. Here we procured supplies, and there were even a few fowl to be found. This same day, on leaving there to pursue our voyage, we saw the mouth of another great river on the left, which emptied into the one we were navigating. Its water was as black as ink, and for this reason we gave it the name of Río Negro. This river flowed so abundantly and with such violence that, for more than twenty leagues, it formed a streak down through the other water, the one water not mixing with the other. This same day we saw other villages that were not very large.

On the next day, which was Trinity, the Captain and all the rest celebrated the holiday in a fishermen's quarters in a village on a hillside. Here much fish was found, which was a help and a great comfort for our Spaniards, because many days had passed since they had had such lodgings. This village was situated on a high spot back from the river as if on the frontier facing other tribes who made war on them, because it was fortified with a wall of heavy timbers. At the time that our companions climbed up to this village to seize food, the Indians decided to defend it and took up a strong position inside that enclosure, which had only one gate, and they set to defending themselves with very great courage. However, as we saw that we were in difficulty, we determined to attack them and so, in accordance with this resolution, the attack was launched through the gate. Entering without any loss, our companions fell upon the Indians and fought with them until they dispersed them, and then they collected foodstuffs, of which there was an abundance.

On Monday we continued on our way, passing by large settlements and provinces, procuring food as best we could whenever we lacked it. On this day we made port at a medium-sized village, where the inhabitants let us come right up to them. In this village there was a very large public square, and in the center of the square was a hewn tree trunk ten feet in girth. Carved in relief on it was a walled city with its inclosure and a gate. At this gate were two very tall towers, having windows, and each tower had a door, the two facing each other, and at each door were two columns. This entire structure that I am telling about rested upon two very fierce lions, which turned their glances backwards as though suspicious of each other, holding between their forepaws and claws the entire structure, in the middle of which was a round open space. In the center of this space was a hole through which they offered and poured out *chicha* for the Sun, for this is the wine which they drink, and the Sun they worship and consider as their god. In short, the construction was well worth seeing, and the Captain and all of us, marveling at such a great thing, asked an Indian whom we seized here what that was, or as a reminder of what they kept that thing in the square? The Indian answered that they were subjects and tributaries of the Amazons and that the only service which they rendered them consisted in supplying them with plumes of parrots and macaws for the linings of the roofs of the buildings of their places of worship; and that all their villages were of that kind, and that they had that thing there as a reminder, and worshiped it as the symbol of their mistress, who rules over all the land of the aforesaid women.

There was also on this same square a not very small house, within which were many vestments of feathers of various colors, that the Indians put on to celebrate their festivals and to dance when they wished to rejoice before this aforesaid hewn tree trunk; it was there that they offered up their sacrifices with their wicked purpose.

We soon left this village and came to another large one which had a similar hewn tree trunk and symbolic device such as has been mentioned. This village put up a strong resistance, and, for a period of more than an hour, they did not let us land. In the end we did so and, as the Indians were numerous and were increasing in number every hour, they would not surrender; but, seeing the damage being inflicted upon them, they decided to flee. Then we had an opportunity, though not for very long, to procure a certain amount of food, because already the Indians were returning towards us. Our Captain did not permit us to wait for their attack, inasmuch as we could gain nothing by trading, and so he ordered us to embark and go on, and that is what was done.

Having departed from here, we passed by many more villages where, like a warlike people, the Indians stood waiting for us, ready to fight, with their arms and shields in their hands, crying out to us, why were we fleeing, for they were waiting for us? But the Captain did not wish to attack where he saw that we could win no honor, particularly as we had a certain amount of food on hand. Whenever there was some on hand, nowhere would he risk his life and those of the companions, and that is why, in some places, we fought, they from the land and we from the water. Whenever the Indians were in great numbers, they formed a wall and our arquebuses and crossbows inflicted damage upon them, and so we passed on, leaving them with the information just mentioned (i.e., what we could do to them).

On Wednesday, the day before Corpus Christi, the seventh of June, the Captain gave orders to make port at a small settlement on the aforesaid river, and so it was seized without resistance. There we found much food, particularly fish, of which there was such a variety and so plentiful that we could have loaded our brigantines up well. This fish the Indians had drying, to be transported into the interior to be sold. All our companions, seeing that the village was a small one, begged the Captain to celebrate Corpus Christi there, since it was the eve of such a great festival. The Captain, as one familiar with the ways of the Indians, said that they must not speak of such a thing because he had no intention of doing it; though the village seemed small to them, it had a large outlying district whence the inhabitants could come to give aid and inflict injury upon us. Rather, he was of the opinion that we should go on as we were accustomed to doing and get to the wilderness to sleep; and our companions again asked as a favor that he celebrate Corpus Christi there. The Captain, seeing that all were urging the request, consented to what they requested, though against his will. So we stayed in this village resting until the hour of sunset. . . .

The Fight with the Amazons

The following Wednesday we captured a village which stood in the bend of a small stream on a very large piece of flat ground more than four leagues long. This village was laid out along one street and had a square half way down, with houses on both sides, and there we found a great deal of food. This village, because it was of the sort already stated, we named Pueblo de la Calle (i.e., Village of the Street).

On the following Thursday we passed other villages of

medium size, and made no attempt to stop there. All these villages are the dwellings of fishermen from the interior of the country. In this manner we were proceeding on our way, searching for a peaceful spot to celebrate and to gladden the feast of the blessed Saint John the Baptist, herald of Christ, when God willed that, on rounding a bend of the river, we should see on the shore ahead many villages, and very large ones, which shone white. Here we came suddenly upon the excellent land and dominion of the Amazons. These villages were forewarned and knew of our coming, in consequence whereof the inhabitants plunged into the water to meet us, and in no friendly mood. When they had come close to the Captain, he would have liked to induce them to accept peace, and so he began to speak to them and call them; but they laughed, and mocked us and, coming close, told us to keep moving and they added that down below they were waiting for us, and that there they were to seize us all and take us to the Amazons.

The Captain, angered at the arrogance of the Indians, gave orders to shoot at them with the crossbows and arquebuses, so that they might reflect and become aware that we had the wherewithal to assail them. In this way damage was inflicted on them and they turned back towards the village to spread the news of what they had seen. As for us, we did not stop approaching the villages. Before we were within half a league of putting in, many squadrons of Indians were along the edge of the water, at intervals. As we kept going ahead, they gradually came together and drew close to their living quarters. In the center of this village there was a great horde of fighters, in a well-formed squadron, and the Captain gave the order to have the brigantines beached right where these men were, in order to go look for food. And so it came about that, as we began to come in close to land, the Indians started to defend their village and to shoot arrows at us. As the fighters were in great numbers, it seemed as if it rained arrows; but our arquebusiers and crossbowmen were not idle, because they did nothing but shoot. Although they killed many, the In-

dians did not become aware of this for, in spite of the
damage done to them, they kept at us, some fighting and
others dancing. Here we all came close to perishing because, as there were so many arrows, our companions had
all they could do to protect themselves from them, without
being able to row. Consequently, they did so much damage
to us that, before we could jump out on land, they had
wounded five of us, of whom I was one. They hit me in one
side with an arrow, which penetrated my torso and, if it had
not been for the thickness of my clothes, that would have
been the end of me.

In view of the danger that we were in, the Captain began
to cheer up the men at the oars and urge them to make
haste to beach the brigantines. Though with hard work, we
finally succeeded in beaching the boats and our companions
jumped into the water, which came up to their chests.
Here a very serious and hazardous battle was fought, because the Indians mixed in among our Spaniards, who defended themselves so courageously that it was wonderful
to behold. This fight lasted more than an hour, for the
Indians did not lose spirit; rather, it seemed as if it re-
doubled, even though they saw many of their own number killed. They stepped over their bodies and merely kept
retreating and coming back again.

I want it to be known why these Indians defended themselves in this manner. It must be explained that they are the
subjects of, and tributaries to, the Amazons, and our coming being known to them, the Indians sent to them to ask
help, and as many as ten or twelve of them came, for we
ourselves saw these women, who were there fighting in front
of all the Indian men as women captains. They fought so
courageously that the Indian men did not dare to turn
their backs, and anyone who did they killed with clubs right
there before us. This is the reason why the Indians kept up
their defense for so long. These women are very white and
tall, and have very long hair, braided and wound about
the head. They are very robust and go about naked, but
with their privy parts covered, with their bows and arrows

in their hands, doing as much fighting as ten Indian men. Indeed, there was one woman among them who shot an arrow a span deep into one of the brigantines, and others less deep, so that our brigantines looked like porcupines.

To come back to our own situation and to our fight: Our Lord was pleased to give strength and courage to our companions, who killed seven or eight (for these we actually saw) of the Amazons, whereupon the Indians lost heart, and they were defeated and routed with considerable damage to their persons. Because many warriors were coming from the other villages to give aid and, as they were bound to turn back on us, since already they were again uttering war cries, the Captain ordered the men to get into the boats with very great haste, for he did not wish to jeopardize the lives of all. So they got into the boats, not without some trouble, because already the Indians were beginning to fight again. Besides this, a great fleet of canoes was approaching on the water, and so we pushed out into the river and got away from the shore. . . .

Customs of the Amazons

That night we managed to get to a place to sleep, now outside of this whole settled region, in an oak grove which was on a large flat space near the river, where we were not without fearful apprehensions, because Indians came to spy on us. Toward the interior there were many well-populated districts and roads leading into it, for which reason the Captain and all the rest of us stayed on guard, waiting for whatever might happen to us.

In this stopping-place the Captain took aside the Indian captured farther back, because he now understood him by means of a list of words that he had made, and asked him of what place he was a native? The Indian answered that he was from that village where he had been seized. The Captain asked him what the name of the overlord of this land was, and the Indian replied that his name was

Couynco, that he was a very great overlord, and that his rule extended to where we were. That, as I have already said, was a stretch of one hundred and fifty leagues. The Captain asked him what those women were who had come to help them and fight against us? The Indian said that they were certain women who resided in the interior of the country, a seven-day journey from the shore, and that it was because this overlord Couynco was subject to them that they had come to watch over the shore. The Captain asked him if these women were married; the Indian said they were not. The Captain asked him about how they lived; the Indian replied first that, as he had already said, they were off in the interior of the land and that he had been there many times and had seen their customs and mode of living. As their vassal he was in the habit of going there to carry the tribute whenever the overlord sent him. The Captain asked if these women were numerous; the Indian said that they were, and that he knew by name seventy villages, and named them before those of us who were there present, and he added that he had been in several of them. The Captain asked him if the houses in these villages were built of straw; the Indian said they were not, but of stone and with regular doors and that from one village to another went roads closed off on both sides and with guards stationed at intervals along them so that no one might enter without paying duties. The Captain asked if these women bore children; the Indian answered that they did. The Captain asked him how, not being married and with no man residing among them, they became pregnant? He said that these Indian women consorted with Indian men at times. When that desire came to them, they assembled a great horde of warriors and went off to make war on a very great overlord whose residence is not far from the land of these women; by force they brought the men to their own region and kept them for the time that suited their caprice. After they found themselves pregnant they sent the men back to their country without doing them any harm. Afterwards, when the time came for them to have children, if they gave birth to male children, they killed them and sent them to their fathers; if female children, they raised them with great solemnity and instructed them in the art of war. He said furthermore that, among all these women, there was one ruling mistress who subjected and held under her hand and jurisdiction all the rest, which mistress went by the name of Coñori. He said that in their possession was a great wealth of gold and silver and that, in the case of all the mistresses of rank and distinction, their eating utensils were nothing but gold or silver, while the other women, belonging to the plebeian class, used a service of wooden vessels, except what was brought in contact with fire, which was of clay. He said that in the capital and principal city in which the ruling mistress resided there were five large buildings which were places of worship and houses dedicated to the Sun, which they called *caranain,* and that inside, from half a man's height above the ground up, these buildings were lined with heavy wooden ceilings covered with paint of various colors, and that in these buildings they had many gold and silver idols in the form of women, and many vessels of gold and of silver for the service of the Sun; and these women were dressed in clothing of very fine wool, because in this land there are many sheep of the same sort as those of Peru; their dress consisted of blankets girded about them from the breasts down, in some cases merely thrown over the shoulders, and in others clasped together in front, like a cloak, by means of a pair of cords. They wore their hair reaching down to the ground at their feet, and upon their heads were placed crowns of gold, as wide as two fingers, and their individual colors. He said, in addition, that in this land, as we understood him, there were camels that carried the inhabitants on their backs, and he said that there were other animals, which we did not succeed in understanding about, which were as big as horses and which had hair as long as the spread of the thumb and forefinger, measured from tip to tip, and cloven hoofs, and that people kept them tied up; but that there were few of these. He said that there were in this land two salt-water lakes, from which the women obtained salt. He related that they had a rule to the effect that, when the sun went down, no male Indian was to remain anywhere in all of these cities, but that any such must depart and return to his district. He said, in addition, that many Indian provinces bordering on them were held in subjection by the Amazons and made to pay tribute and to serve them, while with other provinces they carried on war, in particular with the one which we have mentioned, and that they brought the men of this province there to have relations with them. These Amazons were said to be of very great stature and white and numerous, and he claimed that all that he had told here he had seen many times as a man who went back and forth every day. All that this Indian told us and more besides had been told to us six leagues from Quito, because there were a great many reports concerning these women, and, in order to see them, many Indian men came down the river one thousand four hundred leagues. Likewise, the Indians farther up had told us that anyone who should take it into his head to go down to the country of these women was destined to go a boy and return an old man. The country, the captive Indian said, was cold and there was very little firewood there, and it was rich in all kinds of food; also he told many other things and said that every day he kept finding out more, because he was an Indian of much intelligence and very quick to comprehend; and so are all the rest in that land, as we have stated. . . .

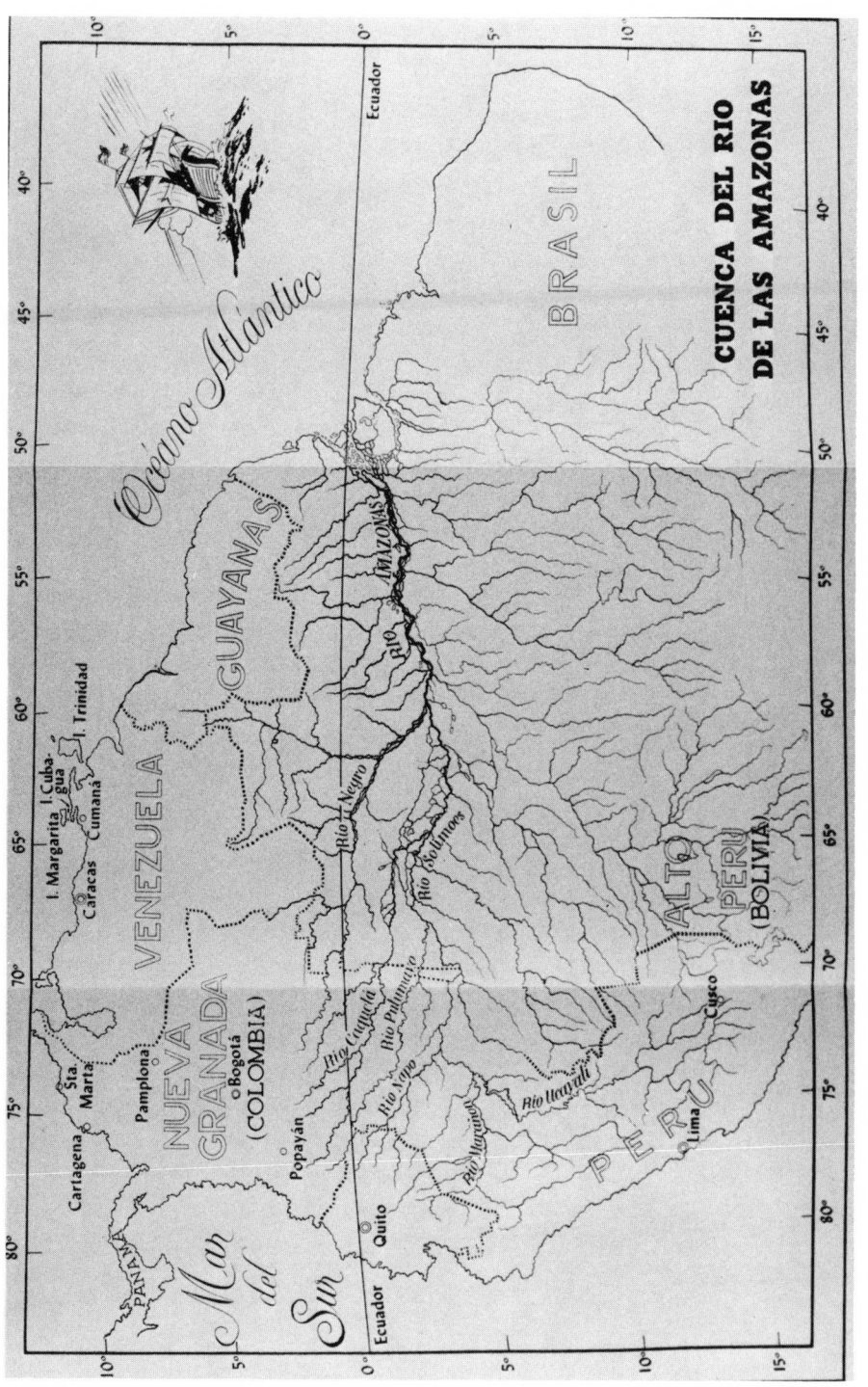

Tha Amazon Basin

A.Palacio Re.
B.Cathedral.
C.Cafa de Cabildo.
D.Cafa Arpt.
F.Uniuerfidad.
G.Alameda.

Las Dos cafas eftan Sañidos por
ce Vna funcion cuas ce Retinta partes
poer La Plana.

Ylir yma Cte trasumente ti ceia

A View of Mexico City in 1628

⟞ 3 ⟝

Robert Tomson's Voyage to the West Indies and Mexico (1555-1558)

In the light of the Spanish Crown's announced policy of excluding foreigners from its New World dominions, it is surprising to learn that an Englishman, Robert Tomson (?–1587), was living in Mexico City in 1557, and even more surprising that a Scotsman had already been residing there for twenty years. It is surmised that Tomson's presence there at this time was the result of an apparent easing of the restrictive practices of Spanish authority, which resulted from the marriage of the Spanish king, Philip II, to Mary Tudor of England. Tomson, a native of Hampshire, England, had traveled to Seville, where he lived in the home of an English merchant whom he had accompanied to New Spain in 1555. His account of shipwreck, description of Mexico City, and report of an auto de fe, in which he was a victim of the Holy Office of the Inquisition, form an especially interesting narrative of a foreigner in sixteenth-century Mexico.

Reprinted from *An English Garner: Voyages and Travels Mainly During the 16th and 17th Centuries,* Vol. I, edited by C. Raymond Beazley, F.R.G.S. (New York: Cooper Square Publishers, 1964), pp. 10–23. Originally appeared as "Robert Tomson of Andover, Merchant. Voyage to the West Indies and Mexico, 1556–1558 A.D.," in Richard Hakluyt, *Principal Navigations, Voyages . . .* (1589).

. . . So that we departed from the islands of the Canaries in the month of October, the aforesaid year [1555], eight ships in our company, and so directed our course towards the Bay of New Spain [Gulf of Mexico];* and, by the way, towards the island of Santo Domingo, otherwise called Hispaniola; so that, within forty-two days [i.e., *in December*] after we departed from the islands of Canaries, we arrived with our ship at the port of Santo Domingo; and went in over the bar, where our ship knocked her keel at her entry. There our ship [rode] before the town; where we went on land, and refreshed ourselves sixteen days.

There we found no bread made of wheat, but biscuit brought out of Spain, and out of the Bay of Mexico. For the country itself doth yield no kind of grain to make bread withal; but the bread they make there is certain cakes made of roots called *cassava;* which is something substantial, but it hath an unsavoury taste in the eating thereof. Flesh of beef and mutton, they have great store; for there are men that have 10,000 head of cattle, of oxen, bulls and kine, which they do keep only for the hides: for the quantity of flesh is so great, that they are not able to spend the hundredth part. Of hog's flesh there is good store, very sweet and savoury; and so wholesome that they give it to sick folks to eat, instead of hens and capons: although they have good store of poultry of that sort, as also of guinea cocks and guinea hens.

At the time of our being there the city of Santo Domingo was not of above 500 households of Spaniards; but of the Indians dwelling in the suburbs, there were more. The country is, most part of the year, very hot; and very full of a kind of flies or gnats with long bills [*mosquitos*], which do prick and molest the people very much in the night when they are asleep, in pricking their faces and hands and other parts of their bodies that lie uncovered, and make them to swell wonderfully. Also there is another kind of small worm, which creepeth into the soles of men's feet,

* Material in brackets was inserted by Raymond Beazley.

and especially of the Indians and children which use to go barefoot, and maketh their feet to grow as big as a man's head, and doth so ache that it would make one run mad. They have no remedy for the same, but to open the flesh, sometimes three or four inches, and so dig them out.

The country yieldeth great store of sugar, hides of oxen, bulls and kine, ginger, *cañafistula*, and *salsaparilla*. Mines of silver and gold there are none; but in some rivers, there is found some small quantity of gold. The principal coin that they do traffic withal in that place is black money, made of copper and brass; and this they say they do use, not for that they lack money of gold and silver to trade withal out of the other parts of [West] India, but because, if they should have good money, the merchants that deal with them in trade would carry away their gold and silver, and let the country commodities lie still. And thus much for Santo Domingo. So we were, coming from the isles of Canaries to Santo Domingo, and staying there until the month of December, which was three months.

About the beginning of January [1556], we departed thence towards the Bay of Mexico and New Spain; towards which we set our course, and so sailed twenty-four days, till we came within fifteen leagues of San Juan de Ulúa, which was the port of Mexico of our right discharge.

And being so near our said port, there rose a storm of northerly winds which came off from *Terra Florida;* which caused us to cast about into the sea again for fear lest that night we should be cast upon the shore before day did break, and so put ourselves in danger of casting away. The wind and sea grew so foul and strong that, within two hours after the storm began, nine ships that were together, were so dispersed, that we could not see one another.

One of the ships of our company, being of the burden of 500 tons, called the "Hulk of Carion," would not cast about to sea, as we did but went that night with the land, thinking in the morning to reach the port of San Juan de Ulúa; but missing the port, went with the shore, and was cast away. There were drowned of that ship, seventy-five

persons, men, women, and children; and sixty-four were
saved that could swim, and had means to save themselves.
Among those that perished in that ship was a gentleman
who had been President the year before in Santo Domingo,
his wife and four daughters, with the rest of his servants
and household.

We, with the other seven ships, cast about into the sea,
the storm enduring ten days with great might, boisterous
winds, fogs, and rain. Our ship, being old and weak, was so
tossed that she opened at the stern a fathom under water,
and the best remedy we had was to stop it with beds and
pillows; and for fear of sinking, we threw and lightened
into the sea all the goods we had, or could come by; but
that would not serve.

Then we cut our mainmast, and threw all our ordnance
into the sea, saving one piece which, early in a morning,
when we thought we should have sunk, we shot off; and,
as it pleased GOD, there was one of the ships of our company near unto us, which we saw not by means of the
great fog; which hearing the sound of the piece, and understanding some of the company to be in great extremity,
began to make towards us, and when they came within
hearing of us, we desired them "for the love of GOD! to
help to save us, for that we were all like to perish!" They
willed us "to hoist our foresail as much as we could, and
make towards them; for they would do their best to save
us"; and so we did.

And we had no sooner hoisted our foresail, but there
came a gale of wind; and a piece of sea struck in the foresail, and carried away sail and mast all overboard: so that
then we thought there was no hope of life. And then we
began to embrace one another, every man his friend, every
wife her husband, and the children their fathers and mothers, committing our souls to Almighty GOD, thinking never
to escape alive. Yet it pleased GOD, in the time of most
need, when all hope was past, to aid us with His helping
hand, and caused the wind a little to cease; so that within
two hours after, the other ship was able to come aboard us,

and took into her, with her boat, man, woman and child, naked without hose, or shoes upon many of our feet. . . .

So we departed out of our ship, and left it in the sea. . . .

Within three days after, we arrived at our port of San Juan de Ulúa, in New Spain.

I do remember that in the great and boisterous storm of this foul weather, in the night there came upon the top of our mainyard and mainmast, a certain little light, much like unto the light of a little candle, which the Spaniards called the *corpos sancto,* and said "It was Saint Elmo" whom they take to be the advocate of sailors. At which sight, the Spaniards fell down upon their knees and worshipped it: praying GOD and Saint Elmo to cease the torment, and save them from the peril they were in; with promising him that, on their coming on land, they would repair unto his chapel, and there cause masses to be said, and other ceremonies to be done. The friars (did) cast relics into the sea, to cause the sea to be still, and likewise said *Gospels,* with other crossings and ceremonies upon the sea to make the storm to cease: which, as they said, did much good to weaken the fury of the storm. But I could not perceive it, nor gave any credit to it; till it pleased GOD to send us the remedy, and delivered us from the rage of the same. His name be praised therefore! . . .

The 16th of April in *anno* 1556, we arrived at the port of San Juan de Ulúa in New Spain, very naked and distressed of apparel and all other things, by means of the loss of our foresaid ship and goods; and from thence we went to the new town called Vera Cruz, five leagues from the port of San Juan de Ulúa, marching still by the sea shore: where we found lying upon the sands a great quantity of mighty great trees, with roots and all, some of them four, five, or six cart load, by estimation; which, as the people told us, were, in the great stormy weather which we endured at sea, rooted out of the ground in *Terra Florida* right against that place (which is 300 leagues over the sea), and brought thither.

So that we came to the town of Vera Cruz where we remained a month. There John Field chanced to meet an old friend of his acquaintance in Spain, called Gonzalo Ruiz de Córdova, a very rich man of the town of Vera Cruz; who (hearing of his coming thither, with his wife and family; and of his misfortune by sea) came unto him, and received him and all his household into his house, and kept us there a whole month, making us very good cheer; and giving us good entertainment, and also gave us, that were in all eight persons, of the J. Field's house, double apparel, new out of the shop, of very good cloth, coats, cloaks, shirts, smocks, gowns for the women, hose, shoes, and all other necessary apparel; and for our way up to the city of Mexico, horses, mules, and men; and money in our purses for the expenses by the way, which by our account might amount unto the sum of 400 crowns.

After we were entered two days' journey into the country, I, Robert Tomson, fell sick of an ague: so that the next day I was not able to sit on my horse but was fain to be carried upon Indians' backs from thence to Mexico.

And when we came within half a day's journey of the city of Mexico, John Field also fell sick; and within three days after we arrived at the city, he died. And presently sickened one of his children, and two more of his household people who within eight days died. So that, within ten days after we arrived at the city of Mexico, of eight persons that were of us of the company, there remained but four of us alive: and I, Robert Tomson, at the point of death, of the sickness that I got on the way, which continued with me for the space of six months [till October 1556]. At the end of which time, it pleased GOD to restore me my health again, though weak and greatly disabled.

Mexico was a city, in my time, of not above 1,500 households of Spaniards inhabiting there; but of Indian people in the suburbs of the city, there dwelt about 300,000 as it was thought, and many more. This city of Mexico is sixty-five leagues from the Gulf of Mexico and seventy-five leagues from the South sea [the Pacific Ocean]; so that it standeth in the midst of the main land, betwixt the one sea and the other.

It is situated in the midst of a lake of standing water, and surrounded round about with the same save, in many places, going out of the city, are many broad ways through the lake or water. This lake and city are surrounded also with great mountains round about, which are in compass above thirty leagues; and the city and lake of standing water doth stand in a great plain in the midst of it. This lake of standing water doth proceed from the shedding of the rain, that falleth upon the mountains and so gathers itself together in this place.

All the whole proportion of this city doth stand in a very level ground; and in the midst of the city is a square, of a good bow shot over from side to side. In the midst of the square is a high Church, very fair and well built all through, but at that time not half finished.

Round about the square, are many fair houses built. On the one side are the houses where Montezuma, the great King of Mexico that was, dwelt; and now there lie always the Viceroys that the king of Spain sendeth thither every three years. In my time there was for Viceroy a gentleman of Castille, called Don Luis de Velasco.

And on the other side of the square, over against the same, is the Bishop's house, very fairly built; and many other houses of goodly building. And hard by the same are also other very fair houses, built by the Marquís de la Valle, otherwise called Hernando Cortés who was he that first conquered the city and country. . . .

The city of Mexico hath streets made very broad and straight that a man being in the highway at one end of the street may see at the least a good mile forward; and in all the one part of the streets of the north part of their city, there runneth a pretty lake of very clear water, that every man may put into his house as much as he will, without the cost of anything but of the letting in.

Also there is a great ditch of water that cometh through the city, even into the high square; where come, every

morning, at break of the day, twenty or thirty canoes of
the Indians which bring in them all manner of provisions
for the city that is made and groweth in the country: which
is a very good commodity for the inhabitants of that place.
And, as for victuals in the city, beef, mutton, hens, capons,
quails, guinea cocks, and such like, are all very good cheap;
as the whole quarter of an ox, as much as a slave can carry
away from the butcher's, for five *tomines,* that is, five *reales*
of silver; and fat sheep at the butcher's, for three *reales,*
and no more. Bread is as good cheap as in Spain; and all
other kinds of fruits, as apples, pears, pomegranates, and
quinces, at a reasonable rate.

The city goeth wonderfully forward in building of Friar-
ies and Nunneries, and Chapels; and is like, in time to
come to be the most populous city in the world, as it may
be supposed.

The weather is there always very temperate. The day
differeth but one hour of length all the year long. The
fields and woods are always green. The woods are full of
popinjays, and many other kind of birds, that make such
a harmony of singing and crying, that any man will rejoice
to hear it. In the fields are such odoriferous smells of flowers
and herbs, that it giveth great content to the senses.

In my time, were dwelling and alive in Mexico, many
old men that were of the Conquerors, at the first conquest
with Hernando Cortés: for, then, it was about thirty-six
years ago, that the country was conquered.

Being something strong, I procured to seek means to
live, and to seek a way how to profit myself in the country
seeing it had pleased GOD to send us thither in safety.

Then, by the friendship of one Thomas Blake, a Scottish-
man born, who had dwelt, and had been married in the
city above twenty years before I came to the city [i.e., *before 1536*], I was preferred to the service of a gentleman,
a Spaniard dwelling there, a man of great wealth, and of
one of the first conquerors of the city, whose name was
Gonzalo Serezo: with whom I dwelt twelve months and
a half [i.e., *up to November 1557*]; at the end of which,

I was maliciously accused by the Inquisition for matters of religion.

And because it shall be known wherefore it was, that I was so punished by the clergy's hand; I will, in brief words, declare the same.

It is so that, being in Mexico [City], at table, among many principal people at dinner, they began to inquire of me, being an Englishman, "Whether it were true that in England, they had overthrown all their Churches and Houses of Religion; and that all the images of the saints of heaven that were in them, were thrown down and broken, and burned, and [that they] in some places stoned highways with them; and [that they] denied their obedience to the Pope of Rome: as they had been certified out of Spain by their friends?"

To whom, I made answer, "That it was so. That, indeed, they had in England, put down all the religious houses of friars and monks that were in England; and the images that were in their churches and other places were taken away, and used there no more. For that, as they say, the making of them, and the putting of them where they were adored, was clean contrary to the express commandment of Almighty GOD, *Thou shalt not make to thyself any graven image,* etc.: and that, for that cause, they thought it not lawful that they should stand in the church, which is the House of Adoration."

One that was at the declaring of these words, who was my master, Gonzalo Serezo, answered and said, "If it were against the commandment of GOD, to have images in the churches; that then he had spent a great deal of money in vain; for that, two years past [i.e., *in 1555*] he had made in the Monastery of Santo Domingo in the city of Mexico, an image of Our Lady, of pure silver and gold, with pearls and precious stones, which cost him 7,000 and odd *pesos*"; which indeed was true, for I have seen it many times myself where it stands.

At the table was another gentleman who, presuming to defend the cause more than any one that was there, said,

"That they knew well enough, that they were made but of stocks and stones, and that to them was no worship given; but that there was a certain veneration due unto them after they were set up in church: and that they were set there with a good intent. The one, for that they were Books for the Simple People, to make them understand the glory of the saints that were in heaven, and a shape of them; to put us in remembrance to call upon them to be our intercessors unto GOD for us: for that we are such miserable sinners that we are not worthy to appear before GOD; and that using devotion to saints in heaven, they may obtain at GOD's hands, the sooner, the thing that we demand of Him. As, for example," he said, "imagine that a subject hath offended his King upon the earth in any kind of respect; is it for the party to go boldly to the King in person, and to demand pardon for his offenses? No," said he, "the presumption were too great; and possibly he might be repulsed, and have a great rebuke for his labor. Better it is for such a person to seek some private man near the King in his Court, and to make him acquainted with this matter, and let him be a mediator to His Majesty for him and for the matter he had to do with him; and so might he the better come to his purpose, and obtain the thing which he doth demand. Even so," saith he, "it is with GOD and His saints in heaven. For we are wretched sinners; and not worthy to appear or present ourselves before the Majesty of GOD, to demand of Him the thing that we have need of: therefore thou hast need to be devout! and have devotion to the mother of God, and the saints in heaven, to be intercessors to GOD for thee! and so mayest thou the better obtain of GOD, the thing that thou dost demand!"

To this I answered, "Sir, as touching the comparison you made of the intercessors to the King, how necessary they were, I would but ask of you this question. Set the case, that this King you speak of, if he be so merciful as when he knoweth that one or any of his subjects hath offended him; he send for him to his own town, or to his own house or place, and say unto him, 'Come hither! I know that thou hast offended many laws! if thou dost know thereof, and dost repent thee of the same, with full intent to offend no more, I will forgive thee thy trespass, and remember it no more!' " Said I, "If this be done by the King's own person, what then hath this man need go and seek friendship at any of the King's private servants' hands; but go to the principal: seeing that he is readier to forgive thee, than thou art to demand forgiveness at his hands!

"Even so is it, with our gracious GOD, who calleth and crieth out unto us throughout all the world, by the mouth of His prophets and apostles; and, by His own mouth, saith, 'Come unto me all ye that labor and are over laden, and I will refresh you!' besides a thousand other offers and proffers, which He doth make unto us in His Holy Scriptures. What then have we need of the saints' help that are in heaven, whereas the LORD Himself doth so freely offer Himself for us?"

At which sayings, many of the hearers were astonished, and said that, "By that reason, I would give to understand that the Invocation of Saints was to be disannulled, and by the laws of GOD not commanded."

I answered, "That they were not my words, but the words of GOD Himself. Look into the Scriptures yourself, and you shall so find it!"

The talk was perceived to be prejudicial to the Romish doctrine; and therefore it was commanded to be no more entreated of. And all remained unthought upon, had it not been for a villainous Portuguese that was in the company, who said, *Basta ser Inglés para saber todo esto y mas,** who, the next day, without imparting anything to anybody, went to the Bishop of Mexico and his Provisor, and said that "In a place where he had been the day before was an Englishman, who had said that *there was no need of Saints in the Church, nor of any Invocation of Saints.*" Upon whose denouncement I was apprehended for the same words here

* You only need to be an Englishman to know all this and a lot more—*I. A. L.*

rehearsed, and none other thing; and thereupon was used as hereafter is written.

So, apprehended, I was carried to prison, where I lay a close prisoner seven months [*till July 1558*], without speaking to any creature, but to the gaoler that kept the said prison, when he brought me my meat and drink. In the meantime, was brought into the prison, one Augustine Boacio, an Italian of Genoa, also for matters of religion; who was taken at Zacatecas, eighty leagues to the northwestward of the city of Mexico.

At the end of the seven months [i.e., *in July 1558*], we were both carried to the high Church of Mexico, to do an open penance upon a high scaffold made before the high altar, upon a Sunday, in the presence of a very great number of people who were, at least, 5,000 or 6,000. For there were some that came one hundred miles off to see the *auto,* as they call it; for that there was never any before, that had done the like in the country: nor could tell what Lutherans were, nor what it meant; for they never heard of any such thing before.

We were brought into the Church, every one with a *san benito* upon his back, which is half a yard of yellow cloth, with a hole to put in a man's head in the midst, and cast over a man's head: both flaps hang, one before, and another behind; and in the midst of every flap a Saint Andrew's cross, made of red cloth, and sewed in upon the same. And that is called *San Benito.*

The common people, before they saw the penitents come into the Church, were given to understand that we were heretics, infidels, and people that did despise God and His works, and that we had been more like devils than men; and thought we had had the appearance of some monsters or heathen people: and when they saw us come into the Church in our players' coats, the women and children began to cry out and made such a noise, that it was strange to hear and see, saying, that "They never saw goodlier men in all their lives; and that it was not possible that there could be in us so much evil as was reported of us; and that we were more like angels among men, than such persons of such evil religion as by the priests and friars, we were reported to be; and that it was a great pity that we should be so used for so small an offense."

So that we were brought into the high Church, and set upon the scaffold which was made before the high altar, in the presence of all the people, until *High Mass* was done; and the Sermon made by a friar concerning our matter: putting us in all the disgrace they could, to cause the people not to take so much compassion upon us, for that "we were heretics, and people seduced of the Devil, and had forsaken the faith of the Catholic Church of Rome"; with divers other reproachful words, which were too long to recite in this place.

High Mass and Sermon being done, our offenses (as they called them) were recited, each man what he had said and done: and presently was the sentence pronounced against us, that was that

> Augustine Boacio was condemned to wear his *San Benito* all the days of his life, and put into perpetual prison, where he should fulfil the same; and all his goods confiscated and lost.
>
> And I, Robert Tomson, to wear the *San Benito* for three years; and then to be set at liberty.
>
> And for the accomplishing of this sentence or condemnation, we must be presently sent down from Mexico to Vera Cruz, and from thence to San Juan de Ulúa, which was sixty-five leagues by land; and there to be shipped for Spain, with straight commandment that, upon pain of 1,000 ducats, every one of the ship Masters should look straightly unto us, and carry us to Spain, and deliver us unto the Inquisitors of the Holy House of Seville; that they should put us in the places where we should fulfil our penances that the Archbishop of Mexico had enjoined unto us, by his sentence there given.

For the performance of the which, we were sent down from Mexico to the seaside, with fetters upon our feet; and there delivered to the Masters of the ships to be carried for Spain, as is before said. . . .

And I, for my part, kept still aboard the ship, and came into Spain; and was delivered to the Inquisitors of the Holy House of Seville, where they kept me in close prison till I had fulfilled the three years of my penance [i.e., *till about 1561*].

Which time being expired, I was freely put out of prison, and set at liberty.

Being in the city of Seville, a cashier of one Hugh Typton, an English merchant of great doing, by the space of one year [i.e., *till about 1562*]; it fortuned that there came out of the city of Mexico, a Spaniard, Juan de la Barrera, that had been long time in the Indies, and had got great sums of gold and silver. He, with one only daughter, shipped himself for to come to Spain; and, by the way, chanced to die, and gave all that he had unto his only daughter, whose name was María de la Barrera.

She having arrived at the city of Seville, it was my chance to marry with her. The marriage was worth to me £2,500 in bars of gold and silver, besides jewels of great price. This I thought good to speak of, to show the goodness of GOD to all them that trust in Him; that I, being brought out of the Indies in such great misery and infamy to the world, should be provided at GOD's hand, in one moment, of more than in all my life before, I could attain unto by my own labor.

After we departed from Mexico, our *San Benitos* were set up in the high Church of the city, with our names written in the same, according to their use and custom; which is and will be a monument and a remembrance of us, as long as the Romish Church doth reign in that country.

~⧉ 4 ⧈~

Journey of Francesco Carletti to South America and Mexico (1594-1596)

―――――•◆•―――――

Italians were conspicuous navigators and travelers to the New World from the time of Columbus to the end of the colonial period. One of the earliest to circumnavigate the globe as a passenger in a series of ships, rather than in a single vessel, was the Florentine merchant Francesco Carletti (1573–1636), who, from May 1594 to March 1596, visited what he called "the West Indies," that is, both Americas, specifically Cartagena in present day Colombia, Panama, Peru, and Mexico. Subsequently, he extended his commercial tour to the Asiatic Islands and mainland, finally returning to Italy in 1606. Carletti was exclusively a trader seeking a fortune by dealing in slaves as well as in merchandise, but he had a good eye for the realities of travel conditions and the customs of the countries he visited. In a series of "chronicles," written in a simple, straightforward style, he reports his observations with a certain detachment and objectivity.

Reprinted from Francesco Carletti, *My Voyage Around the World*, translated by Herbert Weinstock, by permission of Pantheon Books, a Division of Random House, Inc., and Methuen & Co., Ltd. Copyright © 1964 by Random House, Inc.

Cartagena to Panama City

We stayed in the city of Cartagena until August 12, 1594, almost constantly ill of a most malignant fever, and it was not a small grace on the part of God that we were not buried there, seeing that so many of the others died, particularly among those who had come with us and in the ships of the fleet. Of these latter it is a certain thing that more than half die each year as soon as they reach that land or that of Nombre de Dios, a place much more damaging to health and having a pestiferous air. . . .

Putting together the little that remained to us of return from the slaves sold, we invested it in merchandise that had arrived there from Spain in the fleet, which had come in during the month of February of that year. With that, we embarked, having the idea of transporting it to the city of Nombre de Dios, located toward the west on that same coast, at ten degrees, 230 miles distant from Cartagena. It was at that time the port to which the ships of the fleet from Spain usually went to unload their merchandise, which then, having been transported overland to Panamá, the port of the other shore of the sea of noon, called the Sea of the South, was shipped in other vessels to the province of Peru, as we wished to do with ours. . . .

Nombre de Dios consisted entirely of wooden houses situated in a place as unhealthful and conducive to sickness as can be imagined. It was uncomfortable and lacked all commodity for living, all necessities having to come from outside and by sea because its surroundings consisted of nothing but the densest forest and unhappy, uninhabitable deserts. In that city of Nombre de Dios we stayed perhaps fifteen days, most inconveniently and in extreme want of everything necessary for living—especially bread, which no one could find, so that instead of it we ate that which the Indians make of maize, which we call Turkish grain.

But what was worse was that at night we could not defend ourselves from the mosquitoes, which molested us terribly, those of that place not only occurring in great quantity, but also being much more troublesome than our mosquitoes and producing much more poisonous punctures. And this is true throughout the Indies to such an extent that in many places the people abandon those regions for a time and in other districts anoint the whole body with certain juices from bitter herbs in order to defend themselves from those tiny animals. Also in that city of Nombre de Dios there is an uncounted quantity of frogs and toads frightening because of their size. They are met with at every step through all of the streets and they get under people's feet, it being the opinion that they rain down from the sky, or rather, that they are born when the water falls and touches that arid land, which might better be called burned. Also, there are many bats of a very strange nature even though they are formed like ours. At night, the houses being made entirely of wood, they easily enter the rooms and bedrooms, windows and doors always being kept open because of the great heat.

And while the people sleep, these bats come in to find them and, flitting around the beds, make a soft breeze. Without one's feeling it, they bite one at the extreme ends of the fingers and toes or on the forehead or the ears. And then they feed on that tiny piece of flesh which they bear away and on the blood sucked out with it. And there is no way to protect oneself from them, for because of the great heat no one lies covered or enclosed within his bed, so that many people, wanting to hear them and so frighten them off when they come, hang many strings of leaves up around the bed, in the space between one post and another. And when the bats fly into these, they make a noise and are frightened off, so that either one hears them or they go away and do not molest those who are asleep.

Then we embarked again with our merchandise in certain small boats propelled by oars. These are steered and commanded by black slaves, who, twenty-five of them to each boat, navigate along that coast, staying close to shore for sixty miles, and then enter a body of fresh water called the Río de Chagres, the mouth of which lies at ten degrees toward the north. With those small boats, one goes up that river against the current, with unspeakable fatigue and in incredible danger because in many places it is very shallow. And if the weather is dry, one nevertheless must expect rain, which at that season infallibly follows from noon onward each day, with incredible noise and the terror of lightning and thunder and heavenly rumbling, in such a manner that I may say that one feels all that more terrifying there perhaps than in any other part of the world. Or, at least, it is more fearsome than any I ever have heard anywhere else I have been.

What is more, many stones fall, those which we call thunderbolts, mixed with fire and water, descending in sudden downpours so great that they very swiftly bring on floods, against which it is necessary to struggle with the poles if one is to advance and win one's way until that torrent shall have passed. And if, out of bad fortune, the small boat should be stove in or one should be placed in peril in some other manner, it would be impossible to save the people. No place to land appears along the river, the banks of which, from time to time, are closed in and barred by forests so thick and formed of such huge trees that one can neither land there nor find a foothold on shore. All to the contrary, the growth of those same branches forms a bank so impenetrable that it is impossible in any way whatever to reach shore, where the sun's rays cannot penetrate, not to speak of men. It is believed—in fact, it is held completely certain—that those same trees never have been cut down or penetrated by anyone. It is not known whether there are paths or roads to follow, and it is believed that time alone is renewing the trees, as happens with other things in this corruptible universe.

Those forests include a large proportion of areas that remain fresh and green throughout the year and, it is said, are full of various animals—in particular, wild swine and mandril cats or, as they are called, apes. These, throughout the night, make themselves heard in a strange, big noise that seems, in that solitude and forest thickness, to be a roar issuing from the Inferno. They say that those apes, in order to pass from one side of the river to the other, link themselves together by their tails, taking hold of one another. Then, emerging on the tops of the trees, they cling to the branches, which, as has been said, project. Then, having let themselves dangle from the branches, the one lowest down launches himself by means of their all swaying together and tries to gain a foothold on the opposite bank of the river, or to catch hold of the other branches and pull all the others over behind him. And they do this when fleeing or overcoming the current of the river, which is very great.

Finally we navigated that river for nineteen days. Living was very difficult because of lack of bread, instead of which I had to eat some of the bananas mentioned above, which are roasted while green and cooked under embers after being peeled.

Then we reached a place called the House of Crosses, where His Majesty has certain warehouses, for the reception of merchandise, which is transported thence little by little on muleback to the city of Panama, distant from that Casa de Cruces or warehouse by fifteen miles, and from Nombre de Dios sixty miles, traveling across the land that prevents the Atlantic and the Sea of the South from joining. And because in that season it does nothing but rain, as happens all over the Torrid Zone, and especially in its northern part, in the four months of May, June, July and August, and because the route is so bad that nothing worse can ever be imagined, they put all of the merchandise into certain bundles or small parcels. These are put together so that each weighs no more than one hundred pounds, so that each of the beasts can carry two of them despite the terrible route, which they can cover, with great difficulty, in fourteen or fifteen hours. During that time, the beasts move along constantly sunk in mud up to their bellies. It is so narrow that if two of them meet, it is possible only with great difficulty for them to step to one side and pass. Both sides of the path are wild, shut-in, solid forest containing no path other than this one, which was made by hand to permit passage.

The drivers who lead the mules all are black slaves, naked and going along behind, constantly sunk in the mud up to mid-thigh, beating the beasts. And this labor is performed only by them, being a fatigue and torment that never could be borne by white men or done by others the way they do it, on foot. But not even they last long in it, but soon die, miserably paralyzed and covered with sores, which in that climate become incurable with a little scratching because of the heat and the excess of humidity of the region. And the beasts too very often are left behind, skinned along the way, there where their loads likewise remain even, as often happens, if they are of silver or of gold. But these are in no danger of being stolen, there being no place to bear them off to. So they must perforce be returned to Panamá, whence they come, or taken to Nombre de Dios, to which that same path leads.

The rest is all a thicket of impenetrable forests. Besides which, throughout all the West Indies one finds this happiness, that there one encounters neither assassins nor people who commit robbery on the way or even in the houses. And one can go from one place to another with silver and with gold, as they say, in hand without carrying arms of any sort for defending oneself. For the Indians do not carry them either, . . . and the Spaniards do not give themselves over to the infamy of robbing, not even those who have been known as disreputable men in Spain, but who, it is observed, having reached the Indies, are completely changed in character, becoming virtuous and trying to live civilly. . . .

But to return to the subject of the bundles, I say that, in order to protect them from the rain, which is certain to come on that very day, they wrap the bundles up in certain leaves that they call *biao*, which Nature has provided and caused to grow there very large and therefore suitable for such a need. By them, each bundle is protected from the water. And for three *escudos*, two of these bundles, forming a load, are transported from the House of Crosses to Panamá. We had ours transported that way, and with them each of us on a mule that had no mountings or bridle other than a saddle and a halter held in the hand. We traveled the fifteen miles with such weariness and misery that we thought never to reach the desired city of Panamá. Yet on the very evening of the day on which we set out from Casa de Cruces, we arrived, soaked and melancholy. And that was in September, 1594.

The city of Panamá is situated on the other side of that strip of land which divides the Atlantic ocean from the Pacific. And it is distant from the equatorial line by nine and one half degrees toward the north. It is the noblest port of call for everything that goes to and comes from the regions of Peru. All the silver and gold brought back from those regions is unloaded there, and this usually amounts each year to three or four million gold *escudos*. And thence it is taken now to Porto Bello, on the shore of the other sea, whence, loaded onto the King's galleons, it is borne to Havana, a port and fortress situated on the island of Cuba, opposite the mainland of Florida, at twenty-two and one half degrees of the northern part and distant 850 miles, more or less, from the port of Porto Bello. Thence, thereafter, together with other treasures arriving from the provinces of New Spain and other parts of the Indies, these things finally are transported to Seville, in Spain.

The houses of this city of Panamá are made of wood, and the men who live in them all are Spanish merchants who are very rich, especially in cattle. And some of the men there cannot count their cattle, which are too great in number. The city, which is governed by a number of judges who make up a tribunal that they call the Audiencia Real, is without other outsiders or any sort of men except the slaves who serve the Spaniards. Of those slaves, all of whom are blacks, many have fled to a strong location in the midst of those forests, where, so as not to be oppressed, they have founded and constructed a settlement. And the Spaniards are content to let them live in their manner, in that liberty which they have taken, under the condition that they remain peaceful and do no harm and do not receive new fugitives into their settlement.

This port of Panamá is marvelous for the enormous flood and ebb of that sea which, when retiring, leaves bare three or four miles of that coast. And then the new water returns with such fury every twelve hours—taking six hours to wane and six to wax—that a man on a running horse could escape only with great difficulty from the waves at the beginning of that flood. For that reason, large ships cannot remain in that port, but stop at the islands that they call Las Perlas, so named because of the fishing that they do in that sea, about forty-five miles distant from Panamá. Then, wanting to take on cargo for Peru, they approach another island, which they call Pericos, named so because of certain small parrots that are born there in abundance. That island is much closer and handier to the city of Panamá.

There we stayed until November, 1594, enjoying the veal that, in abundance and at very low prices, they also eat on the Sabbath Day and three days each week during Lent— that is, Sunday, Tuesday, and Thursday—by permission of the Church. This is permitted because of the lack in that place of fish and of every other sort of Lenten food. No sorts of vegetables grow there. Everything is brought in from outside, even the wheaten flour for making bread, which comes from Peru and is cheaper when it reaches there than that which is brought from Spain. This is a result of the great expense in transporting it by land from Porto Bello to Panamá. . . .

Voyage from Panama City to Lima, Peru

. . . We embarked from Panamá City at the beginning of November, 1594, together with our merchandise on one of those ships which are arranged and suitable for making such voyages, but are different from other ships because, in order to reach Peru, it is necessary to sail constantly against the wind, keeping the bow close to the wind. For in that sea no wind but the south wind, sirocco, which the Spaniards call south, southeast, and southwest winds, breathes throughout the entire year. Including day and night, we were advancing little by little, twelve or fifteen miles traveled during a day, and this by making a turn toward the land during the daylight, another turn out to sea by night. In that voyage of no more than 1,200 miles, one puts in no less than two months and a half of time. And because of its being such wearisome navigation, for any merchandise except metals one pays as freight fifteen and sixteen *giulii* for every twenty-five sixteen-ounce pounds.

Not all ships are good for making these voyages, but only those built especially for this navigation. These are very wide from the middle toward the prow and narrow toward the poop. And they are entirely flat, without any kind of super-structure, and are open above the first deck from the middle of the mainmast down, so that it is impossible to stow in that space the boat which ships customarily carry and have on covered decks, a thing which cannot be done with these ships because it would impede the navigation. For, permitting the wind to enter, it would prevent the ship from advancing. And that is the reason why, on these ships, it is not possible to be comfortably protected on deck, except for the captain and the other few who have the poop. The rest of the passengers, no matter who they are, must remain uncovered day and night throughout that voyage.

And that was our fate, to be on top of our cases. There, because the rainy season still was not completely over, we suffered the greatest torment and insupportable discomfort, to such a degree that my father took gravely sick and would have died if the courtesy and charity of a friend who accommodated him in the covered space he had, had not freed him from it. But the rains lasted only a few days for, as we passed to the other side of the equinoctial line toward the Antarctic and drew close to the continent of the land of Peru, they suddenly stopped. This both because the rainy season had passed and because, in that area, for a distance of a thousand miles along the sea, it never rains at any time of the year. And only in those months when the sun, being in its southern band, returns toward the equinoctial line, beginning at the end of December and continuing till March, is the sky covered with thick clouds from which is distilled a sort of dew so fine that they call it *garúa* and we would call it sailors' fog or wasted mist. But inland, fifteen or twenty miles within that entire area located between the Tropic and the abovementioned line, it rains a lot during that period when the sun is traversing that region.

Along the aforesaid coast, the inhabitants are not obliged to cover their houses with tile to protect themselves from the rain, but only with certain mats woven from cane and covered with earth, which shelter them from the air and from the sun. And therefore the houses of the city of Lima are made from crude bricks not plastered on the outside. Nor is it the custom to make the houses high, but all low and of only one story, and not of hard stones, as they could be built if the people wished. And the reason why they do not do so is the great and terrifying earthquakes, which are felt with the greatest frequency throughout all those regions, where whole cities are ruined by such catastrophes. In that year of 1595, when I was in Lima, came one so great that, we being at table eating supper, everything was turned upside down. And, terrified by such awful events, we all fled into the streets, as all the others do, retiring to open spaces and into the gardens and plazas so as to avoid the ruins of the houses and other buildings, in which they all live on the ground floors. But this earthquake caused no damage, and lasted only a short time.

Turning back to the navigating, I say that on that route one makes stops and takes on provisions all along that coast, the harbors of which are inhabited by native Indians, now Christians subjected and tributary to the Spaniards. From them, with our ship at anchor, we took on provisions, especially at two places. At a port called Santa, where I disem-

barked with some Spaniards on certain rafts of seven or
eight timbers tied together, lighter than cork and eight or
nine arms long, which those Indians use when fishing, moving them by means of oars, which they handle like ladles,
and also by sails. With those rafts they take to the ships
that pass there various supplies of the region, such as fish,
hens, pigs, sheep, calves, and many fruits of the region, and
in particular certain roots called *patatas* [potatoes], white
in color. These, when boiled or roasted under embers, have
a better, more delicate and agreeable flavor than our chestnuts, and can be served in place of bread. They bring bread
made of maize flour, in cakes as thin as leaves and toasted,
so that one seems to be eating something like our long wa-
fers and very pleasing to the taste.

There I saw two things that seemed as marvelous to me
as I had been told in advance that they would be: that
there were certain wells of water from the surface of which
is dug a grease or bitumen something like liquefied pitch,
but much greasier, thin and liquid. The Spaniards use this
for tarring and smearing the ropes and shrouds of their
ships. A huge quantity of this bitumen (asphalt) is taken
out, thus making a profit for the owners of the land that
generate it. The other marvel was a tooth as large as a fist
and a tibia or leg bone longer than half a man. Those two
things, the tooth and the tibia, the Indians said, came from
a huge man who had died there; and they asserted that in
other times there had been a large quantity of such men
who had arrived as strangers and then had been undone
and killed by the many natives of the region, receiving that
treatment for their bad behavior and the ill-omened ways
with which they had used the Indians. But be that as it may,
I saw one thing and the other, and they seemed to me to be
of the human sort, as the Indians asserted them to be.

Later I returned to the ship with the others. That same
evening, again unfurling our sails to the wind, we continued
our voyage, always coasting along the land. Then we did
not stop until another port, called Paita, farther on, at
about the midway point of the entire route, a place five

degrees from the equinoctial line toward the Antarctic pole. It lies in a benign climate of the purest, most brilliant, and most limpid sky that can be seen or imagined, and it has air so mild that the inhabitants, not being driven by it, are content to live on the sand, into which they drive bunches of cane bound together in the manner of basket-work, making from them the walls and then forming with them the rooms of their poor houses. These they later cover with mats or with the leaves of trees, thus protecting themselves from the sun and from the brightness of the air. In that air, shining in its clarity, the moon is clearer and renders more light than in any other part of the world whatever which I have seen, and in such a way that a common saying in that region for a man wanting to affirm that something is not to be doubted is: "It is clearer than the moon of Paita." In its splendor and brilliance it equals the light of the sun, and this comes about because of the reflection from the fields of sand which are there.

We stayed eight days in that place at exactly the time of the full moon, and thus saw its effect, which certainly was a wonderful thing. We were provided with every sort of refreshment; things abound there, especially salted fish of many kinds, all of them good, which are taken on there as merchandise and carried to the city of Lima to be sold. Many of our passengers landed at the place, it being possible to go on from there overland easily, even though it is necessary to pass through a sandy desert for three or four days. For that reason, one must carry drink and food for oneself and for the animals. As for the rest, it is a safe region and inhabited only by peaceful Indians who are subject and tributary to the Spaniards. But we, returning to our ship, were pleased to pursue our voyage by sea. And without any further stop, we arrived at the port of Lima, called Callao, two miles away, located twelve degrees toward the austral pole from the equinoctial line.

The city, also called "of the Kings," is situated alongside a stream called the Rimac, from which it takes its name. There, in all majesty, as the chief man of the entire province, resides the viceroy, sent from Spain to govern that kingdom for three years, during which he is paid three or four hundred thousand escudos. And very often the viceroy, who has governed Mexico, headquarters of the kingdom of New Spain, succeeds to the government of the city of Lima, headquarters, beginning, and end of all the traffic of that area. In that city live and remain many households of important Spanish gentlemen and merchants. They live with more cleanliness and splendor than in any other part of the West Indies, being served by male and female black slaves, usually bought when they do not know either how to speak or how to do anything, and therefore at a price of four hundred escudos each. Of such slaves, as fancy strikes them, they sometimes buy a female, not beautiful but knowing how to do something, for seven or eight hundred escudos. And while I stayed there I saw a dealer in wine and foods buy one for the abovementioned low price.

But on festive days it is stupefying to see those blacks as they go about superbly dressed in silk and with pearls, and even with gold. And the dances that they assemble together to do in the plazas of the city are no less pleasing to the eye. Of even greater wonder is to see the grandeur and splendor of dress of the wives of the Spaniards, and of everything else that denotes vainglory. The amounts of silver and gold, the expenditures and ostentation, all are so large that any who lack a capital of fifty or one hundred thousand escudos are given no thought, being unable to measure up to the grandness of the others, and from that point on are called peddlers rather than merchants, by a saying of the region.

All over the city and in all the shops, one constantly sees silver in great quantities. And there is no cobbler who does not eat off it, for all of it from the mines of Potosí and all the other provinces comes there. Many merchants, having a treasure of three and four hundred bars and ingots of silver, each worth about five hundred *escudos,* pile them up and then, spreading mattresses on them, use them as beds for sleeping. These same merchants often purchase huge quantities of goods coming from Spain, and of all kinds mixed together, spending from one to two hundred thousand escudos, and doing so with greater security and ease than one of us buys a bit of salad. They accept these things as packed, without seeing either their quality or their condition, and depend for both measure and weight or quantity upon the documents and notes of whoever sells the merchandise to them. And they agree to the price and promise to pay a certain percentage of profit above cost and expenses on the part of the merchant selling to them. At other times, when the merchandise is well assorted and includes things good for these regions—such as linen fabrics, woolens, silk and gold stuffs, which are the chief ones —they buy, as they call it, at the impost price. This is an ancient method of valuation used with every sort of merchandise, to which they further add, above the stated amount of the valuation, ten or twelve per cent according to the assortment and quantity there may be of the less desirable things that have a higher impost and of those which are better and have a lower one. This is the way that they contract for the stuff and merchandise that come from Spain. In return for this, they take away from these provinces of Peru nothing but silver and gold, there being no other sort of goods.

Foodstuffs are very costly there, especially fresh fish, this from lack of anyone to go to fish for it, as the Spaniards hold fishing to be a vile thing to do, and the Indians cannot carry it on, being so few—and becoming fewer and fewer from day to day because of the ill treatment accorded to them. Those who remain seem not to care, and if nonetheless they do go to fish, they do it under duress and by order of justice. In the morning they come from their houses, each carrying on his head a bunch of a certain variety of very small reeds, a sort that grows alongside rivers or in marshes. These are bound together like sheaves of straw that are thick at one end and thin at the other, six or seven arms long. Thus bundled together, a sheaf is put into the water. An Indian gets onto each sheaf, some-

times astride and sometimes seated with his legs pulled in
and crossed. And with a certain paddle in hand, pushing
his sheaf forward while it serves him as a little boat to go
wherever he most wishes, each of them often travels ten or
fifteen miles across that sea, fishing with nets and with
hooks. And they look like marine monsters. And they make
their catches and quickly go back to shore, where they sell
what fish they have brought to those who there are await-
ing them. Each of them then recovers his sheaf from the
water, takes it to his house, and there unbinds it, laying
the reeds out in the air to dry. Then they bind them together again as before.

That is the reason why fish are so costly. Hens, further,
are worth ten or twelve *giulii* each, and their eggs cost half
a *giulio* each, that half-*giulio* being the smallest money
worth anything, even though silver quarter-*giulii* exist. But
with these one scarcely can buy a little salad—of which, as
of every other variety of garden produce, there is an abundance, especially of lettuce of marvelous size and with leaves
incomparably longer than ours, and an infinity of local
fruits of strange qualities and shapes, having the most diverse tastes and names. . . . Those of us who reached there
in the month of January, 1595, ate melons, figs, and grapes,
all in perfection and in good condition And in the province of Cuzco it is always said that grapes are to be found
fresh upon the vines, which bear fruit at different times of
the year according to the sort and situation of the land,
the air in which they are cultivated, and the way of har-
vesting them at different times and seasons, it being possible to do that when one wishes because it is always spring
and summer, never winter.

There are also trees, and in particular fig trees like ours,
which in one year produce fruit twice, once on the side
facing toward the north, once on the other side, facing
toward the south. And this is said to be because of the
movement that the sun makes, for in that climate it shifts
the shadows twice each year as it goes and comes between
the equinoctial line and the Tropic of Capricorn. Finally,

they can have all the things as they wish them at any time
of the year because it always is the same season. Similarly,
they bring in a fine supply of quince-pears that are very
good if eaten raw, but much better as made into a confec-
tion; and also melons that are exquisite and of the same
variety as ours. And no one leaves there without having
found them excellent. That results, I think, for its never
raining in that region and from the strength of the sun,
which nonetheless is tempered by the water that they bring
from the rivers, irrigating with it the fields and whatever
land they want to use for their sowings and other cultivation. The crops, again, become fattened by those waters,
which come from the mountains, most often turbulently
because up there it rains a lot. . . . As for maize, which is
the general food of the natives throughout those Indies, it
is gathered four or five times a year.

Additionally, this whole kingdom abounds today in wines
and oil because of the cultivation of vines and olive trees,
introduced there by the Spaniards, which thrive admirably
there. During the period when I was there, they produced
so much wine that it not only sufficed for the need of that
region, but also accommodated the province of Mexico and
other regions where it is not produced because of the rains
that occur during the four months and which do not permit
them to irrigate or to mature grapes well enough to make
wine from them. . . .

So there is no other drink there than the one made
from maize, which comes to be bearable. The people of
that region call it *chicha*, and they make it from maize
ground up and soaked and then cooked in the water with
which it has been infused, a very dirty thing if it is true
that the maize first is pulled apart by the teeth and then
masticated by old women with slobbering mouths. Be that
as it may, the truth is that this drink is disagreeable to the
sight and worse to the taste, though of much substance and
nourishment, and of such strength and smokiness as to be
more intoxicating than wine made from grapes, which in
that region they harvest exactly at the time when among

us the vines are pruned. And the wine is exactly like that of Spain, and they produce so much of it that in order to make room for the new at the time of the vintage, they throw away the old, so to speak. That the gathering should be done at a different time from ours is not to be marveled at, as it all is caused and governed by the sun, the generating father of all things, which in those months visits and makes his home between the equinoctial line and the Tropic of Capricorn. At the very time when this causes autumn and winter among us, to them on the contrary it brings spring and summer.

Finding myself in those regions during that season, I passed the most comfortable, pleasant, and delectable Lent that could be imagined because of the convenience of the many fruits and greens that come in that period of penitence, during which places for making devotions are not lacking anywhere in the city, which has a cathedral church with its archbishop and other members of the clergy. There are the Jesuits, the Franciscans, the Dominicans, and the Augustinians, all of whom—in fine churches, and with sumptuousness and reverence—administer the Holy Sacraments to the Spaniards who are in that region, and do it with the commodity and order already mentioned.

Further, they do not lack jennet horses of the Spanish breed for their use and recreation. And they also have other sorts of beasts, both mules and asses, for their needs, and in such unnumbered quantities that in the province of Chile, located thirty-five degrees toward the Antarctic pole, they do not count the number of these animals, and whoever wants them goes into the country and catches them, and they cost nothing beyond the business of taming them. There, also, they have beasts of burden native to the region, which the Spaniards very wrongly call *carneros*—that is, rams—but Indians call llamas. When I saw these, they at once seemed to me to resemble small camels in everything except the lack of a hump, as they have the neck, the head, and the feet of those animals, but altogether are smaller in both body and strength. Their flesh is good to

eat, their wool for making cloth for the Indians. These are
very domestic animals, simple and peaceful, but so extraor-
dinarily stubborn and headstrong that they will move along
only in their own way and at their own wish. Feeling weary,
or having some other humor, they throw themselves down
to lie on the ground even if they have burdens on their
backs, and it is impossible to make them get up again even
if one wants to kill them, such is their obstinacy. And for
that reason a custom has arisen in that region of saying to
a stubborn person: "You are a llama."

These animals are employed in transporting light loads,
of one hundred pounds in weight, from one place to another, and especially to carry the coca from Cuzco to Potosí.
This is a leaf that the Indians keep constantly in their
mouths, chewing it together with a small amount of ground
lime, which they always carry at their belts in an animal
horn, having this leaf there also, wrapped in a rag. They
say that chewing this leaf gives them strength and vigor,
and such is the superstition and faith that they have in it
that they cannot work or go on trips without having it in
their mouths. And, on the contrary, having it, they work
happily and walk a day or two without refreshing themselves otherwise or eating anything other than what they
swallow of the saliva brought on by chewing the leaves. I
have seen these leaves on sale in the aforementioned city
of Lima, and they are like those of the almond, but much
greener in color and somewhat smaller.

Having made a trial of chewing the leaf, I found—and
believe—that it has no flavor beyond a certain delicacy and
oiliness that make it into an unguent as one masticates it.
They tell it as certain that more than thirty or forty thousand escudos worth of this coca is consumed each year, and
most of it is bought by the Indians who labor and dig out
silver in the mines of Potosí, in which five thousand Indians
and more work uninterruptedly, day and night. And they
will not go in without that leaf, and so must have both
their mouths and their pockets full. And they must have
rubbed their picks with the leaf out of vain superstition,

because it seems to them to give strength to iron as it does to men. . . .

And to finish with the city of Lima, I say that it is a very rich place because of the innumerable mines of silver and gold which are in that region, and in particular those of the mountains of Potosí, nine hundred miles distant from that city, being down twenty-two degrees from the Tropic of Capricorn. . . .

The region is healthful enough because of the climate, which is so warm and dry that one never finds water by digging in the ground. For that reason, they bring water into this city of Lima in open canals for use in their gardens. These canals, then, running through all the streets, also serve for irrigation, and thus for keeping down the dust and thereby rendering the streets fresh. And, public fountains for the purpose of drinking are not lacking in the plazas and all the other pleasant spots of the city. In the churches there, the dryness being so great, in order to bury the dead it is necessary to throw a quantity of water over the grave so that the earth, thus dampened, may be able to consume the body more quickly and leave room for others. This dryness gives rise to a certain variety of small animals that are generated in the rooms of the houses like fleas, and jump like them, though for the rest they have the shape of worms. These, insinuating themselves between the nails and the flesh of the toes, bore in little by little, nibbling at the flesh as a borer does at wood. There they grow so fat that very often they cause a sore that brings about loss of the toes before one notices that the damage has been done and is incurable. And this occurs because they enter when they are very small, and therefore make a hole so tiny that it scarcely is seen or even felt. These little animals are called chiggers, and they especially attack those who go barefoot. To free oneself from them it is necessary, once they have been detected, to pay careful attention to digging these little animals out diligently from the toes or wherever they may be, being careful not to break them, as when broken they spread in the sore a quantity of eggs from which so many are born that it no longer is possible to dispose of their seed. But if one digs them out whole and without crushing them, one is easily cured if afterwards one places in the hole a little ink, which thus is used as a medication.

In that city we sold all our merchandise. And having converted it into some bars of silver of seventy or eighty pounds each, we began to think of leaving that place, where we had been from the month of January until that of May, 1595, and of going on to the kingdom and provinces of New Spain. There we thought to buy merchandise with the aforesaid silver.

Arrival at Mexico City

We departed from Acapulco and went overland with our silver to the City of Mexico. Along the road we reached a river, and because there is no accommodation for crossing it, neither a bridge nor a ferry, it was necessary for us to do what others do. We placed ourselves on a mass of thick, dry gourds, bound together with a netting of cane. On that we placed the saddle of our horse, which swam across. On that saddle we sat down. Then four of those Indians, one at each corner of the raft of bound gourds, swam, pushing it and directing it to the opposite bank of the river and breaking through that current of water. This is a thing no less perilous than tedious, and especially for the great quantity and value of goods that pass there each year. Nevertheless, it must be done, and even the viceroy passes by there with the same difficulty and danger when he goes from Mexico to embark at that port of Acapulco and pass over to governing Peru.

We reached the City of Mexico in a few days. It is located at twenty degrees toward the north from the equinoctial, in a place as beautiful and delightful and abundant in every deliciousness as could be imagined or seen in the whole world. The city is well located, and also is built in the modern style by the Spaniards, with the houses of stone and lime, almost all of them with a sidewalk, along the straight, wide streets. These, crossing one another, form very beautiful and perfect squares, with three or four very ample and beautiful plazas, and with fountains there and in places easily available to the public. And finally, it is decorated and crowded with those conveniences that Nature and industry can concede to a well-planned city.

Furthermore, there are many canals of water which flow by diverse routes and enter the lake on which the city is based. And on them the people come and go, conducting their daily lives and everything else of which they have need with much comfort. Above these canals they make fields on branches woven together (*chinampas*), thus recovering land that has fallen to the bottom of the lake. For that reason they move these fields from one place to another, now into the shade, now into the sun, as they please or have need to do. And there they cultivate diverse things with much artfulness. And overland arrives everything that the fleets from Spain bring to Vera Cruz, port of the northern sea, which is distant from the City of Mexico another 240 miles. Thus the city is equidistant from the two seas, the South and the North, that is, the Atlantic and the Pacific.

Also, there are very beautiful churches and convents, in particular of the Augustinian monks. Because of inadvertence on the part of the first founders of their church, it is almost submerged to the height of a man, the foundation not having been placed on timbers, as it should have been. And that same thing has befallen all the other churches, including those of Santo Domingo and San Francisco. But it has not happened to that of the Society of Jesus, the Jesuits having arrived later and, using the experience of what had occurred to the others and joining it to their own shrewdness, having found a way to rest their building on timbers stuck into the water of the lake. And it is built of a certain spongy stone, pink in color and very light in weight (*tezontle*), almost like that of the buildings of Leghorn, but much harder. And in my time they were proceeding with their College, a very sumptuous and beautiful structure, as is that inhabited by the viceroy, located on one of the plazas in which there is also the cathedral, which had not been completed in my time. There one still sees a tablet formed from a huge, thick stone worked in a round shape on which are carved various figures in half-relief, and with a small gutter in the middle through which ran the blood of men who here were sacrificed in the times of the Mexican nobles in honor of their idols, of which one sees the remains still throughout the city, walled up in the exterior walls of the buildings erected by the Spaniards, placed there to express the triumph of their foundation.

Finally, to say in a few words everything that occurs to me, I say that in this very beautiful city everything and every good is to be had in supreme perfection and abundance, especially jennet horses of the Spanish race, these because of the benefit from a certain grass that grows in the lake. It resembles rushes, but is stumpy and very tender, and it is green all year. And because of it, the jennets are as plump as could be desired.

Near the City of Mexico is another very large city, today called Santiago, which is entirely inhabited by Indians, who are greatly diminishing in numbers in that area. When I was there, they were dying off rapidly from a certain illness. After having been a little ailing, they lost their blood through their noses and dropped dead, a catastrophe visited only upon them, not upon the Spaniards. The latter, through the bad treatment that they give the Indians, also are a cause of their dying off. Coming from Acapulco, I saw along the way that they used them to carry their things, loading them like beasts. And when they reached some hamlet or walled place or village—of which many were to be found all along that road, but most of them without inhabitants—they wanted every one of their needs to be served and taken care of, as the Indians are forced to take care of them by order and commandment of the administration of that region.

For that reason, no inns being found, it is ordered in each place where there is a population of Indians that a house be set aside and stocked with everything that may serve simply to lodge and feed the travelers. The house is said to be "communal," but not a single person lives in it. A traveler having arrived, he summons the chief Indian of that people, who is called the *toppile*. And he appears with great speed and submissiveness, and punctually does whatever is commanded, which is to bring food for the men and their mounts. Frightened by the Spaniards' threats, he sees that this is done, ordering from among his Indians here one thing and there another—that is, you or someone bring the bread, you the wine, you the meat, you the straw, and you the oats. And thus the other things as well, so that in a trice everything is put in order and taken to the communal house. And then very often when the accounts are figured, instead of giving the Indians money in payment, they give evil words and worse deeds. Thus, through this and other inhuman treatment, God allows their end. And it is believed that within a short time all of them will have died out, as has occurred on the island of Santo Domingo and in other places that were thickly populated when Columbus discovered them, but now remain deserted, quite without inhabitants. . . .

BALSA DE GUAYAQUIL
dibujada con sus proporciones.

B. Proa.
C. Popa.
D. La Ramada ò Casa.
E. Cabria que sirve de Palo.
F. Bolinero.
G. Guara.
G. Remo que sirve de Guar y Timon.
H. La Cozina.
I. Botijas de Aguada.
K. Botijas de Aguada.
K. Proas ò Obenques.
L. Barbacoa ò Culvert.

A flat-bottom boat made in Guayaquil for travel
along the coast of South America.

II

Seventeenth Century

Inhabitants of Peru in typical dress,
with a two-wheeled cart in the background.

✺ 5 ✺

Anonymous Description
of Peru
(1600-1615)

*The road from viceregal Lima on the coast to Cuzco
in the Andean highlands was the main traveled highway of South America throughout the colonial centuries, and its most detailed description is contained
in an anonymous account of a Portuguese Jew discovered early in this century in the National Library
at Paris. By ingenious deductions from internal evi-
dence and notarial records, a distinguished Peruvian
historian positively identifies the author as Pedro de
León Portocarrero, a merchant who traveled and
lived in Peru, chiefly Lima, for over a decade, from
1600 or 1601 to 1615.* It is a lively, spontaneous account, by a victim of the current anti-Semitism in
Spanish lands who probably wished to reveal to alien
interests the vulnerability of the prosperous Peruvian
viceroyalty. While the description of Lima society is
strongly critical, other testimony tends to confirm his
strictures. Less subjective are the illuminating details
of travel conditions on the Lima-Cuzco road, its route,
and the topographical features of the country.*

Portions of this account appeared in *Revista del Archivo Nacional
del Perú*, 17, 1 (1944), 3–44, and are translated by the editor. The
entire narrative is available in *Descripción del Virreinato del
Perú, Crónica inédita de comienzos del Siglo XVII*. Edición,
prólogo, y notas de Boleslao Lewin (Rosario, Argentina, 1958).
 * Guillermo Lohmann Villena, "Una incógnita despejada. La
identidad del Judío Portugués," *Revista Histórica* (Lima, Peru:
1967), vol. 30, 26–93—*I. A. L.*

Lima Society

It is characteristic of the people of Lima and of Peru in general to boast that they bow to no one, even the richer and more powerful. Haughty and inordinately proud, they brag of having a lofty lineage and of being gentlemen of high estate. So pronounced is this mania that, when a humble artisan of Spain comes to this southern continent, he promptly acquires grandiose ideas; he believes at once that his ancestry entitles him to mingle with the best of society. Because of these false concepts and silly notions, many of these newcomers become dissolute and unwilling to work. The luckier ones manage to marry into wealthy families, whereupon they acquire even bigger ideas and assume aristocratic titles. I knew several of these social climbers whose personal enemies and their own blunders exposed them as quite ordinary and insignificant persons. This sort of thing happens because such people refuse to recognize each other's claims; consequently, there are many who envy another's good fortune and, at the slightest slip, cause his downfall.

There are also poor but haughty fellows; they can't bite but they can bark loudly. With heads low they go about sniffing for prey; they have no desire to subordinate themselves, nor is there any reasoning with them. Individuals of that sort are called "soldiers," not because they really are soldiers, but because they go hither and yon with a pack of cards in their hands and lose no opportunity to gamble with anyone they come across. If, by chance, they run into a novice or tenderfoot who is not very bright or whose suspicious nature does not extend to the possibility of a stacked pack of cards, they cheat him out of his money and possessions; sometimes they even win his horse or mule from under him. They are consummate tricksters whose only concern is to master the art of deception.

Many people of that sort are running about Peru, and they are mostly hostile to the rich. They are ever ready for

riots, disturbances, and untoward events in the realm, for
these are occasions when they can steal and run off with
things that they cannot hope to acquire except by such
disruptions of law and order. They have absolutely no desire to be useful. They go about well-dressed, for some
Negro or Indian woman, or several Spanish women—and
not necessarily the poverty-stricken ones, either—clothe and
feed them because these men are their partners by night
and brawling companions by day. Those same women hire
old people who are weak because of age to act as squires,
accompanying them to Mass and on social calls. These
vagabonds outnumber respectable people in Peru and they
are too many to find work for. From stories heard daily of
experiences that others have had with these ne'er-do-wells,
few householders want them as servants. Instead, they hire
Negroes, and so these Spaniards roam about, getting a living any way they can.

A different and less numerous breed take to soldiering,
since every year recruits are sent from Lima to Chile. This
type is not so clever, nor so free and easy in the art of
flattery, and they lack the means to wander from one region
to another like tramps. Usually they are slightly more dis-
posed to accept employment, especially in the exercise of
arms, by which they can live off the king's bounty. This
element marches off with banners flying to fight against the
Araucanian Indians after receiving 200 pesos in Lima with
which to buy clothes. In this way the country is rid of
them and troops are available to make war on the indomi-
table Araucanians. Few ever return to Peru.

If the men are arrogant and haughty, the women are
conceited and presumptuous; since they are good-looking
and pride themselves on being clever and wise, they regard
themselves as nobler than Cleopatra, Queen of Egypt. So far
as being spendthrift and lascivious, they quite resemble her;
all are fond of clothes and even more of eating, and all
want to be social equals. There are, however, inequalities
and divergences among them. Where suitable resources are
lacking, lovers make up the difference. They do not bother

with impoverished paramours, for there are always plenty
of available Negro and Indian women for them. Since these
hussies always have finery and luxuries, they like to display
themselves strolling about in public. If their husbands become aware of the life they are leading and try to bring
them to account, then the faithless wives start screaming.
If their legal mates press matters hard, the women resort
to stratagems to bring about a separation. They clamor for
divorce and forsake their husbands. During my stay I knew
of more than twenty separation suits instituted before the
archbishop and his provisor by women who wanted to avoid
living with their legal mates. In one instance the woman's
husband was worth over 500,000 pesos. With only the desire to satisfy their carnal appetites, the sole thought of
these women is to pursue pleasure and they never reflect
on what may happen to them later. All who tread this path
come to a bad end as experience daily proves.

There are many kinds of such people. They have little
talent and less disposition to work; dissipation has made
them flabby but they are always ready for occasions of
gaiety, of which there is no lack. Aristocratic ladies partici-
pate in these festive diversions and any of them who are
inept in small talk or who wear less conspicuous finery are
considered distinctly *declassée*. Therefore they practice beforehand how they will talk so as to draw attention, and
they plan the effects that they will produce. Because of their
greed and vices and the fact that few really know each
other, they lose all fear of God and are devoid of a sense
of shame. There is no guile or deceit that they do not practice: a father does not spare his child, a woman her husband,
a brother his sister. Like the Indians, they unabashedly take
up with any woman whatever when they are drunk, and
the Spaniard stops at nothing whatever it may be . . .

Then what a lot of faked miracles! I once saw a soldier
who had come from Chile. He pretended he was crippled
in both legs and went to an empty chapel of the Dominican monastery for a nine day vigil. At the end of that period he sprang up, leaped about, and ran around like a

person with no afflictions at all, falsely alleging that St. Dominic had cured him. A public procession celebrated this assumed miracle, but it was soon realized that the soldier was merely a big cheat and a liar.

On another occasion I saw an old hag flogged, branded as a criminal, and paraded in a public *auto* of the Inquisition for having fooled the most aristocratic ladies of Lima with her tricks of sorcery. I also witnessed the burning of sodomites at the stake, including a captain of high repute.

The Negroes and Indians are more barbarous than before they came in contact with the Spaniards because then there was no one to corrupt them. Now they are full of superstition, practice witchcraft, and have commerce with the Devil, whom the Indians call *supay*. I saw Indians punished in an *auto* of the Inquisition, which is illegal by strict command of the king and the Pope; only secular courts have jurisdiction over their crimes. Numerous idols formerly worshiped by the Indians were burned in a huge bonfire of that *auto de fe*, while Indians were flogged and had their heads shaven, which, to them, is the greatest disgrace. The Negroes are much given to rascality and are so perverse that even the Devil can't deal with them!

I speak of these matters broadly, but I could do so in detail. I report these things so that the disreputable and dishonest dealings of the different groups may be recognized and comprehended, for they stop at nothing and have little fear of God. Any land or people who do not fear the Lord can only come to a bad end; everything in this world has its limits.

Lima and Peru generally have people from well-known cities, towns, and villages of Spain. There are representatives of the Portuguese, Gallicians, Asturians, Basques, Navarrese, Aragonese, Valencians, natives of Murcia, French, Italians, Germans, Flemish, Greeks, people from Ragusa, Corsicans, Genoese, Mallorquins, Canary Islanders, English, Moors, and immigrants from India and China; also, there are a great many mixed elements. They all differ in origin, in social circumstances, and in temperament. The

Basques and the men from Extremadura are especially hostile to each other, because the latter conquered Peru, while today the Basques are the wealthiest in this realm and occupy the best offices of the crown. Consequently, the Extremadurans are at odds with them, and a deep enmity prevails. Furthermore, the poor, as is ever the case in the history of mankind, hate the rich.

Since the Creoles, the American born Spaniards, have little fondness for work, they are quite vain about their aristocratic pretensions. Many dabble in theological studies and become clergymen and friars, while their womenfolk go into nunneries. Since most nuns in the convents are assured of board and clothes, they have no inclination to venture forth and take risks anywhere to earn a living. If these Creoles had no contact with people coming from Spain, they would surely relapse into barbarism and ignorance. Every corner of every street in Lima has a *pulperia,* which is a food and wine shop, and every one of them is prosperous because they make a huge profit on everything sold. Lima has kilns for glass-blowing and the manufacture of clay crockery, earthen jugs, jars, and all kinds of tableware for the poor. But no one, however poor, is without a piece of silver of some kind, or without a Negro man or woman servant. In the restricted Indian quarter of Lima, a monthly *mita* takes place. This is a system of drafting forced labor by viceregal decree to work on the farms and in the truck gardens of owners who pay three *reales* a day. During the summer the lowland Yungas Indians perform this obligatory service, and the highland natives do so in the winter. These natives cannot avoid this labor draft because local magistrates are duty bound to impose it and the officials in charge of the Indians must carry it out.

Lima's commercial activity is considerable both by land and by sea. All manufactured products and crops of the realm come to this center, and merchandise goes out from it overland and by water to every part of Peru, to the Kingdom of New Granada, to Tucumán, and to the

Kingdom of Chile. Annually 100,000 pesos' worth of goods
go at the king's expense to the military forces in Chile.
Ships sail from the seaport of Callao with wines to Nicara-
gua and to ports along the whole coast of Guatemala. From
December to April merchants come from all over Peru to
trade in Lima; some send merchandise back to their local
communities, while others forward bars of silver to Spain
and then return home.

Lima and the Peruvian lowlands are subject to frequent
earthquakes. On the afternoon of Saturday, October 19,
1609, I experienced a tremor that knocked down over 500
houses in a brief space of time, and not a single one escaped
being cracked open like a pomegranate. The damage to
the cathedral alone was estimated at 200,000 pesos. I happened to be in the town of Ica fifty leagues from Lima on
November 26, 1605, when an earthquake lasting a quarter
of an hour destroyed many buildings. Arica, the seaport of
Potosí, was suddenly jolted, the sea swept in, houses col-
lapsed and were covered by sand. Its inhabitants managed
to escape by taking refuge on a hill adjoining the town.
The royal warehouses and storehouses of wine were flooded,
and damage was great all along the coast. When earth
tremors shake Lima, everyone rushes into the middle of
the streets, into the public squares, patios, and yards. The
highlands are less subject to earthquakes.

While Lima and Peru in general have people of evil
disposition, they also have good, God-fearing souls who
are honorable, kind, and anxious to do good. But I must
report that, during my fifteen years in Lima, over sixty
merchants went bankrupt. The smallest business failure
amounted to over 100,000 pesos, while others totaled more
than 200,000 pesos. The many bankruptcies resulted from
buying a lot of merchandise on credit, which remained un-
sold; when it was turned over to other dealers, also on
credit, they, in turn, were unable to pay. Excessive expenditures and dishonest employees were also factors con-
tributing to these bankruptcies. Thus it is that everything
is variable in the Indies and nothing is fixed or stable.

God alone is steadfast and His words are truth. He leads us along paths of righteousness and away from all evil, guiding us along the road to divine service. Amen.

The Journey from Lima to Apurimac

. . . After leaving Lima on the road leading to the highlands, one travels steadily east. The Ceneguilla Valley is four leagues due east, and there one proceeds to Chontayllo, an Indian village nine leagues from the sea, which is the whole length of the valley. Scattered about are orchards, cattle ranches, and farms that raise corn, wheat, cucumbers, melons, and other products in abundance, that are harvested in March and April. Much of Lima's firewood comes from this valley. A wealthy chieftain, who owns splendid orchards and gardens, lives in Chontayllo. The fruit of this valley tastes better than the fruit around Lima because the climate is more even.

After crossing the river the road leads to an Indian community called Sisicayo, ten leagues from the capital. Numerous Indian hamlets lie in valleys and on mountain sides within its jurisdiction. From this upland locality one goes upstream, recrossing a river several times, with woods and fruit trees along the way; two leagues of hard going through good and bad stretches bring one to highland Chorillo, an Indian village thirteen leagues from Lima, so called because a nearby stream abruptly drops from a mountain through a gorge over a quarter of a league wide that is cut in a solid mass of rock. The region of heavy rains and thunderstorms begins at Chorillo.

The next place is Guadachería, an Indian hamlet and prosperous farming community. Beyond it several Chapiungas Indian villages are visible in valleys. This locality is known as "Between Hot and Cold" because the chill of the highland hardly reaches it and the heat of the lowlands causes no discomfort; its climate is temperate with rainfall. Potato, wheat, corn, and other crops grow here.

A series of rises and descents bring the traveler to a small *tambo,* or inn, called *Lo Caliente* because it is situated at the beginning of a bleak tableland, the highest part of which bears the name Pariacaca; it is twenty-two leagues from Lima, mostly uphill. Here some travelers become light-headed, feeling a dizzy motion like that experienced by those who go to sea for the first time, and they stagger as if they were drunk; others, however, suffer no effects at all. The snow-topped mountains here are so lofty that they seem to touch the sky.

This stretch is the most strenuous and dreaded in all Peru because it is always stormy and its terrain includes marshy grounds, ponds, streams, high precipices, and difficult passes. The road forks at the beginning of this upland area, one branch of which climbs a staircase, as it is called, because of a series of stone steps; if the mules slip, they tumble into a deep lagoon. It leads to Tunraura, an Indian community in the Jauja Valley, near which the Marañón River flows under a stout stone bridge.

The other branch, called the lower road, crosses a broad stream. At this point the traveler disappears into a large opening in the rocks and journeys underground for more than a league. On re-emerging, he recrosses the river by a natural bridge and comes to some high crags called Pachacaca. With a great roar the river then vanishes again into an opening of a cliff. The rocks there form a huge cavity where travelers camp for the night, their sleep broken by the thunderous crashing of the stream. A dozen or so can make a bed beneath an overhanging rock. Their campfire burns wood that they must bring along, together with enough food and drink. These mountains provide no firewood or food so every traveler comes supplied. If the group is large, personal servants, muleteers, and their mounts sleep in the snow.

All through Peru's mountains are many vicuñas, an animal that produces fine bezoar stones.* As it grazes in

* These were stones found in the entrails of animals and were thought to have great medicinal qualities. An interesting account

the open country, it often feeds on noxious weeds and
grass. When it senses that it is poisoned, the vicuña in-
stinctively knows the plant that is an antidote; this it
looks for, finds, and is then cured. This herb tends to
stimulate the growth of the bezoar stone formed in the
animal's entrails, where it keeps enlarging as long as
the vicuña lives. These stones are plentiful in Peru and
command a good price. Vicuña wool is soft, smooth, and
fine like a beaver's, and it is used for hats and other objects. Its flesh is edible and better than mutton; by drying
it in the sun and wind, unsalted jerked meat is made
resembling dried beef. When combined with peppers,
potatoes, and corn, it makes a tasty and nutritious stew

------

of them is in a curious sixteenth-century work of Nicolás
Monardes. A discussion of the bezoar stone appears in a reprint
of an English translation made in that same period: Stephen
Gaselee (ed.), *Joyfull Newes out of the Newe Worlde writtene
in Spanish by Nicolas Monardes Physician of Seville and
Englished by John Frampton, Merchant, anno 1577*, 2 vols.
(London, New York, 1925), I, 135–139. In Vol. II, p. 25, there
is a section "Of the bezaar (*sic*) stones of the Peru," which
reads in part: "Our Occidentall Bezaar stones have greate
vertues, principallye they doe remedie manye persones, whiche
bee sicke of the Harte . . . in all kinde of Venom, it is the
moste principall remedie that we knowe nowe, and that whiche
hath doone best effect, in many that have been poysoned,
whiche have taken it as well by Venome taken at the mouthe as
by bitinges of venomos wormes, whiche are full of poyson. It doth
truely a marveilous and manifest worke, unto them that have
dronke water standying in a stinkyng lake, beyng infected with
beastes and varmentes whiche are full of poyson. . . ."
A similar belief existed in the United States in the so-called
"madstone" briefly discussed in Gerald Carson, *The Old Country
Store* (New York: E. P. Dutton, 1954), p. 122–123. "What is a
madstone? When a small, hard object lodged in a deer's stomach,
it was sometimes surrounded by a calcium deposit to form a
smooth, round stone, the madstone. . . . The virtue of the
stone was that when applied to the bite of a dog, it told whether
or not the dog was mad. If the stone would not adhere, the dog
did not have rabies. If the dog was infected, or in cases of snake
bite, spider bite, or bee stings, the madstone was popularly
believed to bring relief and drive out poison"—*I. A. L.*

called *locro.* The vicuña, which is about the size of a goat, wanders wild and is swifter and more graceful than any other animal. Whoever catches them does so without interference by anyone. When the Indians wish to entertain local magistrates and other important personages, they organize a hunt called a *chaco.* They gather in large numbers and surround four or six leagues of hills and plains; then they slowly close in on the vicuñas and other animals until they capture them with their hands or, if they prefer, by beating their prey with sticks. The Indians are so overwhelming in numbers that their victims are unable to escape. This kind of a hunt provides great entertainment and enjoyment.

Many *guanacos,* a kind of llama, run wild in the mountains of Peru; neither this species nor the vicuñas breed in the lowlands. The *guanacos* are much larger than our sheep, being taller and longer; the head tops a long neck and its wool is excellent; it is either white or dark brown. They are the best and most profitable livestock in the world because they carry loads up to seven *arrobas* with the same kind of harness as other beasts of burden. There are droves of over 400 or 500; in the lowland they carry wine, each one two jars weighing seven *arrobas* and conveyed in panniers made of *icho,* a strong grasslike matweed or *esparto* grass which abounds in the mountains. They transport wheat, corn, flour, and almost anything else. The greatest distance that they can travel when loaded is two or three leagues a day, but they go over any kind of a trail, however rough or bad, and carry burdens across rivers, however wide they may be. If they tire along the way, the only thing to do is to let them rest. No matter how hard you beat them, they won't get up until they feel rested. When one takes a notion to flee, it darts off more swiftly than a horse.

The wool of the *guanacos* and llamas makes fine bedcovers and delicate, costly fabrics in exquisite colors; it also supplies coarse clothing for the Indians, and bezoar stones are in their entrails. The flesh is edible and slightly sweet, and the hide is usable, so the animal really costs nothing. Six to twelve pesos will buy one, but the hide and flesh alone repay the owners who often have six thousand of them. Some transport only *coca* in the Andes and to Potosí. There are even some that travel ten leagues a day over flat land with a load of eight *arrobas*. Many deer and *vizcachas*, which are like hares, likewise abound in these mountains. With so many meadows to pasture in, cows and sheep are plentiful. The high tablelands are covered with snow that quickly melts in the valleys and lowland plains.

The way from Pachacaca is through these bare mountains to a cattle ranch called Velausteguí for an overnight stop. Continuing through valleys and along a river bank, the traveler comes to the famous Jauja Valley; then he crosses the deep-flowing Marañón River, either by a ford, or on a raft, or by the Atunjauja Bridge, and arrives at the Indian town of Huancayo.

The Jauja Valley is world renowned and many are the stories told about it. Altogether it has fourteen Indian communities. It is a large district with Franciscan and Dominican monasteries for the instruction of the natives. Fine wheat and corn grow in abundance; it produces the best bacon in the realm; it has big flocks of hens that give eggs, and also fruit such as peaches; all these products are destined for the Lima market forty leagues away. The Indians maintain a large wayside *tambo* for travelers here; there are none in the Pariacaca Mountains because no one can live up there. Beyond Huancayo, however, inns are located along the whole travel route, spaced at intervals of five or six leagues. These are known as royal hostels because the crown maintains them.

Indians brought to these establishments under forced labor provide personal services to wayfarers. As soon as a traveler reaches an inn, the Indian in charge hastens to put at his disposal a servant whose uncompensated duty is to fetch water, firewood, peppers, salt, and *icho* for bedding. While one Indian attends the traveler and guards his goods, others look for hens and whatever he asks for, and they take his mules away to pasture, bringing them back the next morning. If the traveler feels generous, he pays the Indians some amount; if not, he goes on his way. This service is available at all *tambos;* at some stops there are only Indian women because their menfolk are otherwise engaged. By a decree of Francisco de Toledo, a former viceroy of Peru, a penalty of four pesos and nine reales was imposed on any Spaniard who violated a native woman.

These Indians are the most timid and cowardly people in the world; they tremble at the sound of a Spaniard's voice, and one whiteman is enough to put a hundred to flight. They will do nothing asked of them, whether good or ill, unless they are beaten. They are much given to witchcraft and drunkedness; when drunk they lie with their mothers, sisters, and daughters, and make propositions to every female, and the latter are as bad as the males. On giving birth it is the Indian mother's custom to wash themselves and the child in cold water. They are a wretched, craven people, small in size and ugly. Those living in the Jauja Valley are better looking. They go on drunken sprees; when they travel, many lead their mounts by hand and walk with packs on their backs. They worship the devil, whom they call *supay;* they confess that they know he is evil, but they pay homage so that he will do them no harm. The Jauja Valley lies between two lofty mountains.

The next stop is at the Arcos *tambo,* and the route continues along the steep banks of the Marañón River to Casina with its attractive orchards. Following closely along this river through some bad stretches, it is crossed on a stone bridge. At this point a road turns off, leading to Huancavelica with its rich mines of quicksilver. This metal is carried to all of Peru's silver mines, and the entrance to the pit from which it is taken is a half league from the town. They load it on llamas that carry the mercury to the seaport of Chincha, whence it is shipped to Arica and brought overland to Potosí and other silver mines. Called Oropesa de Huancavelica, it is sixty leagues from Lima; it has 2,000 houses for Spaniards, and 3,000 for Indians, many of whom work in the pits. Merchants and others who trade in the town are always on hand, for it is a prosperous center and buying and selling go on continually. It has monasteries, a cathedral, and Indian parishes, and its chief magistrate is always a nobleman; it has a royal treasurer and an accountant. Browsing in the fields and mountains surrounding the locality are herds of cows and sheep that produce excellent butter, plenty of cheese, and their flesh makes fine jerked beef. The sugar crop is large in the deep ravines through which the Marañón flows, since frost never reaches that depth, which fact also accounts for the highly productive ranches and varied fruits. Heavy thunderstorms, rains, and snow feature this area; the soil is very fertile.

On the opposite side of the river flowing by the town is a level plain near a high hill from which gushes a hot spring called Puquio; every one who bathes in it likes to enjoy its warmth. God has endowed this water with the special property of solidifying. It must not be supposed, however, that all the water is thus transformed, for a considerable volume flows out of the spring and runs off to join the river. The water that is desired to become a solid is channeled into a large enclosure or hollow made especially for this purpose. Soon the water caught there becomes a hard slab, which is cut and shaped. Everything in the town is made of this solid material, which is yellow in color and somewhat soft.

Chocolococha, whose Spanish name is Castrovirreina, is fourteen leagues from Huancavelica, and its rich silver mines have metal of every degree of fineness. The best quality is worth 2,380 *maravedis,* the highest price; all others are less. This mine yields at least nine hundred bars of silver that are marked and stamped with the royal seal and have a value of a thousand pesos of eight reales each. Besides these ingots much silver is melted and made into silverware by craftsmen who rob the king of his royal fifth, that is, one part in five. As a matter of fact the mine operators pay only a tenth, as the veins are thin and hard to work. They are located high in the snow-covered mountains two leagues from town. Llamas transport the ore to silver refining mills on a small stream near the settlement. This ore is in the form of rocks, the best of which is dark blue or a brownish white. As firewood is scarce, it is melted in ovens heated by *icho* and llama droppings which are abundant all over the mountains.

After heating the ore millstones, kept wet by water from the river, grind it to a powder; it is then dropped into troughs and mixed with water and quicksilver. The mercury absorbs all the silver, leaving a residue of mine dust. Dealers buy these leavings and repeat the process, extracting what is called black silver. Despite persistent efforts, no way to refine this material has been discovered; should they ever be successful, it would yield unlimited wealth. The mercury is drawn off from the silver by heating, after which it has no further use; the silver takes the form of lumps, some as big as loafsugar. To convert them into bars they are placed in clay crucibles and, when melted, are poured into vats and dropped into cold water. Then they are brought to the Crown's officials, who stamp and number them, indicating the degree of fineness, and put aside the royal fifth. The numbers stamped go from one to a thousand, and even six thousand; they start with the first day of the year and continue to the last. By this system the officials keep an account of the silver bars of each mine every year; none can be stolen or lost, because it is discovered when its owner declares that it is missing. Purchasers also put their brands on the ingots, and the bits of silver that drop off the latter become the property of the assayer.

Castrovirreina has about five hundred dwellings for Spaniards and many more for the Indians. A governor, a person of high rank who acquires a fortune here, represents the Crown. Trade is brisk and merchants have well-stocked stores. Many excellent wines come up from the plains and, even if of poor quality at the place of origin, they improve greatly on reaching the mountains. This is the coldest highland in all Peru, but the soil is good and the inhabitants are sturdy. Vermin does not thrive here, and lice, fleas, mice, spiders, mosquitoes, chiggers, or snakes are unknown, nor are there troublesome animals. Pregnant Spanish women must go to the warm lowlands to give birth, because the penetrating cold of this bleak highland has caused many deaths. The more precautions taken against the cold, the less good they do; it is so icy cold that the wines freeze. They can hang a slaughtered bullock in the doorway and consume it unsalted a little at a time; even if the meat remains there a whole year, it does not spoil.

The road out of Castrovirreina leads to Ica, Pasco, Chincha, and Lima over a cold highland to Huamanga, a city on the main route. On turning back toward Huancavelica, the way is through three lagoons of fresh water, that is to say, one travels on land with lakes of great depth on either side. When the wind blows, it whips up waves as big as ocean surf; each lake is a full league long. On passing a silver mill the road skirts another lake under exceedingly high, snow-capped mountains that are more awesome than any others in the world; they are part of the Pariacaca chain.

This road goes through a swamplike marsh in which the unwary will bog down in the soft ground. The open country is deceptive to anyone unacquainted with it, and an Indian guide is highly essential. Then craggy rocks are reached called *vizcachas* because these rodents are so numerous there that they literally cover them. Next the road drops into valleys and continues through meadows with great herds of grazing llamas that belong to the crown; they are used to transport quicksilver. It is best to travel through this region in the summertime because quagmires, swampy marshes, and rivers make the journey difficult in winter . . .

After crossing the Marañón River by a stone bridge, the traveler soon passes over the stream from Huancavelica and follows a rough road up a steep slope to the Picois *tambo*. From that point of vantage one beholds a vast, bewildering maze of lofty mountains from which there seems to be no way out. A few Indian hamlets dot the slopes, and the

Marañón River flows so far below that it resembles a small silver thread. Beyond Picois one comes upon some rugged rocks called "The Friars" because they are so tall and slender that they look like men. The Huancavelica road joins here and goes on to the Porcos *tambo*. Indian communities lie scattered about the mountain sides.

A descent of two and a half leagues brings an island in sight in the middle of the Marañón River. Called Huamanga Island, it has many Indian villages and lead mines. The Marañón runs east until it carves out this island, whereupon it swings west. At the foot of an incline a suspension bridge stretches across a river which joins the Marañón. . . . This structure invariably sags into the water, making it necessary to unload the mules and carry the merchandize across on the backs of Indians and Negroes. When the flow is low the stream is forded. The road then goes on to the Azángaro *tambo;* on the right hand—no, I mean the left hand—is a district composed of the hamlet of Guanta and other Indian communities. If the rivers are fordable, the packtrain proceeds through Vinagua Valley. It is a cheerful dale with fine ranches, many orchards, hunting preserves, and cattle that belong to owners in Huamanga. The latter city is a prosperous trading center situated in a fertile region where wheat and corn grow in abundance; everything raised in Peru is here available. Cattle, oxen, and sheep are everywhere plentiful and cheap in these mountains and their valleys through which rivers wind. Huamanga has a chief magistrate, a bishop, monasteries belonging to the four religious orders in Peru, convents of nuns and Theatins, and dwellings of noble gentlemen. It is seventy-eight leagues from Lima.

Vilcas, an Indian village, is reached by plodding up and down inclines past several native communities, past Doña Teresa's ranch, and past many dairy farms, and by fording streams. It is allegedly the highest cultivated land in Peru. Here there are vestiges of large buildings erected in Inca times. The cut stones that are superbly fitted together in the walls are the most remarkable in the world.

Many villages lie in this district from which one descends a long gradient to the Uramarca River, one of the biggest tributaries of the Marañón. It is forded in summer and crossed by a suspension bridge in winter. Sugar canebrakes thickly line this river, from which one climbs up to the Uramarca *tambo*. The trail then passes several Indian communities and dairy farms, and Andaguailas the Great, as the valley is called in Peru, is reached after passing a small native hamlet. There are many such settlements in its jurisdiction, and an abundance of wheat, corn, and sugar grows along its streams. It is, in fact, a very prosperous district.

The *tambo* at Pingos is reached after passing several ranches and then, plodding up a long incline, one arrives at Guancarama, famous for its manufacture of sandals for the rest of Peru. Journeying over hill and dale and through several ravines, the traveler comes to the *tambo* at Cochacajas. A rough descent of two leagues brings him to where wheat and corn are raised, and then across the Abancay River on a stone bridge. This point is the beginning of the Abancay Valley, with its dense growth of sugar canebrakes and of many other products; its *tambo* is twenty-four leagues from Cuzco. Overhanging this renowned valley is a lofty, snow-covered mountain with, so it is alleged, rich, unworked veins of silver. Moving on, with high hills and deep valleys continually visible, the Indian village and *tambo* at Curaguasí are reached, whereupon the traveler descends to the magnificent river of this province, said to flow more swiftly than any other in Peru.

From the Great Chasm and Bridge
of Apurimac to Cuzco

The great, sheer rock of Apurimac and its bridge are the two most formidable and dangerous passages in the entire route from Lima to Cuzco. A small force could easily hold off an army of men there. The river, rushing with great volume and tremendous force, dashes against the chasm wall, which rises smooth and unbroken to a vast height like an enormous rampart. On top of this huge cliff a roadway was gouged out by iron tools; here a gigantic mass of stone rears up over four leagues [sic], and passage over its rock face is impossible. More than four hundred steps cut in descending order in this chasm wall are like a staircase; a beast of burden can stop to rest on each step which is so narrow that a low wall guards the outer edge to keep man or beast from falling into the river; it is a very narrow space indeed.

High, forest-covered mountains are on the other side of the river, and enormous rocks, rugged crags, and abrupt precipices render this terrain utterly impassable. But the Incas had a good trail through these forbidding stretches, for they used to take their pleasure and ease in a ravine at the river's edge four leagues away from the chasm and its bridge. It is known positively that there is much gold scattered about that ravine because, at certain seasons of the year, good swimmers have crossed the river and brought back nuggets of fine quality as big as walnuts. The rushing waters sweep through such rugged land, where both banks are high cliffs, that no one dares cross over except at the greatest risk, and bad stretches prevent travel overland.

The bridge is the product of much engineering skill. The rocky crags provide an abutment, while a pier of stone and mortar resting on a pedestal supports the other end. This column stands alone because it was impossible to construct a stone or wooden buttress over the deep, swiftly flowing river. This bridge is 180 paces long. To construct it they used huge beams of heavy timber a third of a *vara* thick seasoned for two years and carefully cut and squared. Long, heavy, and stout spikes were driven through them to make a solid sort of framework, with three of the beams underneath as a floor, over which heavy planking was laid. A beam was placed on either side, making the structure safe and sound. The bridge always shakes whenever it is used. Because of the danger of too great a weight laden beasts are not allowed on it but are led over bareback one at a time.

Long packtrains of tough, sturdy mules, sixty to eighty in number, slowly plod over this long route from Lima to Cuzco, carrying merchandise. An Indian or Negro muleteer is in charge of every ten animals. Owners of these freight carriers have an agreement with Lima shippers to the effect that, at this Apurimac pass, at every suspension bridge, and at every river in flood, the bales and cases of goods are shifted to the backs of Indians and Negroes. Consequently, all mules are unloaded at the places stipulated; if any freight is lost, the carriers must pay for it.

Many efforts have been made and piles of rocks and other materials have been assembled to build a bridge over this river, but all attempts were unsuccessful, although the engineers were competent. With an equal lack of success they have tried to open a passage through a small mountain to deflect the river, but the craggy rocks were too massive and impregnable. An official is in charge at the Apurimac chasm and its bridge to keep it in repair. To pay for its maintenance, a tax is imposed on all goods transported over it. The official I met there was a Fleming. It is because the chasm and its bridge are so famous in Peru that I dwell upon it at such length.

Beyond this river lies the province of Aimaraes, an exceedingly rough mountain area peopled by Indians. Vilcabamba, with its mines of low grade silver, is north of this stream which empties into the Marañón. Annually, five hundred bars of silver are extracted there. Many Indian communities lie scattered about this region, to which Spanish merchants come to sell their goods, while others go prospecting. The king's magistrates strictly forbid all but a few Spaniards from living in these Indian villages because of abuses committed against their inhabitants by Spanish vagrants. These petty merchants are called peddlers; some of them hawk as much as 40,000 pesos' worth of wares.

On leaving behind the Apurimac bridge, the Cuzco road

passes a *tambo,* above which are Mollapata and other Indian hamlets, and then it comes to Limatambo. There are impressive remains here of the elaborate structures built in the times of the Incas; these valleys have good soil. Quijana, an Indian community, is the beginning of level country with splendid fields where a good deal of wheat and other crops grow. It is one hundred and forty leagues from Lima to Cuzco over rugged mountains, through deep valleys and ravines, and along steep precipices, up and down hill all the way. The entire trail is narrow, but great care is taken to keep it in repair because of the many packtrains and travelers using it.

Indians, a mestizo, and a Spaniard in Peru.

◄§ 6 ҿ►

Visit of
Antonio Vázquez de Espinosa
to Cajamarca, Peru
(1615)

———————◄•●•►———————

*A widely traveled Spanish observer of the seventeenth-
century New World was a Carmelite friar, Father
Antonio Vázquez de Espinosa, author of a detailed*
Compendium and Description of the Western Indies,
*which remained unpublished until 1942. Chiefly geo-
graphical, his long work describes places visited in
Spain's oversea realms from 1612 to 1621, in parts of
which he spent varying periods of time. Born late in
the sixteenth century at Jérez de la Frontera, he
studied for the priesthood and was eager to spread
the Faith in the New World. After about two years
in Mexico and Central America and nearly six more
in different parts of South America, he apparently
returned to Middle America during a final two years.
Meanwhile, he had recorded his observations of all*

Vázquez briefly portrays this community in the *Compendio y
Descripción de las Indias Occidentales por Antonio Vázquez de
Espinosa, transcrito del manuscrito original por Charles Upson
Clark*, Vol. CVIII of the Smithsonian Miscellaneous Collections
(City of Washington, 1948), libro quarto del distrito de la
Audiencia de Lima, capítulo 6, párafos 1182–1188. The passage
has been translated by the editor. An English version of the
entire work by Charles Upson Clark was published by the
Smithsonian Institution in 1942.

localities visited. By 1622 he was back in Spain, where death claimed him in 1630 before he completed his Compendium and Description *for publication.*

In 1615 he had lived for a while in Cajamarca, Peru, scene of the ransom and execution of the Incan leader Atahualpa by Francisco Pizarro in the conquest of Peru.

Thirty-six leagues east of Trujillo, the town of Cajamarca lies in the heart of the mountains on the western slope of a valley that is four leagues long and, at intervals, more than two leagues wide. It is on an almost east-west line and climatically it is cold owing to its altitude in the mountain range. Corn, wheat, and potatoes grow in abundance, though occasionally subject to heavy frosts. A small stream flows through this valley, and about a league from the town are the Baths of the Incas that are so famous throughout Peru. It was there that Atahualpa, the king, his chieftains and overlords were assembled when Francisco Pizarro came to Cajamarca in December 1531, and it was there that the Spanish conqueror made a prisoner of the Inca monarch, as the chroniclers of the Indies relate.

Amid these baths are attractive houses and covered pools built by the Incas. Conduits bring warm water from thermal springs, which are very hot even though no live volcanoes are nearby, and they also bring cold water to temper the baths. About an harquebus-shot distance away is a small pond of steaming water, into which, according to a seemingly well-founded legend, the Indians tossed an immense treasure of precious metals in the form of jewels, vessels, and receptacles on perceiving what the Spaniards had done and on realizing the invaders' greed for gold and silver. Several curious or, rather, avaricious individuals have attempted to drain these waters into the river in an effort to locate this treasure. Their efforts, however, were unsuccessful owing to inadequate facilities and methods. For the sick and infirm these baths are most beneficial and health-giving. As I was in poor health in 1615, I bathed there frequently and it pleased God to restore me completely. In gratitude I went to the missions among the Motilones and Tabalosos Indians to preach our Holy Faith.

Between Cajamarca and the Baths of the Inca is a kind of public walk or path about a league long with rows of poplars and other leafy trees neatly planted on either side. The valley is too cold for a natural forest covering, and it is all quite flat and bare. The town of Cajamarca is extensive with its inhabitants scattered over a wide area. Its streets are straight and well formed; it is, in my opinion, the largest Indian community in all Peru. Its big, imposing Franciscan convent provides religious instruction, and there the Indians receive the Holy Sacraments. The viceroys invariably appoint a chief magistrate for the locality, who is duly authorized by his Majesty and the Council of the Indies. Customarily this office is bestowed upon the official sent by the new viceroy to bring word of his own predecessor's departure. Cajamarca has many workshops for weaving woolen stuff and ribbed fabrics. They are the property of the *encomenderos,* or Spanish overlords, whose Indians do all the work. More than a hundred Spaniards live in this community, which has many shops and markets owned by merchants and traders. Cajamarca is a large emporium whose thriving commerce places it on the main traveled route through the mountains from Quito and the northern provinces on one hand, and from Cuzco, Potosí, and the whole southern region on the other hand. Accordingly, this Indian community and its town council have a large, well-built, and capacious inn to lodge transient muleteers and traders. It has an innkeeper, constables, and an ample staff of Indians to serve the Spaniards who stop there. This hostelry is on the big central square; on the opposite side is the *Guayrona,* an aggregation of substantial, imposing lodgings for traveling dignitaries. These establishments are well managed and, for due compensation, town officials take prompt and efficient care of their guests' every need.

Adjoining this institution is the magistrate's house, where many Indians work for him, making special fabrics of a delicate weave called *cumbe*. These textiles are costly and valuable for they are adorned with embroidered figures, hunting scenes, and other curious designs. The wool of the vicuña and of the llama is woven in intricate patterns and myriad colors. Indian children do this handiwork, which is so fine and exquisite, by using needles made of chicken-bones or sheep bones carefully ground and sharpened. It is truly remarkable to see them produce such delicate crafts-manship in these fabrics, and in the many other things that they make.

Artisans of every kind abound in this locality, including scribes, singers, and a choirmaster to train them. These choir members are like prebendaries who attend church daily to pray to Our Lady and assist in the celebration of the Mass. At these holy services they play flageolets and other musical instruments, a widespread practice in the Indies. Ordinarily, those who take part are the sons of native chieftains and overlords, who greatly prize this par-ticipation, regarding it as a high honor.

A street separates the magistrate's establishment on the square from the local Indian chieftain's dwelling, which is near the convent. Inside his house is the large room that Atahualpa declared he would fill with gold as his ransom. The Indian chieftain indicated to me the mark on the wall to which the treasure would reach, and he also showed me where the Incan king was kept a prisoner. The large room had no ceiling and its walls were huge, well-fitted blocks of masonry. It was about forty feet long and the mark up to which Atahualpa had promised to heap the gold was about an *estado* and a half [2¾ yards?] from the ground, or about as high as a man of medium stature could reach with a poniard or a dagger. According to what this Indian chieftain, Don Felipe, told me, that room remains unchanged and will always remain so to commemorate the imprisonment and execution of Atahualpa after the arrival of the Spaniards in December 1531. The death of the Incan king occurred in March 1532. The bishop was attempting to assign a local priest for the Spaniards here in this town.

Near the village of San Marcos in the southern part of the district, there is a suspension bridge of fiber or woven osiers like willow. It crosses the wide flowing stream which, joining the Balsas River fed by still other tributaries, rushes through the Cajamarca Valley. The bridge is formed by two cables a little longer than the width of the river and made of tightly woven fiber and as thick as a man's thigh. These are attached to a stout tree or a rock at a convenient place on the river and the other two ends are carried over to the opposite bank. There they are stretched until taut and are then fastened. Many tightly-bound bundles of sticks or bunches of rattan are placed crosswise to form a grid or wattle. About a yard high on either side of the bridge, two ropes reach across, supported by struts to form the balustrade of a hand railing which permits travelers to cross safely. Such, then, is a suspension bridge. They sway a good deal when one passes over them but are perfectly safe. The Indians build several other kinds of bridges over streams but they never had, nor knew how to construct, bridges of stone with arches like ours.

Let the foregoing suffice to describe the Cajamarca district, adding only that, on top of most hills overlooking the valley and near the town, the Incas used to have many storage places for corn, potatoes, and other foodstuffs used by their armies and also for the benefit of the poor; these storehouses are still standing. Several silver mines such as the San Cristóbal are in the vicinity. They also raise cattle, pigs, deer, and vicuña, and in the entrails of the latter they find bezoar stones (see pages 105–106).

The eastern extremity of the Cajamarca district extends almost twenty leagues to the Balsas River, which flows in great volume far below between sheer crags where it is exceedingly cold while it is quite warm at the water's level.

Rafts serve as a ferry across this stream; they are made of logs, usually from the pawpaw trees that are plentiful along the river's banks. To make a crossing the Indian men or their women customarily carry a log of light balsa wood under their arms or over their shoulders which they drop into the water. They then either sit or lie at full length upon it and float quite safely to the opposite shore. I was astonished to see little Indian girls doing this, but I was also happy to observe this procedure and thus know what to do in similar circumstances. Often on later occasions I have followed this example when I had to cross a river or stream.

The territorial extent of Cajamarca constitutes a jurisdiction that is too large for the bishopric of Trujillo. For the spiritual needs of the area it might well be divided to form another unit as, indeed, the city of Chachapoyas and neighboring provinces have been requesting. The latter places in this respect are at a great disadvantage because they are so distant that bishops are unable to visit and make confirmations there. If Chachapoyas had a bishop the Tabalosos Indians would be brought into the fold of the Faith. They number more than 18,000 souls, are eager to be Christians, and they ask for priests. Hence this region and nearby provinces could readily be brought into our Holy Faith.

≪§ 7 ≩≫

Acarete du Biscay's Journey from Buenos Aires to Potosí (1658)

———◆●◆———

French as well as Italian travelers contrived to evade the Spanish ban on foreign visitors to the Crown's New World possessions. When the French Bourbons ascended the Spanish throne in the eighteenth century, Frenchmen enjoyed relatively free access to those lands. In the previous century a certain Acarete du Biscay came from France to Cádiz, from which port he was able to embark in December 1657 for the River Plate region of South America in the guise of a nephew of a Spanish gentleman. In due course he made an extended journey from Buenos Aires across the Argentine Pampas to the city of the famous silver mines at Potosí in modern Bolivia. The writer's interest was clearly commercial, but he took note of social and cultural as well as economic aspects of the Spanish settlements and countryside through which he passed.

This narrative translated into English as *An Account of a Voyage up the Rio de la Plata and Thence over Land to Peru* . . . (London, 1698), and here reproduced in modernized form, records his observations and impressions. Concerning this individual, standard bibliographies and authorities supply no information other than to indicate that the original version *Voyage à Buenos Aires et delá au Perou* was published at Paris in 1672.

The inclination I always had to traveling made me leave
my father's house very young, but I can truly aver that I
was not so much prompted to it out of pure curiosity to
see foreign countries as out of hope to acquire knowledge
and improve my judgment, which for the future might be
helpful to me, not only in my private concerns, but likewise render me more serviceable to my king and country,
which I declare was the chief aim of my voyages. I went
first into Spain, where I tarried long enough to learn
their language, particularly at Cádiz. The fancy took me to
go to the West Indies possessed by the Spaniards, for I
often heard them talk of the beauty and fertility of the
country, and the great riches they draw from thence, but
then I was at a loss how to bring it about, because 'tis very
difficult for a stranger to get into those parts. . . . As the
Spanish ministers, apprehending lest the interruption of
the commerce and the scarcity of European commodities in
Buenos Aires and Río de la Plata might constrain the
inhabitants to traffic with strangers (which 'tis their interest
to prevent as much as they can), thought fit to grant li-
cences to several of their private subjects to trade to the
Indies at their own proper risk. A certain cavalier took one
of them, fitted out a ship at Cádiz, where I abode at that
time; I resolved to go in her, and that the more willingly,
because I had formerly had some dealings with him. He
very friendly consented to let me go under his name for
his nephew, that I might conceal my being a foreigner,
which if known would have stopped my voyage, because in
Spain they allow none but native Spaniards to go in their
ships to the Indies. We set sail about the latter end of
December 1657, in a ship of 450 tons, and in 105 days
reached the mouth of the River de la Plata. . . .

A Description of Buenos Aires

Before I say anything of my journey to Peru, I will set
down what I observed remarkable at Buenos Aires whilst
I tarryed there. The air is pretty temperate, much as 'tis in

Andalusia, but not quite so warm; the rains fall almost as often in summer as winter; and the rain in sultry weather usually breeds divers kinds of toads, which are very common in this country, but are not venemous. The town stands upon a rising ground on the side of the River de la Plata, a musquet shot from the channel, in an angle of land made by a little rivulet called Riochuelo, which falls into the river a quarter of a league from the town; it contains 400 houses, has no enclosure, neither wall nor ditch, and nothing to defend it but a little fort of earth surrounded with a ditch, which commands the river, and has ten iron guns, the biggest of which is a twelve pounder. There the governor resides, who has but 150 Men in garrison, which are formed into three companies commanded by three captains, whom he appoints at will; and indeed he changes them so often that there is hardly a wealthy citizen but has been a captain. These companies are not always full, because the soldiers are drawn by the cheapness of living in those parts to desert frequently, notwithstanding they endeavor to keep them in the service by a large pay, which is per diem four reals, worth 1s. 6d. English, and a loaf which is as much as one man can eat. But the governor keeps 1,200 tame horses in a plain thereabouts for his ordinary service and, in case of necessity, to mount the inhabitants of the place and form a small body of cavalry.

Besides this fort there is a little bastion at the mouth of the rivulet wherein they keep guard. There are but two iron guns mounted upon it, each carrying a three-pound ball; this commands the place where the barks come ashore to deliver or take in goods, which are liable to be visited by the officers of the bastion when they lade and unlade. The houses of the town are built of earth, because there is but little stone in all those parts up as far as Peru; they are thatched with canes and straw and have no stories; all the rooms are of a floor, and are very spacious. They have great courtyards, and behind their houses large gardens full of orange trees, lemon trees, fig trees, apple trees, pear trees, and other fruit trees, with store of herbs, cabbages, onions, garlic, lettuce, peas, beans; and especially their melons are excellent. The soil being very fat and good, they live very commodiously and, except wine, which is something dear, they have plenty of all sorts of victuals, such as beef, veal, mutton, venison, hares, coneys, pullets, ducks, wild geese, partridges, pidgeons, turtles and all kind of wild fowl, and so cheap that one may buy partridges for a penny a piece, and the rest proportionably. There are likewise abundance of ostriches who herd in flocks like cattle and, tho' they are good meat, yet none but the savages eat of them. They make umbrellas of their feathers, which are very commodious in the sun; their eggs are good, and everybody eats of them, tho' they say they are of hard digestion. . . .

The houses of the better sort of inhabitants are adorned with hangings, pictures, and other ornaments and decent moveables, and all that are tolerably well-to-do are served in plate, and have a great many servants, blacks, mulattoes, mestices [mestizos], Indians, cabres, or sambos, who are all slaves. The Negroes come from Guinea; the mulattoes are begotten by a Spaniard upon a black; the mestizos are born of a Spaniard and an Indian, and the sambos of an Indian man and a mestiza, all distinguishable by their color and hair. They employ these slaves in their houses or to cultivate their grounds, for they have large farms stocked with grain in abundance, as wheat, barley and millet, or to look after their horses and mules, who feed upon nothing but grass all the year round, or to kill wild bulls, or, in fine, to do any kind of service. All the wealth of these inhabitants consists in cattle, which multiply so prodigiously in this province that the plains are quite covered with them, particularly with bulls, cows, sheep, horses, mares, mules, asses, swine, deer, and others, insomuch that, were it not for a vast number of dogs who devour the calves and other young beasts, they would overrun the country. They make so great profit of the skins and hides of these animals that a single instance will be sufficient to show how far it might be improved by good hands. The twenty-two

Dutch ships that we found at Buenos Aires were each of them laden with 13,000 or 14,000 bull hides at least, which amount to above 300,000 livers, or 33,500 pounds sterling, bought by the Dutch at seven or eight reals a piece, that is, under an English Crown, and sold again in Europe for twenty-five shillings English at least. When I expressed my astonishment at the sight of such an infinite number of cattle, they told me of a stratagem sometimes made use of, when they apprehend a descent from any enemies, that is matter of greater wonder, and 'tis this; they drive such a herd of bulls, cows, horses and other animals to the shore side that 'tis utterly impossible for any number of men, even tho' they should not dread the fury of those wild creatures, to make their way through so great a drove of beasts. The first inhabitants of this place put everyone their mark upon those they could catch, and turned them into their enclosures, but they multiplied so fast that they were forced to let them loose, and now they go and kill them according as they want them, or have occasion to make up a quantity of hides for sale. At present they mark only those horses and mules which they catch to tame and breed up for service. Some persons make a great trade of sending them to Peru, where they yield 50 patagons a pair.

Most of the dealers in cattle are very rich, but of all the trading people the most considerable are they that traffic in European commodities, many of whom are reputed worth 200,000 or 300,000 crowns. So that a merchant worth no more than 15,000 or 20,000 crowns is looked upon as a mean retailer; of these last there are near 200 families in the town, that make 500 men bearing arms, besides their slaves, who are three times that number, but are not to be reckoned of any defense, because they are not allowed to bear arms. Thus the Spaniards, Portuguese, and their sons (of whom those that are born upon the place are termed Creoles, to distinguish them from the natives of Spain) and some mestizos, are the militia, which, with the soldiers in garrison, compose a body of above 600 men, as I computed them in several musters, for they draw out on horseback three times a year near the town on festival days. I observed there were many old men among them that did not carry fire arms, but only a sword by their side, a lance in hand, and a buckler at their shoulders. They are also most of them married and masters of families, and consequently have no great stomach to fighting. They love their ease and pleasure and are entirely devoted to Venus. I confess they are in some measure excusable in this point, for most of their women are extremely pretty, well-shaped, and clear-skinned, and withal so faithful to their husbands that no temptations can prevail with them to loosen the sacred knot. But then, if their husbands transgress, they are often punished with poison or dagger. The women are more in number than the men. Besides Spaniards, there are a few French, Hollanders, and Genoese, but all go for Spaniards, otherwise there would be no dwelling for them there, especially those that differ in their religion from the Roman-Catholics, because the Inquisition is settled there.

The Bishop's revenue amounts to 3,000 patagons per annum. His diocese takes in this town and Santa Fe, with the farms belonging to both. Eight or ten priests officiate in the cathedral, which is built of earth as well as the houses. The Jesuits have a college; the Dominicans, the Recollects, and the Religious de la Mercy have each a convent. There is likewise a Hospital [poor house], but there are so few poor people in these parts that 'tis of little use.

Journey from Buenos Aires to Peru

I left Buenos Aires and took the road to Córdova, leaving Santa Fe on my right hand, of which place take this account: 'tis a Spanish settlement dependent upon Buenos Aires. The commander is no more than a lieutenant, and does nothing but by order from the Governor of Buenos Aires. 'Tis a little place containing twenty-five houses, without any walls, fortifications, or garrison, distant 80 leagues from Buenos Aires northward, situate upon the River de la Plata. Large vessels might come up to it, were it not for a great bank that obstructs the passage a little above Buenos Aires. Nevertheless 'tis a very advantageous post, because 'tis the only passage from Peru, Chili, and Tucumán to Paraguay, and in a manner the magazine [central warehouse] of the commodities drawn from thence, particularly that herb [yerba mate] already spoken of, which they cannot be without in those provinces. The soil is as good and fertile here as at Buenos Aires, and the town, having nothing remarkably different from what has been observed of Buenos Aires, I leave it, and proceed upon my journey. 'Tis counted 140 leagues from Buenos Aires to Córdova, and because some parts of the road are uninhabited for a long way together, I furnished myself at my departure with what I was informed I should stand in need of. So I set out having a savage for my guide, with three horses and three mules, some to carry my baggage, and the rest to change upon the way when that I rid upon was tired.

From Buenos Aires, to the River Lucan, and even as far as the River Recife, 30 leagues, I passed by several habitations and farms cultivated by the Spaniards, but beyond Recife to the River Salladillo, I saw none. Let it be observed by the way, that these rivers as well as all the rest in the provinces of Buenos Aires, Paraguay, and Tucumán that fall into the River de la Plata are fordable on horseback; but when the rains or any other accident swell them, a traveler must either swim over or else get upon a bundle in the nature of a raft, which a savage hauls over to the other side. I could not swim and so was forced to make use of this expedient twice or thrice when I could not find a ford. The way was this: my Indian killed a wild bull, took the hide off, stuffed it with straw, and tied it up in a great bundle with thongs of the same hide, upon which I placed myself with my baggage; he swam over hauling me after him by a cord tied to the bundle, and then he repassed and swam my horses and mules over to me. . . .

Córdova is a town situate in a pleasant and fruitful plain upon the side of a river, bigger and broader than that I have just spoken of. 'Tis composed of about 400 houses, built like those of Buenos Aires. It has neither ditches, nor walls, nor fort for its defense. He that commands it is governor of all the provinces of Tucumán and, tho' it be the place of his ordinary residence, yet he is wont now and then, as he sees occasion, to go and pass some time at St. Jago [Santiago] de l'Estero, at St. Miguel de Tucumán, (which is the Capital City of the Province) at Salta and at Xuxui [Jujuy]. In each of these villages there is a lieutenant, who has under him an alcalde and some officers for the administration of justice. The Bishop of Tucumán likewise usually resides at Córdova, where the cathedral is the only parish church of the whole town. But there are divers convents of monks, namely of Dominicans, Recollects, and those of the Order de la Mercy, and one of nuns. The Jesuits have a college there, and their chapel is the finest and richest of all.

The inhabitants are rich in gold and silver, which they get by the trade they have for mules, with which they furnish Peru and other parts, which is so considerable, that they sell about 28,000 or 30,000 of them every year, which they breed up in their farms. They usually keep them till they are about two years old, then expose them to sale, and get about six patagons a piece for them. The merchants that come to buy them carry them to St. Jago [Santiago], to Salta, and Jujuy where they leave them for three years, till they are well grown and become strong, and afterwards bring them to Peru, where they presently have sale for them, because there, as well as in the rest of the western part of America, the greatest part of their carriage is upon mules. The people of Córdova also drive a trade in cows, which they have from the country of Buenos Aires, and carry to Peru, where, without this way of subsistence, 'tis certain they would have much ado to live. This kind of traffic makes this town the most considerable in the Province of Tucumán, as well for its riches and commodities, as for the number of its inhabitants, which are counted to be at least 500 or 600 families, besides slaves, who are three times the number. But the generality of them of all degrees have no other arms but a sword and poignard, and are very indifferent soldiers, the air of the country, and the plenty they enjoy, rendering them lazy and cowardly.

From Córdova I took the way of St. Jago [Santiago] de l'Estero, which is 90 leagues distant from it. In my journey I, from time to time, that is, 7 or 8 leagues, met with single houses of Spaniards and Portuguese, who live very solitarily. They are all situate upon small rivulets, some of them at the corners of forests which are frequently to be met with in that country, and are almost all of algarobe-wood, the fruit of which serves to make a drink that is sweet and sharpish, and heady as wine; others of them in open fields, which are not so well stocked with cattle, as those of Buenos Aires. But, however, there are enough of them, and indeed more than needs for the subsistence of the inhabitants, who also make a trade of mules, and cotton, and cochineal for dying, which the country produces. . . .

A Description of the City of Potosí and the Mines There

I was no sooner alighted from my horse at a merchant's house to whom I had been recommended, but I was conducted by him to the President of the Provinces of Las Charcas, to whom the order I carried from the King of Spain was directed, as the Principal Director of his Catholic Majesty's affairs in this province, in which Potosí is situate, which is the place of his ordinary residence, altho' the city de la Plata is the capital. After I had delivered the order to him, I was brought to the *corregidor* [chief magistrate] to deliver that which belonged to him, and afterward to those other officers for whom I brought orders. They all received me very well, particularly the President, who presented me with a chain of gold for the good news I had brought him.

But before we go any farther 'tis convenient I should give some description of the city of Potosí, as I have done of others. The Spaniards call it the Imperial City, but nobody could ever tell me for what reason. 'Tis situate at the foot of a mountain called Arazassou [Aranzazú], and divided in the midst by a river, which comes from a lake inclosed with walls, which lies about a quarter of a league above the city, and is a kind of reserver [reservoir] to hold the water that is necessary for the work-houses of that part of the city, which is on this side of the river over against the mountain, [and] is raised upon a little hill, and is the largest and most inhabited part. As for that part of the city which is on the side of the mountain, there's scarce anything but engines and the houses of those that work in them. The city has neither walls, ditches, nor forts for its defense. There are reckoned to be 4,000 houses well built of good stone, with several floors, after the manner of the buildings in Spain. The churches are well made, and all richly adorned with plate, tapestry, and other ornaments, and above all those of the monks and Nuns, of whom there are several convents of different orders, which are very well furnished. This is not the least populous city of Peru, with Spaniards, mestizos, strangers, and natives (which last the Spaniards call *Indios*), with mulattoes and Negroes. They count there are between 3,000 and 4,000 natural Spaniards bearing arms, who have the reputation of being very stout men and good soldiers. The number of the mestizos is not much less, nor are they less expert at a weapon, but the greatest part of them are idle, apt to quarrel and treacherous. Therefore they commonly wear three or four buff-waistcoats one upon another, which are proof against the point of a sword, to secure themselves from private stabs.

The strangers there are but few; there are some Dutch, Irish, and Genoese, and some French, most of whom are of St. Malo, Provence, or Bayonne, and pass for people of Navarre and Biscaye. As for the Indians, they are reckoned to amount to near 10,000 besides the mulattoes and the blacks; but they are not permitted to wear either swords or firearms, nor [are] their *curacas* and *caciques*, tho' they may all aspire to any degree of knighthood, and to benefices, to which they are often raised for their laudable actions and good services. They are also forbidden to wear the Spanish habit, but are obliged to clothe themselves in a different manner, in a close-coat without sleeves, which they wear next their shirts, to which their band and laced cuffs are fastened. Their breeches are wide at bottom after the French fashion, their legs and feet naked. The blacks and mulattoes, being in the service of the Spaniards, are habited after the Spanish mode and may bear arms, and all the Indian slaves after ten years service are set at liberty, and have the same privileges with the others.

The government of this city is very exact, by the care which is taken by twenty-four magistrates, who are constantly observing that good order be kept in it, besides the *corregidor* and President of Las Charcas, who directs officers after the manner of Spain. It is to be observed that, excepting these two principal officers, as well as Potosí as everywhere else in the Indies, all the people, whether knights, gentlemen, officers or others, are concerned in commerce, of which some of them make so great an advantage that in the city of Potosí there are some reckoned to be worth two, some three, and some four millions of crowns; and a great many worth two, three, or four hundred thousand crowns. The common people, too, live much at their ease, but are all proud and haughty, and always go very fine, either in cloth of gold and silver, or in scarlet, or silk trimmed with a great deal of gold and silver-lace.

The furniture of their houses is very rich, for they are generally served in plate. The wives, both of gentlemen and citizens, are kept very close to a degree beyond what they are in Spain; they never go abroad, unless it be to go to mass, or to make some visit, or to some public feast, and that but rarely. The women here are generally addicted to excess in taking coca. This is a plant that comes from the side of Cuzco, which, when it is made up in rowls [rolls] and dried, they chew as some do tobacco. They are so heated, and sometimes absolutely fuddled by it, that they have no command of themselves at all. 'Tis likewise often used by the men, and has the same effects upon them. They are otherwise very temperate in eating and drinking, tho' they have before dwelt in places well stored with all sort of provisions, as beef, mutton, fowls, venison, raw and preserved fruits, corn and wine, which are brought hither from other parts, and some from a great distance, which makes these commodities dear, so that the meaner sort of people, especially those that have very little beforehand, would find it hard enough to live there, if money were not very plenty, and easy to be got by them that are willing to work.

The best and finest silver in all the Indies is that of the mines of Potosí, the principal of which are found in the mountain of Aranzazú, where, besides the prodigious quantities of silver that have been taken out of veins, in which the metal evidently appeared and which are now exhausted, there is almost as great quantities of it found in places where they had not digged before. Nay, from some of the earth which they threw aside formerly when they opened the mines and made pits and cross-ways in the mountains, they have taken silver and have found by this that the silver has been formed since that time, which shows how proper the quality of this ground is for the production of that metal. But indeed this earth does not yield so much as the mines that are found by veins among the rocks. . . .

The King of Spain does not cause any of these mines to be wrought on his account, but leaves them to those persons that make the discovery of them, who remain masters of them after the *corregidor* has visited them and declared them proprietors, on the accustomed conditions and privileges. The same *corregidor* describes and marks out the superfices of the ground, in which they are allowed to open the mine on the outside; which does not, for all that, limit or restrain their work underground, every man having liberty to follow the vein he has found, the extent and depth of it reaching never so far, tho' it should cross that which another has digged near it. All that the King reserves for himself, besides the duties we shall hereafter speak of, is to give a general direction by his officers for all the work of the mines, and to order the number of savages to be employed in them, to prevent the disorders that would arise if every proprietor of the mines should have liberty to set as many of them to work as he pleased; which would frequently give occasion to those that are most powerful and rich to engross and have so great a number of 'em [savages], that few or none would remain for others to employ to keep their work going forward. For this would be contrary to the King's interest, which is to make provision that there be a sufficient number of slaves for all the mines that are opened. For this end he obliges all the *curacas,* or chiefs of the savages, to furnish every one a certain number, which they must always keep complete, or else are forced to give twice as much money as would have been paid in wages to those that are wanting, [lacking] if they had been present.

Those that are destined for the mines of Potosí don't amount to above two thousand and two or three hundred. These are brought and put into a great enclosure which is at the foot of the mountain, where the *corregidor* makes a distribution of them to the conductors of the mines, according to the number they want. And, after six days constant work, the conductor brings them back the Saturday following to the same place, where the *corregidor* causes a review to be made of them, to make the owners of the mines give them the wages that are appointed them, and to see how many of them are dead, that the *curacas* may be obliged to supply the number that is wanting—for there's no week passes but some of them die, either by divers accidents that occur, as the tumbling down of great quantities of earth and falling of stones, or by sickness and other casualties.

They are sometimes very much incommoded by winds that are shut up in the mines; the coldness of which, joined to that of some parts of the earth, chills them so excessively that, unless they chewed coca, which heats and fuddles them, it would be intolerable to them. Another great hardship which they suffer is that in other places the sulphurous and mineral vapors are so great that it strangely dries them up, so that it hinders them from free respiration. For this they have no other remedy than the drink which is made with the herb of Paraguay, of which they prepare a great quantity to refresh and moisten them when they come out of the mines at the times appointed for eating or sleeping. This drink serves them also for physic to make them vomit and cast up whatever incommodes their stomachs.

Among these savages they ordinarily choose the best workmen to break up the ore between the rocks. This they do with iron bars [crowbars], which the Spaniards call *palancas,* and other instruments of iron; others serve to carry what they dig in little baskets to the entrance of the mine; others to put it in sacks and load it upon a sort of great sheep [llamas], which they call *carneros de la tierra.* They are taller than asses and commonly carry two hundred pound weight; these serve to carry it to the work-houses, which are in the town along the river, which comes from the lake I have spoken of before. In these work-houses, which are a hundred and twenty in number, the ore is refined, of which take the following account:

They first beat it well upon anvils with certain great hammers, which a mill continually keeps at work. When it is pretty well reduced to powder, they pass it thro' a fine sieve and spread it upon the ground about half a foot thick in a square place that is very smooth, prepared for the purpose. Then they cast a great deal of water upon it, after which they, with a sieve, spread upon it a certain quantity of quick-silver, which is proportioned by the officers of the mint, and also a liquid substance of iron, which is prepared by two millstones, one of which is fixed, and the other is continually turning. Between these they put an old anvil, or some other massy piece of iron, which is worn away and consumed with water by the turning millstone, so that 'tis reduced to a certain liquid matter. The ore, being thus prepared, they stir it about and mix it, as men do when they make mortar, for a fortnight together, every day tempering it with water. After this, they several times put it into a tub, wherein there is a little mill which, by its motion, separates from it all the earth with the water, and casts them off together, so that nothing but the metallic matter remains at the bottom, which is afterward put into the fire in crucibles to separate the quick-silver from it, which is done by evaporation. As for the iron substance, that does not evaporate, but remains mixed with the silver, which is the reason that there is always in eight ounces (for example's sake) three-quarters of an ounce or thereabouts of false alloy.

The silver, when thus refined, is carried to the mint, where they make an essay [assay] of it whether it be of the right alloy, after which it is melted into bars or ingots, which are weighed, and the fifth part of them deducted, which belongs to the King, and are stamped with his mark. The rest appertain to the merchant who, in like manner, applies his mark to them and takes them away from thence when he pleases in bars, or else converts them into reals and other money. This fifth part is the only profit the King has from the mines, which yet are esteemed to amount to several millions. But besides this, he draws considerable sums by the ordinary impositions upon goods, without reckoning what he raises upon quick-silver, both that which is taken out of the mines of Huancavelica, which are situated between Lima and Cuzco, and that which is brought from Spain, with which two vessels are loaded every year, because that which is taken out of these mines is not sufficient for all the Indies.

They use divers ways of carriage to transport all the silver that is annually made about Potosí for Spain. First they load it upon mules that carry it to Arica, which is a port on the South-Sea [Pacific], from whence they transport it in small vessels to the fort of Lima, or Los Reyes, which is a fort upon the same sea, two leagues from Lima. Here they embark it with all that comes from other parts of Peru in two great gallions that belong to his Catholic Majesty, each of which carry 1,000 tons and are armed each with fifty or sixty pieces of canon. These are commonly accompanied with a great many small merchant ships as richly loaded, which have no guns but a few *petareroes** to give salutes and take their course toward Panama, taking care always to send a little pinnace 8 or 10 leagues before to make discoveries. They might make this way in a fortnight's time, having always the help of the south-wind, which reigns alone in this sea. Yet they never make it less than a month's voyage, because by this delay the commander of the gallions makes a great advantage in furnishing those with cards that have a mind to play on ship-board during the voyage, which amounts to a very considerable sum, both because the tribute he receives is ten patagons for every pack of cards, and because there is a prodigious quantity of them consumed, they being continually at play, and there being scarce anybody aboard but is concerned for very considerable sums. . . .

Fiesta at Potosí

Three weeks after my arrival at Potosí, there were great rejoicings made for the birth of the Prince of Spain, which lasted for a fortnight together, during which time all

* A *petarero* is a small explosive device which shoots or fires small charges—*I. A. L.*

work ceased throughout the city, in the mines, and in the adjacent places. And all the people great and small, whether Spaniards, foreigners, Indians, or blacks, minded nothing else but to do something extraordinary for the solemnizing of this festival. It began with a cavalcade made by the *corregidor,* the twenty-four magistrates of the city, the other officers, the principal of the nobility and gentry, and the most eminent merchants of the city, all richly clothed; all the rest of the people, and particularly the ladies, being at the windows and casting down abundance of perfumed waters, and great quantities of dry sweetmeats. The following days they had several plays, some of which they call *Juegos de Toros,* other *Juegos de Cannas,* [Cañas] several sorts of masquerades, comedies, balls, with vocal and instrumental music, and other divertisements, which were carried on one day by the gentlemen, another day by the citizens; one while by the goldsmiths, another while by the miners; some by the people of divers nations, others by the Indians, and all with great magnificence and a prodigious expense.

The rejoicings of the Indians deserve a particular remark, for, besides that they were richly clothed, and after a different manner, and that comical enough, with their bows and arrows, they, in one night and morning, in the chief public place of the city, prepared a garden in the form of a labyrinth, the plats of which were adorned with fountains spouting out waters, furnished with all sorts of trees and flowers, full of birds, and all sorts of wild beasts, as lions, tigers and other kinds, in the midst of which they expressed their joy a thousand different ways, with extraordinary ceremonies.

The last day save one surpassed all the rest, and that was a race at the ring, which was performed at the charge of the city with very surprising machines. First there appeared a ship towed along by savages of the bulk and burden of a 100 tons, with her guns and equipage of men clothed in curious habit, her anchors, ropes, and sails swelling with the wind, which very luckily blew along the street through which they drew her to the great public place, where, as soon as she arrived, she saluted the company by the discharge of all her canon. At the same time, a Spanish lord, representing an emperor of the East coming to congratulate the birth of the prince, came out of the vessel attended with six gentlemen and a very fine train of servants that led their horses, which they mounted, and so went to salute the President of Los Charcas. And, while they were making their compliment to him, their horses kneeled down and kept in that posture, having been taught this trick before. They afterward went to salute the *corregidor* and the judges of the field, from whom, when they had received permission to run at the ring against the defendants, they acquitted themselves with great gallantry, and received very fine prizes distributed by the hands of the ladies.

The race at the ring being finished, the ship and a great many other small barks that were brought thither advanced to attack a great castle wherein Cromwell the Protector, who was then in war with the King of Spain, was feigned to be shut up; and, after a pretty long combat of fireworks, the fire took hold of the ship, the small barks, and the castle and all was consumed together. After this a great many pieces of gold and silver were distributed and thrown among the people in the name of his Catholic Majesty. And there were some particular persons that had the prodigality to throw away two or three thousand crowns a man among the mob.

The day following, these rejoicings were concluded by a procession made from the great Church to that of the Recollects, in which the Holy Sacrament was carried, attended with all the clergy and laity. And, because the way from one of these churches to the other had been unpaved for the celebration of the other rejoicings, they repaired it for this procession with bars of silver, with which all the way was entirely covered. The altar where the Host was to be lodged in the Church of the Recollects was so furnished with figures, vessels, and plates of gold and silver, adorned with pearls, diamonds, and other precious stones that scarce ever could anything be seen more rich, for the citizens brought thither all the rarest jewels they had. The extraordinary charge of this whole time of rejoicing, was reckoned to amount to above 500,000 crowns. . . .

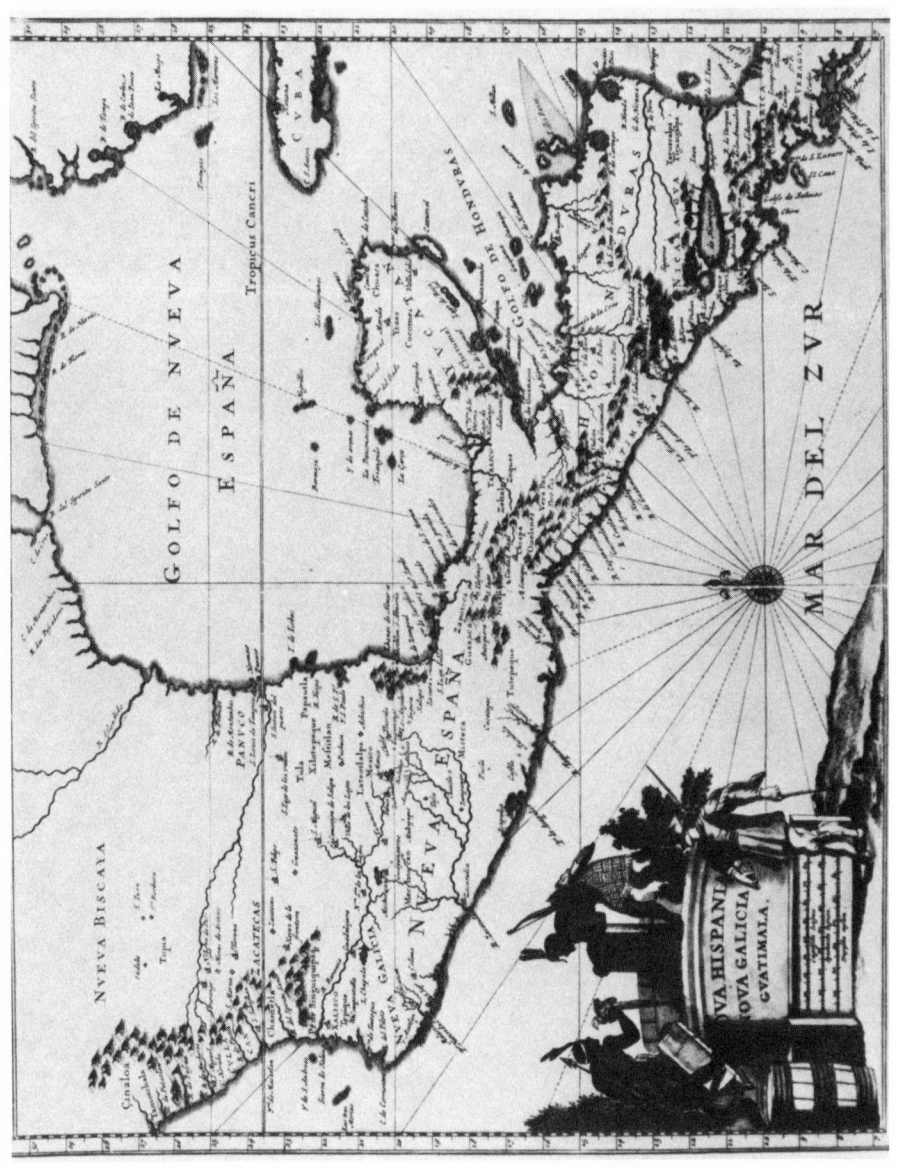

Central America: New Galicia, New Spain, and Guatemala.

⋖ 8 ⋗

The Pacific Crossing
of Gemelli-Careri
(1697-1698)

———◆◆———

Concerning the trans-Pacific voyage from the Philippines to Mexico on the Manila Galleon, *a seventeenth-century historian remarked that it was "the longest, most tedious, and most dangerous voyage in all the seas." Giovanni Francesco Gemelli-Careri, another Italian round-the-world traveler, about whom few biographical facts are available, amply corroborates this assertion in his* Giro del Mondo *(Venice, 1719), which includes an account of his experience in crossing the Pacific Ocean. A well-educated Neapolitan, widely traveled in Europe, he had found it expedient about 1694 to escape political persecution by embarking on a world tour. His journey eastward had brought him to the Philippines, where he boarded the annual galleon to Mexico, leaving Manila in June 1697 and arriving at Acapulco seven months later in January 1698. His journal records observations of the Mariana Islands and recounts the hardships of shipboard life that were familiar to Father de la Torre a century and a half before.*

Excerpts are taken from the English translation in Awnsham and John Churchill, *A Collection of Voyages and Travels,* 4 vols. (London, 1704), Book III, pp. 453–473. Spellings and punctuation have been modernized.

The voyage from the Philippine Islands to America may be called the longest and most dreadful of any in the world, as well because of the vast ocean to be crossed, being almost the one half of the terraqueous globe, with the wind always ahead, as for the terrible tempests that happen there, one upon the back of another, and for the desperate diseases that seize people in seven or eight months lying at sea, sometimes near the line, sometimes cold, sometimes temperate, and sometimes hot, which is enough to destroy a man of steel, much more [than enough to destroy] flesh and blood, which at sea had but indifferent food.

The ship being again laden, and about a thousand jars of water put in by the commander and other officers, we set sail on Friday, June 29th [1697] before noon, in the presence of the colonel. Having sailed two leagues, we came to an anchor within the same bay. On pretense that he wanted water, the commander left behind a Dominican, who had given him five hundred pieces of eight* for his voyage, a Recolet** and a physician he had agreed to keep at his own table, which accident put me into a good little cabin for my bed and equipage [baggage]. Saturday, the last day of June, the wind continuing at south against us, though we had hoisted sail, we soon dropped anchor again. The same we did Sunday, the 1st of July, having sailed but half a league. Monday, the 2nd, stirred not; and Tuesday just weighed and dropped anchor again, the wind continuing contrary both days, with much rain, so that in five days, we scarce sailed three leagues.

Some water being spent, the boat was sent to take in more, near the hill Bataan. Being curious, I went in the boat with the major Vincent Arámbola, a Basque, and landed on a plain, where the arrows of many Negrillos, or island blacks, who were hunting in the woods could reach us. The women and children began to bark like dogs to

* Former silver coins of Spain and Spanish America equal in value to eight reals—*I. A. L.*

** A member of a religious order who gathers church income —*I. A. L.*

drive out the wild beasts before their husbands and fathers, who lay ready in ambush. So, whilst the water was taking in, we stood very fearful, as not being able, with two fire-locks, to oppose hundreds of blacks, armed with bows and arrows, short javelins, and long knives. Wherefore I retired to the boat, without inquiring into the matter of hunting, as Arámbola did. The Filipino sailors belonging to our ship, bringing the water from the wood, were no way molested by the savages, because they are friendly among themselves. Having taken the water, we returned aboard after midnight, more afraid than hurt, having stood upon our guard, not only because of the blacks, but also on account of the unconquered Zambolos who live upon part of that mountain.

Wednesday, July 4th, we stirred not, the wind being contrary. Thursday, 5th, before day, drove along with the tide and very little wind, but the wind then starting up against us, came to an anchor near Mariveles. The governor came aboard in a little *prao,* which is a tree hollowed with two wings on the sides to prevent its oversetting, to bring our captain some fruit, and then went away. Friday, 6th, the same wind continued with those rains, which never fail about Manila. Saturday, 7th, the wind freshening and the rain growing tempestuous, we weighed anchor and brought the ship under the shelter of the hill of Bataan. The same southerly winds and rains continuing, we lay in the same place all Sunday and Monday, the 8th and 9th. Tuesday, 10th, we were towed a little way. Nothing troubled me but the heat, for there was none of the other plague of lice, so frequent in other ships, because, in those parts, they do not breed on Europeans. Search was then made to discover whether there were any jars that, instead of water, were filled with commodities upon pretense of carrying them safer; and several were cast into the sea full of pepper, purselane,* and other goods of value. . . .

* Any number of related weeds having pink, fleshy stems and small round leaves—*I. A. L.*

Of the People, Religion, Fruit, Climate and Wonderful Boats of the Mariana Islands

The chief of the Mariana Islands is Iguana, and therefore a strong castle is built on it, guarded by eighty or ninety men. The second is Sarpana, in which there's also a garrison, but the governor lives in Umatta. They are both flat, so that the ships can come no nearer than within three leagues of them. In Agana there are two colleges, [schools] the one of children, the other of Indian maids, instructed and governed by twelve fathers of the society, and maintained by the king, with an allowance of three thousand pieces of eight a year, besides his bounty for maintenance of the fathers. His majesty generously spends thirty-four thousand pieces of eight a year to keep these islands, the governor's salary being three thousand pieces of eight, and the rest for a major, a hundred soldiers, the Jesuits and colleges aforementioned. All this is sent from New Spain to Manila, with cloth for the soldiers. There is also a small vessel kept to carry all necessaries thither. The houses of the fathers of the society are made of mud walls, because the islands furnish no other materials. Those of the Indians are huts covered with boards, or palm tree leaves like caves. The island is ten leagues in compass, and is six from Sarpana. This is not so large, nor have the Jesuits any house in it, but repair thither as there is occasion. There is a small garrison to curb those barbarous people.

The inhabitants of the Mariana Islands are of a gigantic stature, corpulent, and very strong, and will sometimes clap 500 weight on their backs as if it were nothing. They are great swimmers and dive so swiftly that they will take fish. Before the coming of the Spaniards they lived under a chief, naked, wandering about the mountains. They knew not what fire was, or the use of iron, but did eat raw fish, sometimes rotten, cocoas, and roots, drinking fair water.

There never was, nor is there at present, any selling among them, but only exchange; and should the Spaniards carry never so many pieces of eight, no man would give them a coconut or a hen, and they might starve, did they not give stuff, cloth, or other things those people want in exchange.

No token of any religion has been hitherto found in any of the islands discovered, as several missionaries told me, who had been long there; only an extraordinary veneration for their ancestors, not out of love, but fear, keeping their skulls in their houses, and calling upon them in time of need; by which it appears they have some true notion of the immortality of the soul, and that there is some place for them to reside in, from whence they can do good or harm. Their language is different from that of the Philippines. Their weapon is a spear pointed with the bone of a man's leg, or a sharp stone.

Tho' in these islands the trees are not so large and thick as in the Philippines, yet the soil is proper to produce all things necessary for man's sustenance. Formerly there was nothing but the fruit of the country, and some hens, but afterward the Jesuits and soldiers residing there brought over rice, herbs, and other things from the Philippine Islands. And, as for beasts, horses, cows and swine, they have increased considerably in the mountains. There were not so much as rats, but the ships have furnished them. No venomous creatures at all breed there.

The most wonderful and peculiar fruit of these islands is the *rima*, which serves the natives instead of bread and is very nourishing. The plant is thick and full of leaves, the fruit as big as a man's head, of a date color, but prickly like the *giacca* of Goa; and in the middle is a kernel like a white nut. Boiled or roasted, it serves for bread, and keeps four or six months. The taste is like an Indian fig, or *plantan*. Besides, the mountains abound in cocoa-trees.

The *ducdu* is a tree like the *rima*, and the fruit, which is green without, is like a long pear. The inside pulp is white and soft, sticking to about 15 kernels, which roasted, taste like chestnuts, as do those of the *giacca*. For common food there are abundance of roots, as *ubis, gavas, camotes* and others. The water is very good. The air is better and more temperate than that of Luzon, tho' that island be upon the same parallel with Iguana and Sarpana.

The little boats of these islands are very strange as well for their make as swiftness. They are made of two crooked bodies of trees hollowed, and sewn together with Indian cane. They are about five or six yards long and, because the breadth of them is not above four spans and they would easily overset, therefore they join to the sides pieces of solid timber, which balance them; and, as for passengers, the boat being scarce able to contain three Indian sailors, they therefore lay boards across in the middle, hanging over the water on both sides, where those that will be carried from place to place fit. Of the three sailors aforesaid, one is always in the middle to lade out the water, which certainly comes in over the sides and at the seam; the other two keep one at head and one at stern to move and steer the boat. The sail is like those we call latin [lateen] sails, that is, triangular, made of mat, and as long as the boat, which being therefore easy to overset when the wind is astern, they keep out of it as much as they can. No sort of boat whatsoever can come near them for swiftness, for they run ten or twelve Italian miles an hour. When they are to return from any place, they remove the sail without turning the boat about, so that which was the stern becomes the head, and he that was in the prow, is steersman. If anything is to be mended in the boat, the goods and passengers are set upon the sail, and the boat is presently righted, and turned up if it was overset—things so wonderful the Spaniards themselves can scarce believe them, though they see them everyday. Though these be fit only for a short cut, yet in case of urgent necessity, two set out from Iguana, crossing a sea of 900 Italian miles, to go to the Philippine Islands.

Shipboard Life on the Manila Galleon

The poor people stowed in the cabins of the galleon bound toward the Land of Promise of New Spain endure no less hardships than the children of Israel did when they went from Egypt toward Palestine. There is hunger, thirst, sickness, cold, continual watching, and other sufferings besides the terrible shocks from side to side, caused by the furious beating of the waves. I may further say they endure all the plagues God sent upon Pharaoh to soften his hard heart for, if he was infected with leprosy, the galleon is never clear of a universal raging itch as an addition to all other miseries. If the air then was filled with gnats, the ship swarms with little vermin the Spaniards call *gorgojos,* bred in the bisket [biscuit] so swift that they, in a short time, not only run over cabins, beds, and the very dishes the men eat on, but insensibly fasten upon the body. Instead of the locusts, there are several other sorts of vermin of sundry colors that suck the blood. Abundance of flies fall into the dishes of broth, in which there also swim worms of several sorts. In short, if Moses miraculously converted his rod into a serpent, aboard the galleon a piece of flesh, without any miracle, is converted into wood, and in the shape of a serpent.

I had a good share in these misfortunes due to the boatswain, with whom I had agreed for my diet, as he had fowls at his table the first days, so when we were out at sea he made me fast after the Armenian manner, having banished from his table all wine, oil, and vinegar, dressing his fish with fair [fresh] water and salt. Upon flesh days he gave me *tassajos fritos,* that is, steaks of beef or buffalo dried in the sun or wind, which are so hard that it is impossible to eat them without they are first well beaten like stockfish; nor is there any digesting them without the help of a purge. At dinner another piece of that same sticky flesh was boiled, without any other sauce but its own hardness and fair water. At last he deprived me of the satisfac-

tion of gnawing a good bisket, because he would spend no
more of his own, but laid the king's allowance on the table;
in every mouthful whereof there went down abundance of
maggots and *gorgojos* chewed and bruised. On fish days the
common diet was old rank fish boiled in fair water and salt.
At noon we had *mongos,* something like kidney beans, in
which there were so many maggots that they swam at top
of the broth, and the quantity was so great that, besides the
loathing they caused, I doubted whether the dinner was
fish or flesh. This bitter fare was sweetened after dinner
with a little water and sugar; yet the allowance was but a
small cocoa shell full, which rather increased than quenched
drought. Providence relieved us for a month with sharks
and *cachoretas* the seamen caught, which, either boiled or
broiled, were some comfort. Yet he is to be pitied who has
another at his table, for the tediousness of the voyage is
the cause of all these hardships. 'Tis certain they that take
this upon them, lay out thousands of pieces of eight in
making the necessary provision of flesh, fowl, fish, bisket,
rice, sweetmeats, chocolate, and other things. And the quantity is so great that, during the whole voyage, they never
fail of sweetmeats at table and chocolate twice a day, of
which last the sailors and grummets make as great a consumption as the richest. Yet at last the tediousness of the
voyage makes an end of all; and the more because, in a
short time, all the provisions grew naught, except the
sweetmeats and chocolate, which are the only comfort of
passengers.

Abundance of poor sailors fell sick, being exposed to the
continual rains, cold, and other hardships of the season. Yet
they were not allowed to taste of the good bisket, rice,
fowls, Spanish bread, and sweetmeats, put into the custody
of the master by the king's order to be distributed among
the sick, for the honest master spent all at his own table.
Notwithstanding the dreadful sufferings in this prodigious
voyage, yet the desire of gain prevails with many to venture
through it, four, six, and some ten times. The very sailors,
though they forswear the voyage when out at sea, yet when

they come to Acapulco, for the lucre of two hundred seventy-five pieces of eight the king allows them for the return, never remember past sufferings, like women after their labor. The whole pay is three hundred and fifty pieces of eight, but they have only seventy-five paid them at Cavite, when they are bound for America for, if they had half, very few would return to the Philippine Islands for the rest.

The merchants, there is no doubt, get by this voyage a hundred and fifty or two hundred per cent, and factors have nine in the hundred, which, in two or three hundred thousand pieces of eight, amounts to money. And indeed it is a great satisfaction to return home in less than a year with seventeen or eighteen thousand pieces of eight clear gains, besides a man's own venture, a sum that may make a man easy as long as he lives. Captain Emanuel Argüelles told me that he, without having any employment [investment], should clear to himself that voyage by commissions twenty-five or thirty thousand pieces of eight. It was reckoned the pilot would make twenty thousand pieces of eight, his mates nine thousand each. The captain of the galleon, forty thousand. The master, his mate, and boatswain, who may put aboard several bales of goods, may make themselves rich in one voyage. He that borrows money at fifty per cent may get as much more, without standing to the hazard of losses. The extraordinary gains induce many to expose themselves to so many dangers and miseries. For my own part, these or greater hopes shall not prevail with me to undertake that voyage again, which is enough to destroy a man, or make him unfit for anything as long as he lives.

I have made this digression to show the reader through what thorns men must venture to come at the so much coveted roses of riches. The Spaniards and other geographers have given this the name of the Pacific Sea, as may be seen in the maps; but it does not suit with its tempestuous and dreadful motion, for which it ought rather to be called the Restless. But the truth is, the Spaniards gave it this fine name in sailing from Acapulco to the Philippine Islands, which is performed very easily in three months, without any boisterous motion in the sea, and always before the wind, as was said before. . . .

End of the Voyage

On Saturday, January 19, 1698, in the morning, we found ourselves opposite to the village and port of Coyucca, whose coast being fourteen leagues in length abounds in cocos, cacao, vanillas, and other things. The wind holding fair, we entered the port of Acapulco at the great channel, and came to an anchor there at five in the afternoon. All the night was spent laboring with the anchors to draw the ship up the bay, so that before day the stern was made fast with a rope to a tree; for, though the port be good and safe against all winds, yet being winding like a snail, the wind that is good to come in at the two mouths, one N.W. and the other S.E., is not good to carry a ship up under the shore.

Sunday, January 20, all that were aboard again embraced one another with tears of joy, seeing ourselves in our desired port after a voyage of two hundred and four days and five hours. *Te Deum* was sung in thanksgiving, but our commander had not the goodness to solemnize it with firing some guns, saying the powder would not be allowed him at Manila. The castle was saluted with seven guns, and then answered with three, hanging out its colors.

Inquiring of the pilots how many leagues and degrees we had sailed, I found them of several opinions, and this, because we had not kept our course but plied backward and forward to no purpose. Peter Fernández, a Portuguese, born in the island of Madeira, the chief pilot, said we had run one hundred and twenty-five degrees, and two thousand five hundred Spanish leagues. But Isidore Montes d' Oca of Seville, his mate, would have it to be one hundred and thirty degrees, and about three thousand leagues. In sailing from Acapulco to Manila, it is certain there is none of this needless compass taken, as has been observed before for, having fallen down from bare seventeen degrees to thirteen, they then run upon one and the same parallel quite to Manila, right afore the wind, which carries them in two months and a half, or three at farthest, without any storm. And therefore they run through only one hundred and eighteen degrees which, being from east to west, it is hard to measure the leagues; but the pilots guess them to be about two thousand two hundred Spanish [leagues]. . . .

All Sunday we waited for the king's officers to make their search that we might go ashore. They came three hours before night, and were the castellan, Don Francis Mecca, the *contador,* or comptroller, and the *guarda mayor,* or surveyor, to whom was delivered the register or entry of all that was aboard the galleon (to regulate the king's duties, which amounted to eighty thousand pieces of eight, including the present to the viceroy) and the duplicates of the letters to be sent to Madrid, all to be sent to Mexico with all speed by another express, to make use of them in case the first, sent by the other messenger we said was put ashore, were lost. Having taken an account who I was, they expressed a great deal of civility and offered their service to me. When they were gone, the image of our blessed lady was carried ashore, and I went along with it to the parish church, the galleon in the meanwhile firing all its guns. At night I came back and lay aboard the galleon, that my equipage might not be left to my slave, through whose negligence it might have been damaged. Going ashore upon Monday, I was told that the sentinel which looks toward Peru (there being two on a mountain, whereof this is one, and the other looks toward China) had discovered two ships out at sea, making toward the port. They were supposed to be the admiral and tender of the Peru fleet that came for the Count de Cañete, the new viceroy. I dined with Don Francis Mecca, and before we arose from table we heard a cannon fired. I asked the meaning of it, and he told me it was to signify to the ships that came, if friends, that they might come into the port; if others, to let them understand that the Spaniards were upon their guard and ready to receive them. The castellan sent Major Arámbolo with the boat of our ship to view them and bring an account what they were, because the boats of two vessels belonging to Peru were not fit to go. It is fit I should here stop my pen, that I may with fresh courage continue my voyage in the next, which is the last volume.

❧ III ❧

Eighteenth Century

Three Peruvians drinking *mate*,
popularly called "St. Bartholomew's herb."

⊷ 9 ⊷

Voyage of Amedée Frezier to
South America
(1712-1714)

————◆●◆————

*The eighteenth century witnessed greatly increased
travel to the Hispanic lands of the New World, particularly by Frenchmen. The accession of the Bourbons of France to the Spanish throne in 1700 and the
enlightened despotism of these monarchs facilitated a
series of scientific missions that subsequently published detailed reports of observations on all aspects
of colonial life. An interesting example is Amedée
François Frezier (1682–1773), a French military engineer, who spent the years 1712 to 1714 visiting the
west coast of South America and ports of Brazil. The
resulting book-length account appeared in Paris immediately upon his return and quickly required a
succession of reprintings. Writing with literary distinction, Frezier presents a lively description of social
and cultural life in Lima. Whereas a century before
the Portuguese Jew had tended to bare the sordid
aspects, the Frenchman depicts its more opulent and
aristocratic ways, though in many details their observations coincide. More briefly than when he wrote about*

The popularity of Frezier's narrative almost at once produced
an English translation, *A Voyage to the South Sea and Along
the Coasts of Chili and Peru in the Years 1712, 1713, and 1714.
. . .* (London: J. Bowyer, 1717), from which the following
slightly modernized selections are made.

Peru, he sketches the conditions of existence that he noted in a short stopover at São Vicente, then the capital of colonial Brazil.

Customs and Manners of the Spaniards of Peru

Before we leave Peru, it will be proper, in this place, to say something of what I could observe of the manners of the Creole Spaniards, that is, those born in that country. To begin with religion, I must observe that, like those in Europe, they value themselves upon being the best Christians of all nations. They even pretend to distinguish betwixt themselves and us by that qualification; so that among them it is a very usual way of speaking to say a Christian and a Frenchman to signify a Spaniard and a Frenchman. But without diving into the interior of either, they have nothing of the outward practice of the church discipline, by which they may merit that pre-eminence. . . .

Those people are not only credulous to excess but also superstitious. They add to the beads they wear about their necks some *habillas,* being a sort of sea chestnuts, and another sort of fruit of the like nature, resembling the shape of a pear, called *chonta,* with nutmegs and other such things to preserve themselves against witchcraft and infectious air. The ladies wear amulets about their necks, being medals without any impression, and a little jet hand, a quarter of an inch long, or else made of fig tree wood, and called *higa,* the fingers closed, but the thumb standing out. The notion they have of the virtue of those amulets, or counter-charms, is to preserve themselves from the harm that might be done by such as admire their beauty, which they call, as in English, an evil eye. These preservatives are made larger for children. This superstition is common among the ladies and the meaner people; but there is another which is almost general, and of great moment for avoiding the pains of the other world, which is to take care in this to provide a religious habit, which they buy, to die and be buried in, being persuaded that, when clad in a livery so much respected here below, they shall, without any difficulty, be admitted into Heaven, and cannot be drove into the utter darkness, as the friars give them to understand. . . .

To conclude, tho' such persons [clergy and friars] should with their mouths preach up Christian virtues, what fruit could they produce whilst they give such ill example? If it were upon modesty and meekness, they are impudent in the highest degree. May I presume to say it, most of them are generally armed with a dagger; it is not to be thought that is to murder, but at least to oppose any that should oppose their pleasures or offend them. Should the subject be poverty and the contempt of riches, the most regular of them trade and have their slaves of both sexes. And several churchmen appear in colored cloths adorned with gold, under their usual habit. Should it be humility, they are insufferably proud, a true copy of the Pha[r]isees, who would take place everywhere and be saluted in public places. In short, not satisfied with the low bows made them, they offer their sleeves to be kissed in the open streets and in the churches, whither they go on purpose to disturb the faithful, who are attentive to the sacrifice, to have homage done to their pretended dignity, differing very much therein from the sentiments of the first of the Western monks, St. Benedict, who chose for his religious men the habit of the poor in his time, and St. Francis, a ridiculous habit, to render himself contemptible in the eyes of men. It is well known that, to prevent their meddling with worldly affairs, the King of Spain has been formerly obliged to make use of his authority, and yet he has not prevailed. . . .

In short, I do not, by what I have said, pretend to exclude the worthy and learned people of Peru and Chili. I know there are such among all conditions; there have been some of eminent piety, whom the Church has admitted into the catalogue of Saints. Lima has produced within its territory St. Rose of St. Mary of the third order of St. Dominick. The bishop of that city, Toribius,* a European, sanctified himself there; and they there honor the blessed Francis Solano, a native of Paraguay. But after all, I differ very much from the opinion of the author of the life of the holy Toribius, who says that in all likelihood, Peru will afford heaven more saints than it has given silver to the earth. Virtue seems to me to be more common among the laity than among the friars and the clergy. I make no scruple to say so; it would be a false nicety to spare men who dishonor their profession without control under pretense that they are consecrated to God by solemn vows.

This is what I have to object, as a traveler who observes what is done in the countries where I happen to be, and who deduces, as a consequence from the behavior of such people, that they have little religion in their hearts, notwithstanding their gravity and outward affectation.

If we next examine the character and inclinations of the secular Creoles, we shall find among them, as among other nations, a mixture of good and evil. It is said, that the inhabitants of la Puna, that is, the mountain country of Peru, are well enough to deal with, and that there are very worthy people among them, generous and ready to do a good turn, especially if it can feed their vanity and show the greatness of their souls, which they there call *punto,* that is, point of honor, which most of them value themselves upon, as a qualification that raises them above other nations and is a proof of the purity of the Spanish blood, and of the nobility all the whites boast of. The most beggarly and meanest of the Europeans become gentlemen as soon as they find themselves transplanted among the Indians, blacks, mulattoes, mestizos, and others of mixt blood. That imaginary nobility causes them to perform most of their good actions. I found in Chili that they practiced much hospitality, especially abroad in the country, where they entertain strangers very generously and keep them long enough in their houses without any interest. Thus the little merchants of Biscay and

* Santo Toribio, Archbishop of Lima (1538–1606), canonized in 1726—*I. A. L.*

other European Spaniards travel much, with small expense.

In the great towns and along the coast, we now find that the Creoles are fallen off from those good qualities our first Frenchmen had found among them, and which all men applauded. Perhaps the natural antipathy they have for our nation is increased by the ill success of the trade they have drove with us. This antipathy extends so far as to lessen the affection they ought to have for their king [the Bourbon Philip V], because he is a Frenchman. Lima [and the surrounding mountain area] was at first divided into two parties, and the clergy and friars impudently prayed for his [Philip's] competitor [the Hapsburg claimant to the Spanish throne]. But the Basques scattered about the country, and most of the European Spaniards, being informed of the valor and virtue of Philip V, always exerted their fidelity to him, so that the Creoles, being convinced of their ill-grounded prejudice, began to have an affection for the Holy King, for so they call him. And, tho' there should still remain any obstinate spirits, they will become more cautious, seeing his crown fixed by the unanimous consent of all nations. They are timorous and easy to be governed, tho' dispersed and remote from their superiors, and have a thousand retreats of deserts and plains to escape punishment. And besides, there is no country where justice is less severe, for scarce anybody is punished with death. Nevertheless, they stand in awe of the king's officers. Four troopers, who are no better than messengers, coming from the viceroy, make all men quake at the distance of 400 leagues from him.

As for wit in general, the Creoles of Lima do not want [lack] it. They have a vivacity and disposition to sciences; those of the mountains somewhat less; but both sorts of them fancy they much exceed the European Spaniards, whom among themselves they call brutes. Perhaps this is an effect of the antipathy there is between them, tho' they are subjects of the same monarch. I believe one of the principal reasons of that aversion is because they always see those strangers in possession of the prime places in the state and driving the best of their trade, which is the only employment of the whites, who scorn to apply themselves to arts for which they have no relish.

In other points, they are little addicted to war. The easy tranquillity they live in makes them apprehensive of disturbing their repose. However, they undergo the fatigue of long journeys by land with much satisfaction. Four or 500 leagues traveling through deserts and over uncouth mountains does not fright them any more than the ill fare they meet with by the way; whence may be concluded that they are good for the country they live in.

In relation to commerce, they are as sharp and understanding as the Europeans, but being dainty and slothful and not vouchsafing to deal without there be considerable profit, the Basques and other European Spaniards, who are more laborious, grow rich sooner. The very workmen, who live barely on the labor of their hands, are so indulgent to themselves as not to spare taking the siesta, that is, a nap after dinner; whence it follows that, losing the best part of the day, they do not half the work they might, and by that means make all workmanship excessively dear.

Delicacy and slothfulness seem to be peculiar to the country, perhaps because it is too good; for it is observed that those who have been bred to labor in Spain grow idle there in a short time, like the Creoles. In short, men are more robust and laborious in a poor country than in a fruitful. . . .

The Creoles are generally outwardly composed and do not depart from that gravity which is natural to them. They are sober as to wine, but they eat greedily and after an indecent manner, sometimes all in the same dish, commonly a portion, like the friars. At any considerable entertainment, they set before the guests several plates of different sorts of food successively, and then each of them gives the same to his servants and to those that stand by and are not at the table, to the end, say they, that all may partake of the good cheer. When the Creoles came to eat aboard our ships, where they were served after the French fashion in great dishes placed according to art and symmetry, they boldly took them off to give to their slaves, sometimes before they had been touched. But when the captains durst not make them sensible of that indecency, our cooks, who were jealous of their own labor, did not spare to let them understand that they discomposed the beauty of the entertainment. Not having the use of forks, they are obliged to wash after eating, which they all do in the same basin, and with that general and disagreeable washing-water they do not stick to wash [mind washing] their lips. The meat they eat is seasoned with *axi* [garlic], or pimiento, that sort of spice we have before spoken of, which is so hot that strangers cannot possibly endure it. But that which makes it still worse, is a greasy taste the lard gives to all their cookery. Besides, they have not the art of roasting great joints, because they do not turn them continually as we do, which they admired the most of all our dishes. They make two meals, one at ten in the morning, the other at four in the evening, which is instead of a dinner at Lima, and a collation at midnight. In other places they eat as we do in France.

During the day, they make much use of the herb [yerba mate] of Paraguay, which some call St. Bartholomew's herb, who, they pretend, came into those provinces, where he made it wholesome and beneficial, whereas before it was venomous. Being only brought dry and almost in powder, I cannot describe it. Instead of drinking the tincture, or infusion, apart as we drink tea, they put the herb into a cup, or bowl, made of a calabash, or gourd, tipped with silver, which they call mate. They add sugar and pour on it water, which they drink immediately, without giving it time to infuse, because it turns as black as ink. To avoid drinking the herb which swims at the top, they make use of a silver pipe, at the end whereof is a bowl, full of little holes; so that the liquor sucked in at the other end is clear from the herb. They drink round with the same pipe, pouring hot water on the same herb, as it is drank off. Instead of a pipe, which they call *bombilla*, some part the herb with a silver separation, called *apartador*, full of little holes.

The reluctancy the French have shown to drink after all sorts of people, in a country where many are poxed, has occasioned the inventing of the use of little glass-pipes, which they begin to use at Lima. That liquor, in my opinion, is better than tea; it has a flavor of the herb, which is agreeable enough. The people of the country are so used to it that even the poorest use it once a day, when they rise in the morning. . . .

I have elsewhere observed that the use of this herb is necessary where there are mines, and on the mountains of Peru, where the whites think the use of wine pernicious. They rather choose to drink brandy and leave the wine to the Indians and blacks, which they like very well.

If the Spaniards are sober as to wine, they are not very reserved as to continency. In matters of love they yield to no nation. They freely sacrifice most of what they have to that passion; and, tho' covetous enough upon all other occasions, they are generous beyond measure to women. To add the pleasure of liberty to the rest, they seldom marry in the face of the church; but, to use their own way of expression, they all generally marry behind the church, that is, they are all engaged in a decent sort of concubinage, which among them is nothing scandalous; so far from it, that it is a disgrace not to keep a mistress, upon condition she be true to them. But they are as apt to observe that fidelity as wives do to their husbands in Europe. It is even frequent enough to see married men forsake their wives to adhere to mulattoes and blacks, which often occasions disorders in families. Thus the two ancient ways of marrying still subsist in that country: that of keeping a mistress is very answerable to that which was called by use, and there is some remainder of the other in the ceremony of marriage. The bridegroom puts into the bride's hand 13 pieces of money, which she then drops into the curate's hand. So, in the marriage *per coemptionem*, the bride and bridegroom gave one another a piece of money.

The priests and friars, as I have said before, make no scruple of it, and the public is no farther scandalized than as jealousy concurs, because they often keep their mistresses finer than others, by which the mulatto women are often known. Several bishops, to put a stop to that abuse, every year at Easter, excommunicate all that are engaged to concubines; but, as the evil is universal, and the confessors are parties concerned, they are not severe in that particular. Whence it follows that those people, who are otherwise easily frighted by the church thunderbolts, do not much fear these. The friars evade those strokes, on account that they, not being free, are not looked upon as concubinaries in the utmost forms; and that, besides, they have not the intention to be so. A pleasant solution, the invention whereof must doubtless be assigned to some cunning casuist grounded on *Justinian's Code,* which declares conventions invalid which are made among persons that are not free, and on the wise maxim expounded by those casuists so much cried down in France, *that the intention regulates the quality of the action.* In fine, this custom is so settled, so commodious, and so generally received, that I question whether it can be ever abolished. The laws of the kingdom seem to authorize it, for bastards inherit almost like the lawfully begotten when they are owned by the father; and there is no disgrace inherent to that birth, as is among us, where the crime is wrongfully imputed to the innocent person, wherein we should perhaps be more favorable, if every man were well acquainted with his original.

Tho' the women are not shut up like the Spanish women in Europe, yet it is not usual for them to go abroad by day. But, about nightfall, they have liberty to make their visits, for the most part where it is not expected; for the modestest in open day are the boldest at night, their faces being then covered with their veils, so that they cannot be known, they perform the part which the men do in France.

The method they use at home is to sit on cushions along the wall, with their legs across on an *estrado,* or part of the room raised a step above the rest, with a carpet on it, after the Turkish fashion. They spend almost whole days in this manner, without altering their posture, even to eat; for they

are served apart, on little chests, which they always have
before them to put up the work they do. This makes them
have a heavy gait, without the grace of our French women.

That which they call *estrado,* as was hinted above, is,
as used in Spain, all one end or side of a visiting-room,
raised six or seven inches above the floor, of the breadth of
five or six foot. The men, on the contrary, sit on chairs, and
only some very great familiarity admits them to the *estrado.*
In other respects, the women there have as much liberty at
home as in France. They there receive company with a very
good grace and take pleasure to entertain their guests with
playing on the harp or the guitar, to which they sing. And
if they are desired to dance, they do it with much com-
plaisance and politeness.

Their manner of dancing is almost quite different from
ours, where we value the motion of the arms and sometimes
that of the head. In most of their dances their arms hang
down, or else are wrapped up in a cloak they wear, so that
nothing is seen but the bending of the body, and the activity of the feet. They have many figure dances, in which
they lay by their cloaks or mantles; but the graces they add
are rather actions than gestures.

The men dance almost after the same manner, without
laying aside their long swords, the point whereof they keep
before them that it may not hinder them in rising or cou-
peeing, which is sometimes to such a degree that it looks
like kneeling. . . .

These agreeable accomplishments, which Spanish women
have from their education, are the more moving, because
they are generally attended with a graceful air. They are,
for the most part, sprightly enough; their complexion is
good but not lasting, by reason of their using so much sublimate [a form of make-up], which is contrary to what
Oexmelian says in his History of the Bucaniers. Sublimate,
says he, is also formed, or metamorphosed, tho' not used in
America, because the women there do not paint. They have
sparkling eyes, their discourse pleasant, approving of a free
gallantry, to which they answer wittily, and often with such

a turn as has a taste of libertinism according to our customs. Those proposals, which a lover would not dare to make in France without incurring the indignation of a modest woman, are so far from scandalizing that they are pleased with them, tho' they be, at the same time, far from consenting. Being persuaded that it is the greatest token of love that can be shown them, they return thanks as for an honor done them, instead of taking offense as of an ill opinion conceived of their virtue. By these simple and natural ways we perceive the secret pleasure and satisfaction we receive when we find ourselves courted. This effect of self-love, which is the source of reciprocal affection, is afterward the occasion of disorder, when decency and religion do not put a stop to it. But, without regarding essential duties, humane prudence alone ought to suffice to hinder a man of sense from being taken in the snares of the coquettes of that country, for their obliging behavior is generally the effect of their avarice rather than a token of their inclination. They are perfectly skilled in the art of imposing on the frailty a man shows for them, and engaging him in continual expenses without discretion. They seem to take a pride in ruining many lovers, as a warrior does in having vanquished many enemies. . . .

That misfortune is not the only punishment of those who suffer themselves to be taken. They there often lose the inestimable treasure of health, which they seldom recover, not only because in those temperate climates they make little account of the venereal diseases, notwithstanding which they attain to the longest old age, but also because the scarcity of physicians, who are only to be found in three or four great cities, does not afford them the opportunity of being cured. Some women only patch up their distempers with sarsaparilla, ptisans of mallows,* and other herbs of the country, and especially the use of cauteries, which are looked upon as specifics [remedies], and whereof both sexes alike make provision, which the women so little en-

* A decoction similar to barley water made by boiling down barley and other ingredients—*I. A. L.*

deavor to conceal that, in their serious visits, they enquire
after their issues and dress them for one another. They [the
men] ruin themselves in debauching with the women; and
they themselves observe that, whether it is that God pun-
ishes them for those criminal expenses or, as others think,
that the estates they have are unjustly usurped from the
Indians, they are scarce ever seen to descend to the third
generation. What the father rakes together with much
trouble, and often with much injustice in the administration of governments, the sons do not fail to squander; so
that the grandsons of the greatest men are often the poorest. They are themselves so far convinced of this truth, that
it is become a proverb in Spain: "It thrives no better than
an Indian estate."

The women, as I have said, are the principal cause; vanity
and sensuality render them insatiable as to ornaments and
good feeding. Tho' the make of their habit be of itself
plain enough and not very susceptible of changes in fash-
ions, they love to be richly dressed, whatsoever it costs, even
in the most private places. Even their very smocks, and
fustian waistcoats they wear over them, are full of lace; and
their prodigality extends to put it upon socks and sheets.
The upper petticoat they commonly wear, called *faldellín,*
is open before and has three rows of lace, the middlemost
of gold and silver, extraordinary wide, sewed on silk galoons,
which terminate at the edges. Their upper waistcoat, which
they call *jubón,* is either of rich cloth of gold, or, in hot
weather, of fine linen, covered with abundance of lace, con-
fusedly put on. The sleeves are large and have a pouch
hanging down to the knees. But in Chili they begin to put
down the pouch and cut them more even, after the manner
of boots. If they have a little apron, it is made of two or
three strips of silk flowered with gold or silver, sewn together with laces.

In the cold countries they are always wrapped up in a
mantle, being no other than a misshapen piece of bays
[thick, coarse woolen cloth], one-third longer than it is
broad, one point whereof hangs upon their heels. The best

are of rich stuffs, covered with four or five rows of broad lace, and extraordinary fine. In other respects, their formal dress is the same as that of the Spanish women in Europe, viz. the black taffeta veil, which covers them from the head to the feet. They use that they call mantilla for an undress, to appear the more modest; and it is a sort of cloak, or mantle, round at the bottom, of a dark color, edged with black taffeta. Their dress in the black taffeta veil, a wide upper petticoat of a musk color, with little flowers, under which is another close coat of colored silk called *pollera*. In this dress they go to the churches, walking gravely, their faces so veiled that generally only one eye is to be seen. By this outside a man would take them for vestal virgins, but would be commonly very much deceived. Whilst these women are abroad nothing appears more clean, nothing more composed, or more neat. They have no ornament on the head; their hair hangs behind in tresses. Sometimes they tie ribbons about their head with gold or silver; when the ribbon is broad, adorned with lace, and goes twice about the forehead, it is called *vincha*. The breasts and shoulders are half-naked, unless they wear a large handkerchief, which hangs down behind to the mid-leg, and in Peru serves instead of a little cloak or mantle, called *gregorillo*. They commit not any offense against modesty when they show their breasts, which the Spaniards look upon with indifference, but out of a ridiculous extravagancy they are much in love with little feet, of which they take great notice; and therefore they take extraordinary care to hide them, so that it is a favor to show them, which they do with dexterity.

I do not speak of extraordinary ornaments of pearls and jewels; there must be many pendants, bracelets, necklaces and rings, to reach the height of the fashion, which is much the same as the ancient mode of France.

As for the men, they are now clad after the French fashion, but for the most part in silk cloths with an extravagant mixture of light colors. Out of a sort of vanity peculiar to their nation, they will not own that they have borrowed that mode from us, tho' it has not been used among them any

longer than since the reign of King Philip V. They rather
choose to call it a warlike habit.

The grown men wear the *golilla,* being a little band, not
hanging but sticking out forward under the chin, and a
sword as they do in Spain, excepting the judges and presi-
dents.

The traveling habit in Peru is a coat flashed on both
sides under the arms, and the sleeves open above and below, with button-holes; it is called *capotillo de dos faldas*
[a loose jacket].

The dwellings of the Spaniards in Peru are no way answerable to the magnificence of their garb. Without Lima,
in which place the buildings are handsome enough, nothing
is poorer than the houses; they consist in only a ground
floor, 14 or 15 foot high. The contrivance of the stateliest
of them is to have a court at the entrance, adorned with
porticos of timber work, the length of the building which
is always [a] single [story] in Chili, because of the largeness
the top would require. But on the coast of Peru, they make
them as deep as they please because, when they cannot have
lights from the walls, they make them in the roof, there
being no rain to apprehend. The first room is a large hall,
about 19 foot broad, and between 30 and 40 in length,
which leads into two other chambers, one within another.
The first is that where the *estrado* is to receive company,
and the bed in a nook, in the nature of an alcove, spacious
within and whose chief conveniency is a false door [i.e.
back door] to receive or dismiss company, without being
perceived coming in, tho' upon surprise. There are few of
those beds in the houses, because the servants lie on sheep
skins upon the ground.

The height and largeness of the rooms would nevertheless give them some air of grandeur, did they know how
to make their lights regularly; but they make so few windows that they have always a dusk and melancholy air; and,
having no use of glass, they are latticed with grates of turned
wood, which still lessens the light. The household stuff does
not make amends for the ill contrivance of the building;

only the *estrado* is covered with carpets, and velvet cushions for the women to sit on. The chairs for the men are covered with leather, printed in half relief. There are no hangings but abundance of scurvy pictures made by the Indians of Cuzco. In fine, there are neither boarded nor stone floors, which makes the houses damp, especially in Chili, where it rains much in winter.

The common materials for private buildings are those they call *adobes,* that is, large bricks, about 2 foot long, 1 in breadth, and 4 inches thick, in Chili, and somewhat smaller in Peru, because it never rains there; or else the walls are of clay rammed between two planks, which they call *tapias.* That manner of building was used among the Romans, as may be seen in Vitruvius.* It is not expensive, because the soil is everywhere fit for making of those bricks, and yet it lasts ages, as appears by the remains of structures and forts built by the Indians, which have stood at least 200 years. It is true, it is not so in regard to rain, for they are obliged to cover them in winter on the north side with thatch, or planks. Thus they preserve them in Chili. The public structures are, for the most part, made of burnt bricks, and stone. At La Conception they have a greenish fort of a soft nature; at Santiago they have a stone of a good grain, dug half a league northwest from the city; at Coquimbo they have a white stone as light as a pumice stone; at Callao and Lima they have a stone of good grain brought 12 leagues by land, full of saltpeter, which makes it molder, tho' otherwise very hard; the mole of the port, made in 1694, is built with it. There are in the mountains quarries of the fine limestone, whereof plaster of Paris is made; they only use it to make soap and to stop earthen vessels. All their lime is made of shells, whence it is that the same is only fit to whiten the walls.

As for their taste in architecture, it must be owned that the churches in Lima are well built as to the case only, which is well proportioned, lined with pilasters, adorned

* Marcus Vitruvius Pollio, Roman architect and engineer, first century B. C.—*I. A. L.*

with moldings, and without carved capitals, over which are beautiful cornishes and fine vaults full centered and contracted. But in the decoration of the altars all are confused, crowded and bad, so that a man cannot but lament the immense sums they spend on those gilt disorders. . . .

The Description of the City of São Salvador, or St. Saviour, the Capital of Brazil

The town which our charts call São Salvador, or St. Saviour, is in the language of the country plainly called *Cidade da Bahia,* the City of the Bay. It is in about 12 degrees 45 minutes of south latitude, on an eminence of about 100 fathoms, formed by the eastside of the Bay of all Saints. The access to it is so difficult, by reason of its great steepness, that they have been forced to have recourse to machines for carrying up and letting down of goods from the town to the port.

The plan of the upper town is as regularly drawn as the unevenness of the mountainous soil would permit; but tho' the streets there are straight, and of a good breadth, most of them have so steep a descent that they would be impracticable for our coaches, and even for our chairs.

The rich people, notwithstanding that inconveniency, do not go a foot; being always industrious, as well in America as in Europe, to find means to distinguish themselves from the rest of mankind, they would be ashamed to make use of the legs which nature has given us to walk. They lazily cause themselves to be carried in beds of fine cotton, hanging by the ends to a pole, which two blacks carry on their heads or shoulders; and to be there concealed, and that neither the rain nor the heat of the sun may offend them, that bed is covered with a tester [canopy], to which they hang curtains to be drawn when they please. Thus lying along there at their ease, with the head on a rich pillow, they are carried about more gently than in coaches or chairs. Those cotton hammocks are called *serpentins,* and not *palankins,* as some travelers say.

If this great unevenness of the ground is inconvenient to the inhabitants, it is on the other hand very advantageous to the fortifications. With a small expense this might be made a town morally impregnable; nature has there made ditches and outworks flanking one another, where the ground might be disputed inch by inch. The east side is almost inaccessible, being almost covered by a deep pool, having 15 or 20 fathom water in some places, which lies down in a vale between two hills, the ascent whereof is very steep.

From that pool, which comes very near the sea, on the north side, is a little stream that serves for ships to water.

In short, to approach the town on the south side, the landing must be near the forts I have mentioned, or farther in among the batteries, which are on the coast; which would certainly be very difficult, tho' the opposition were never so small.

The Dutch, in 1624, having taken this place, when under the dominion of the Spaniards, fortified it on the landside with a rampart, or rather a great entrenchment of earth, which enclosed the body of the upper town, the third part of a league in length; which did not prevent the Spaniards' retaking of it the next year, 1625. That enclosure is now quite ruined; it has been neglected to endeavor to fortify the approaches by a number of forts made in several places.

The first, on the south side is the new, or St. Peter's Fort, made of earth, faced with stonework, which they were working upon when we were there. It is a regular square, with 4 bastions, of 20 foot in the face, as much curtain, and 4 fathoms flank; furnished with cannon, which on the one side plays upon the road, but much under metal. About it is a little ditch, five or six fathoms wide.

The second, on the same side nearer the town, is Fort Diego, or James. It is also a square of stonework, without a ditch, with 4 bastions of 8 fathoms in the face. It is a battery of bombs for the road, and serves now for a magazine.

The third is the great powder magazine, called *Casa da Polvora,* or the powder-house. It is also a square of stonework, without a ditch; the bastions of 6 fathoms face, the curtains of 14, and the flanks of 2. It contains 8 distinct magazines, vaulted and covered pyramid-wise, with as many globes on the tops; said to contain 2,000 or 3,000 barrels of powder; but there are often under 100.

The fourth is Fort St. Anthony, on the north, which is directly over the watering-place, of stonework, square like the others, but somewhat larger and better contrived. The bastions have about 16 fathoms face, the flanks 4 or 5, and the curtain 25, with a good ditch. One side of it plays upon the road, but it does not well defend a depth, by which men may come under covert to the counterscarp, and by the same way go to the town. Half a cannon shot from this, toward the N.E., is Fort *Nossa Senhora da Victoria,* the Fort of our Lady of Victory, made of earth, to which I could not go, nor to the others that are farther off, as that of St. Bartholomew, which defends a little harbor, where ships may careen; that of *Montserate,* nor to those at the entrance, before mentioned.

To secure these forts and the town, the King of Portugal maintains six companies of regular forces, uniformly clothed, and not in brown linen, as Dampier* says; that is altered; they are well disciplined and paid. Those I saw were in a very good condition, well armed, and full of fine men; they want nothing but the reputation of being good soldiers.

The city of Bahia, as is well known, is the capital and metropolis of Brazil, and the usual seat of a viceroy. However, the governor has not always that title; witness he that was in our time.

The inhabitants have an outside good enough as to politeness, neatness, and the manner of giving themselves a

* William Dampier (1652–1715), English explorer, pirate, and author—*I. A. L.*

good air, much like the French. I mean the men only, for there are so few women to be seen that but a very imperfect account can be given of them. The Portuguese are so jealous that they scarce allow them to go to mass on Sundays and holidays. Nevertheless, in spite of all their precautions, they are almost all of them libertines, and find means to impose upon the watchfulness of their fathers and husbands, exposing themselves to the cruelty of the latter, who kill them without fear of punishment when they discover their intrigues. Instances hereof are so frequent, that they reckoned above thirty women murdered by their husbands within a year. Fathers show more humanity toward their daughters; when they cannot hide their shame by marrying them off, they turn them out of doors, and then they are at liberty to be common. A fine expedient!

Whether it be the effect of the climate or of our natural bent after that which others endeavor to keep from us by force, there is no need of any extraordinary efforts to be admitted to the last familiarity. The mothers help the daughters to keep out of the sight of their fathers, either through compassion or out of a principle of the law of nature, which enjoins us to do by another as we would be done by. But in short, tho' they did not themselves meet men half way, the scarcity of white women would draw the crowd after them; for nineteen in twenty of the people we see there are blacks, men, and women, all naked, except those parts which modesty obliges to cover; so that the city looks like a new Guinea. In short, the streets are full of none but hideous figures of black men and women slaves, whom delicacy and avarice, rather than necessity, have transplanted from the coast of Africa, to make up the state of the rich and contribute toward the sloth of the poor, who ease themselves of their labor on them, so that there are always about twenty blacks to one white. Who would believe it? there are shops full of those poor wretches, who are exposed there stark naked, and bought like cattle, over whom the buyers have the same power; so that upon slight disgusts, they may kill them almost without fear of punishment, or at least treat them as cruelly as they please. I know not how such barbarity can be reconciled to the maxims of religion, which makes them members of the same body with the whites when they have been baptized, and raises them to the dignity of sons of God, *all sons of the most High.* Doubtless they will not suffer themselves to be convinced of that truth; for those poor slaves are too much abused by their brethren, who scorn that relation.

I here make this comparison, because the Portuguese are Christians who make a great outward show of religion, even more than the Spaniards. For most of them walk along the streets with their beads in their hands, a figure of St. Anthony on their breasts, or hanging about their necks, and with an extravagant furniture of a long Spanish sword on their left, and a dagger almost as long as a short French sword on their right; to the end that when occasion shall offer, neither arm may be useless toward destroying of their enemies. In reality, those outward tokens of religion are very deceitful among them, not only in regard to true probity but even to Christian sentiments; they often serve to conceal from the eyes of the world a great number of Jews; an amazing instance has been seen in that town. A curate, after having for several years behaved himself outwardly to edification, at last made his escape with the sacred ornaments into Holland, to live there as a Jew; for which reason, to be admitted to the clergy, a man must prove himself an old Christian, as they call it, that is, of ancient Christian descent.

The upper town is adorned with several churches, the most remarkable of which is the cathedral, which having the title of St. Saviour, has communicated its name to all the town. Before it is a small open place, like a platform, whence is a prospect of all the bay and several islands, forming an agreeable landscape. Adjoining to that place is the hospital under the name of *Nossa Senhora da Misericordia,* or our Lady of Mercy. On the cathedral depend the two parishes of St. Anthony and St. Peter, and if I mistake not, St. Barbara. To the north of the cathedral is the monastery of the Jesuits, whose church is all built with marble carried from Europe. The sacristy is very beautiful, combined with the next work the buffets [vestry], or places for vesting, the curious wood, inlaying and ivory they are made of, as for a series of little pictures that adorns them. But we must not call the painting on the ceiling fine, being unworthy to be taken notice of by a man of skill. The other churches and monasteries have nothing remarkable. There are Benedictines, Franciscans, Carmelites, Dominicans, Barefoot Augustins, and a monastery of Capuchins, which formerly consisted of all French, but they were turned out during the last wars, to put in Italians. They are there called *os Barbudos,* or the Bearded Friars. I know of but one moastery of nuns, called *as Freiras da Incarnaçao,* or the Nuns of the Incarnation. In the lower town there are other chapels of brotherhoods: St. Barbara, our Lady of the Rosary, and *de Pila*————this last for the soldiers———— *Corpo Santo* for poor people, and the Conception for sailors.

The great trade that is drove at the bay, for the country commodities, make the inhabitants easy. Every year about March, there arrives a fleet of about twenty ships from Lisbon, laden with linen and woolen cloths and stuffs, especially serges, *perpetuanas* [thick woolen material], *bays* [baize], and *sayas* [outer skirts], which the women use for their veils, instead of black taffeta, as the women wear in Spain, which fashion they follow pretty near. The use of that stuff is a piece of modesty forced upon them by the king's order, who prohibits the wearing of silk. The other saleable commodities are stockings, hats, iron, kitchen furniture, but above all, bisket, meal, wine, oil, butter, cheese, etc. The same ships, in exchange, carry back gold, sugar, tobacco, wood for dying called Brazil wood, balsam, oil of *copayva, hypecacuana,* some raw hides, etc.

The town standing on a steep eminence, they have erected three machines for carrying up and letting down of goods to and from the upper town. Of those three, one is at the Jesuits, not only for the public, who pay for the use of it, but also for the use of that community, which is certainly no enemy to trade. Those machines consist of two great wheels like drums, which have one common axle-tree, over which is wound a cable, made fast to a sledge or cart, which is drawn up by blacks, who going in the wheels, wind the cable up the spindle, and to the end that the sledge may meet with no opposition, but come up easily, it slides along a boarded way, reaching from the top of the hill to the bottom, being about 140 fathoms in length.

Besides the trade of European commodities, the Portuguese have another considerable [trade] in Guinea. They carry thither linen cloth, made in the islands of Cape Verde, glass beads, and other trifles, and bring back gold, ivory and blacks to sell at Brazil.

The correspondence with Río de Janeiro, near which are the gold mines of the *Paulistas* [natives of São Paulo], which afford great plenty, still adds to the wealth of the bay. The houses there are well built, the inhabitants handsomely lodged and furnished. The men and women are modest in their habit, because they are wisely forbid wearing of gold or silver lace; but they show their wealth in certain ornaments of massive gold, even on their black women slaves, who are adorned with rich chains several times about their necks, great rings and pendants in their ears, crosses, plates they wear on their foreheads, and other very weighty ornaments of gold.

Contrary to the usual policy of other Crowns, the King of Portugal does not permit strangers to resort thither, to carry away the product of the country, tho' they buy with specie, much less to carry goods to sell or exchange, wherein he is more faithfully served than the King of Spain in Peru. This regulation is grounded on two good reasons: the first, to oblige his subjects to take pains, and by that means procure them all the profit of the commerce; the second and the chiefest, to prevent the duties he has upon all commodities being sunk by the viceroys and governors, for all ships being obliged to come and unlade in his sight at Lisbon, nothing can escape him.

Tho' this Bay of All Saints be a very populous place, where they reckon there are about 2,000 houses, it is not nevertheless a good place for ships to put in, especially in winter, not only because of the great rains it is subject to at that time, but also because provisions are not good there. The meal and wine carried thither from Europe are always the worse for that passage; the beef there is worth nothing; there is no mutton, and fowls are scarce and dear. The fruits of that season, as the bananas, and the oranges, will not keep long at sea, and garden stuff is there almost unknown, either through the supineness of the Portuguese, or because it is a difficult matter to cultivate the same, by reason of the great multitude of pismires which destroy the plants and the fruit almost everywhere, so that they are the bane of agriculture in Brazil.

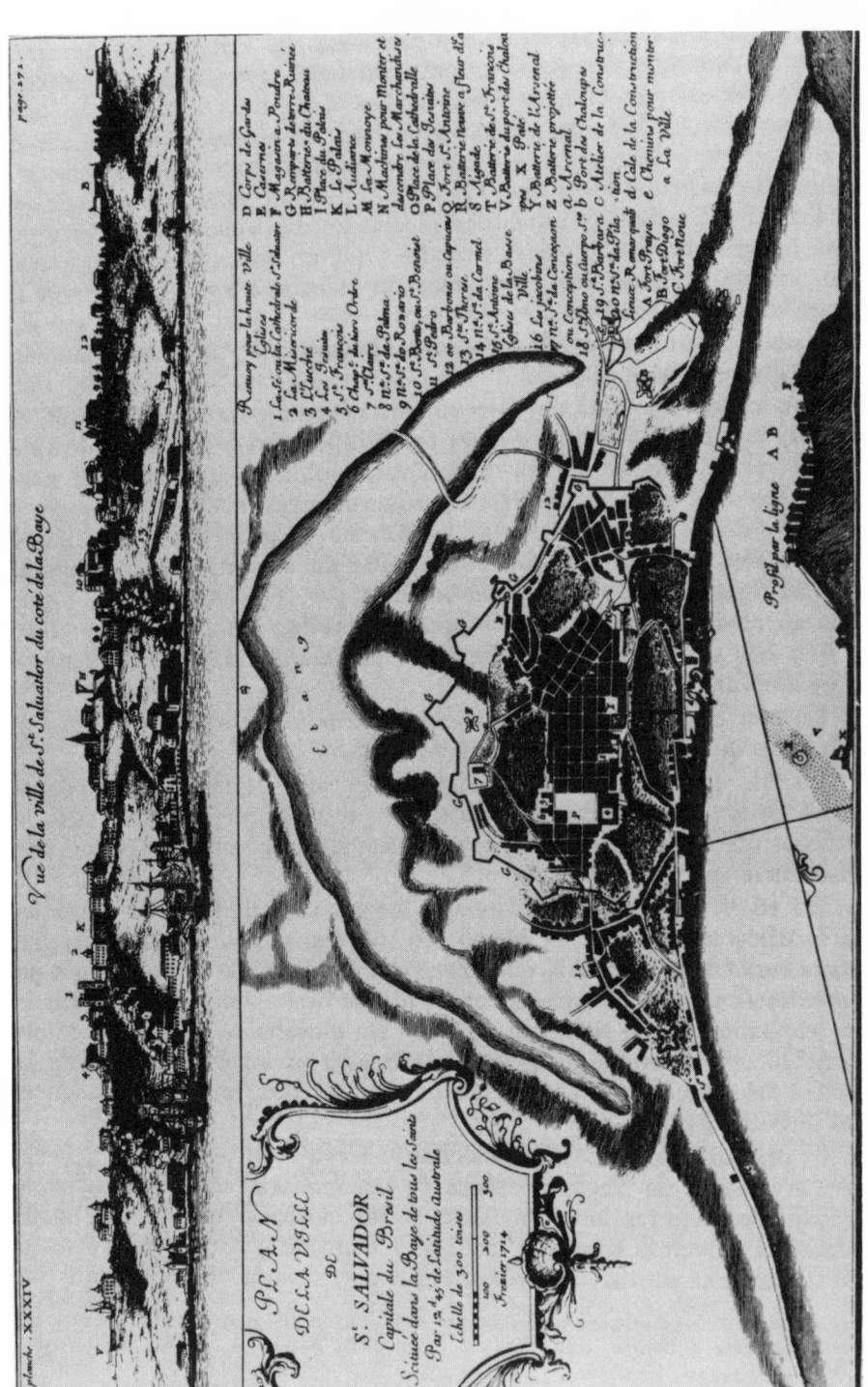

San Salvador, the capital of Brazil in 1714.

৺ 10 ৶

The Expulsion of the Jesuits from Paraguay as Recounted by Louis Antoine de Bougainville (1767)

———◄•►———

While on a voyage around the world, the celebrated French traveler Louis-Antoine de Bougainville (1729–1811) chanced to be in the River Plate region at the time of the expulsion of the Jesuits from the Spanish colonies. He thus witnessed some details of the departure of members of this order from Paraguay in 1767. Earlier military service in Canada during the French defeat at Quebec in 1759 had awakened Bougainville's curiosity about Spanish America. With the dream of planting a colony in the Malvinas or Falkland Islands east of Argentina, he equipped an expedition for this purpose at his own expense. Frustrated in this effort by the cession of French claims to Spain, he then acted upon his government's instructions to sail around the world. His

---

On completing his circumnavigation of the globe, Bougainville published his *Description d'un voyage autour du monde,* 2 vols. (Paris, 1771–1772). Chapter VII gives an account of the Jesuit missions in Paraguay and the events attending their extinction. An English version of this travel narrative made by J. R. Forster promptly appeared in 1772, from which the following extracts are reproduced.

first stop was at Montevideo, in modern Uruguay,
just as the Spanish governor-general was executing
his monarch's command to expel the Jesuits.

Whilst we carried on our preparations for leaving Río
de la Plata, the marquís of Bucarelli made some on his part
to go on the Uruguay [River]. The Jesuits had already
been arrested in all the other provinces of his department,
and this governor-general intended to execute the orders
of his Catholic majesty, in person, in the missions. It de-
pended upon the first steps that were taken, either to make
the people consent to the alterations that were going to
be made, or to plunge them again into their former state
of barbarism. But before I give an account of what I have
seen of the catastrophe of this singular government, I must
speak something of its form. . . .

Indeed, if one casts a general view at a distance upon
this magic government, founded by spiritual arms only,
and united only by the charms of persuasion, what institution can be more honorable to human nature? It is a
society which inhabits a fertile land, in a happy climate,
of which all the members are laborious and none works
for himself. The produce of the common cultivation is
faithfully conveyed into public storehouses, from whence
everyone receives what he wants for his nourishment, dress,
and housekeeping. The man who is in full vigor feeds,
by his labor, the new-born infant; and when time has consumed his strength, his fellow-citizens render him the
same services which he did them before. The private houses
are convenient, the public buildings fine, the worship uniform and scupulously attended. This happy people knows
neither the distinction of rank nor of nobility, and is
equally sheltered against super-abundance and wants.

The great distance and the illusion of perspective made
the missions bear this aspect in my eyes and must have
appeared the same to everyone else. But the theory is
widely different from the execution of this plan of government. . . .

The extent of country in which the missions are situated contains about two hundred leagues north and south, and about one hundred and fifty east and west, and the number of inhabitants is about three hundred thousand. The immense forests afford wood of all sorts; the vast pastures there contain at least two millions of cattle; fine rivers enliven the interior parts of this country and promote circulation and commerce throughout it. This is the situation of the country, but the question now is How did the people live there? The country was, as has been told, divided into parishes, and each parish was directed by two Jesuits, of which one was rector, and the other his curate. The whole expense for the maintenance of the colonies was but small, the Indians being fed, dressed, and lodged, by the labor of their own hands. The greatest costs were those of keeping the churches in repair, all of which were built and adorned magnificently. The other products of the ground, and all the cattle, belonged to the Jesuits, who on their part, sent for the instruments of various trades, for glass, knives, needles, images, chaplets of beads, gun-powder, and muskets. Their annual revenues consisted in cotton, tallow, leather, honey, and above all, in mate, a plant better known by the name of Paraguay tea, or South-Sea tea, of which that company had the exclusive commerce, and of which likewise the consumption is immense in the Spanish possessions in America, where it is used instead of tea. . . .

The Jesuits were occupied with the care of extending their missions when the unfortunate events happened in Europe which overturned the work of so many years, and of so unwearied patience in the New World. The court of Spain, having resolved upon the expulsion of the Jesuits, was desirous that this might be done at the same time throughout all its vast dominions. Cevallos* was recalled from Buenos Aires, and Don Francisco Bucarelli appointed

* Pedro de Cevallos, an energetic governor of Buenos Aires and the first viceroy of the new viceroyalty of the River Plate created in 1776—*Forster*.

to succeed him. He set out, being instructed in the business
which he was intended for, and with orders to defer the
execution of it till he received fresh orders, which would
soon be sent him. The king's confessor, the count d'Aranda,
and some ministers, were the only persons to whom this
secret affair was entrusted. Bucarelli made his entry at
Buenos Aires in the beginning of 1767.

When Don Pedro de Cevallos arrived in Spain, a packet
was dispatched to the marquís of Bucarelli with orders
both for that province and for Chili, whither he was to
send them over land. This vessel arrived in Río de la
Plata in June 1767, and the governor instantly dispatched
two officers, one to Peru, and the other to Chili, with the
dispatches from court directed to them. He then sent his
orders into the various parts of his province where there
were any Jesuits, viz. to Córdova, Mendoza, Corrientes,
Santa Fe, Salta, Montevideo, and Paraguay. As he feared
that, among the commanders of these several places, some
might not act with the dispatch, secrecy, and exactness
which the court required, he enjoined, by sending his orders to them, that they should not open them till a certain
day, which he had fixed for the execution, and to do it
only in the presence of some persons whom he named, and
who served in the highest ecclesiastical and civil offices
at the above-mentioned places. Córdova, above all, interested his attention. In that province was the principal
house of the Jesuits, and the general residence of their
provincial. There they prepared and instructed in the
Indian language and customs those who were destined to
go to the missions and to become heads of colonies; there
their most important papers were expected to be found.
M. de Bucarelli resolved to send an officer of trust there,
whom he appointed the king's lieutenant of that place,
and on whom, under this pretext, he sent a detachment of
soldiers to attend.

It now remained to provide for the execution of the
king's orders in the missions, and this was the most critical

point. It was dubious whether the Indians would suffer
the Jesuits to be arrested in the midst of the colonies,
and this violent step must at all events have been supported by a numerous body of troops. Besides this, it was
necessary, before they thought of removing the Jesuits,
to have another form of government ready to substitute
in their stead, and by that means to prevent confusion and
anarchy. The governor resolved to temporize, and was contented at that time to write to the missions that a *corregidor* and a *cacique* from each colony should be sent to him
immediately, in order to communicate the king's letters to
them. He dispatched this order with the greatest quickness,
that the Indians might already be on the road and beyond
the missions before the news of the expulsion of the Jesuits
could reach thither. By this he had two aims in view; the
one, that of getting hostages of the fidelity of the colonies
when the Jesuits would be taken from thence; the other,
that of gaining the affection of the principal Indians by
the good treatment he intended for them at Buenos Aires,
and of instructing them in the new situation upon which
they would enter; for, as soon as the restraint would be
taken away, they were to enjoy the same privileges and
have the same property as the king's other subjects.

Every measure was concerted with the greatest secrecy
and, though people wondered that a vessel should arrive
from Spain without any other letters than those for the
general, yet they were very far from suspecting the cause
of it. The moment of the general execution was fixed to
the day when all the couriers were supposed to have arrived at their different destinations, and the governor
waited for that moment with impatience, when the arrival
of the two small three-masted ships with lateen sails of
the king from Cádiz, the *Andaluz* and the *Adventurero,*
was near making all these precautions useless. The governor-general had ordered the governor of Montevideo
that, in case any vassels should arrive from Europe, he
should not allow them to speak with any person whatso-

ever before he had sent him word of it; but one of the two small sailing vessels, being in a forlorn situation at the entrance of the river, it was very necessary to . . . give her all the assistance which her situation required.

The two small vessels had sailed from Spain after the Jesuits had been arrested there, and this piece of news could by no means be prevented from spreading. An officer of these ships was immediately sent to M. de Bucarelli and arrived at Buenos Aires the 9th of July, at ten in the evening. The governor did not lose time; he instantly dispatched orders to all the commanders of the places to open their former packets of dispatches, and execute their contents with the utmost celerity. At two of the clock after midnight, all the couriers were gone, and the two houses of the Jesuits at Buenos Aires invested, to the great astonishment of those fathers, who thought they were dreaming when roused from their sleep in order to be imprisoned and to have their papers seized. The next morning an order was published in the town, which forbade, by pain of death, to keep up any intercourse with the Jesuits, and five merchants were arrested, who intended, it is said, to send advices [dispatches] to them at Córdova.

The king's orders were executed with the same facility in all the towns. The Jesuits were surprised everywhere, without having the least notice, and their papers were seized. They were immediately sent from their houses, guarded by detachments of soldiers, who were ordered to fire upon those that should endeavor to escape. But there was no occasion to come to this extremity. They showed the greatest resignation, humbling themselves under the hand that smote them, and acknowledging, as they said, that their sins had deserved the punishment which God inflicted on them. The Jesuits of Córdova, in number above a hundred, arrived toward the end of August at the Encenada, whither those from Corrientes, Buenos Aires, and Montevideo came soon after. They were immediately embarked and the first convoy sailed, as I have already said, at the end of September. The others, during that time, were on the road to Buenos Aires, where they should wait for another opportunity.

On the 13th of September arrived all the *corregidores* and a *cacique* of each colony with some Indians of their retinue. They had left the missions before anyone guessed at the reason of their journey there. The news which they received of it on the road had made some impression on them but did not prevent their continuing the journey. The only instruction which the rectors gave their dear proselytes at parting was to believe nothing of what the governor-general should tell them: "Prepare, my children," did everyone tell them, "to hear many untruths." At their arrival they were immediately sent to the governor, where I was present at their reception. Thy entered on horseback to the number of a hundred and twenty and formed a crescent in two lines. A Spaniard, understanding the language of the Guaranís, served them as an interpreter. The governor appeared in a balcony; he told them that they were welcome, that they should go to rest themselves, and that he would send them notice of the day which he should fix in order to let them know the king's intentions. He added, in general, that he had come to release them from slavery and put them in possession of their property, which they had not hitherto enjoyed. They answered by a general cry, lifting up their right hands to heaven and wishing all prosperity to the king and governor. They did not seem discontented, but it was easy to discover more surprise than joy in their countenance. On leaving the governor's palace, they were brought to one of the houses of the Jesuits, where they were lodged, fed, and kept at the king's expense. . . .

At my departure from Buenos Aires, the Indians had not yet been called to an audience of the general. He was willing to give them time to learn something of the language and to become acquainted with the Spanish customs. I have been several times to see them. They appeared to me of an indolent temper and seemed to have that stupid air so common in creatures caught in a trap. Some of them were pointed out to me as very intelligent but, as they spoke no other language but that of the Guaranís, I was not able to make any estimate of the degree of their knowledge. I only heard a *cacique* play upon the violin, who, I was told, was a great musician; he played a sonata, and I thought I heard the strained sounds of a serinette. Soon after the arrival of these Indians at Buenos Aires, the news of the expulsion of the Jesuits having reached the missions, the marquís de Bucarelli received a letter from the provincial, who was there at that time, in which he assured him of his submission and of that of all the colonies to the king's orders. . . .

It was expected that, in seizing the effects of the Jesuits in this province, very considerable sums of money would be found; however, what was obtained that way amounted to a mere trifle. Their magazines [warehouses] indeed were furnished with merchandise of all sorts, both of the products of the country and of goods imported from Europe. There were even many sorts which could not have a sale in these provinces. The number of their slaves were considerable and, in their [convent] at Córdova alone, they reckoned three thousand five hundred.

I cannot enter into a detail of all that the public of Buenos Aires pretends to have found in the papers of the Jesuits. The animosity is yet too recent to enable me to distinguish true imputations from false ones. I will rather do justice to the majority of the members of this society who were not interested in its temporal affairs. If there were some intriguing men in this body, the far greater number, who were sincerely pious, did not consider any thing in the institution besides the piety of its founder, and worshiped God, to whom they had consecrated themselves in spirit and in truth. I have been in-

formed, on my return to France, that the marquís de
Bucarelli set out from Buenos Aires for the missions, the
14th of May, 1768, and that he had not met with any ob-
stacle, or resistance, to the execution of his most Catholic
majesty's orders. . . .

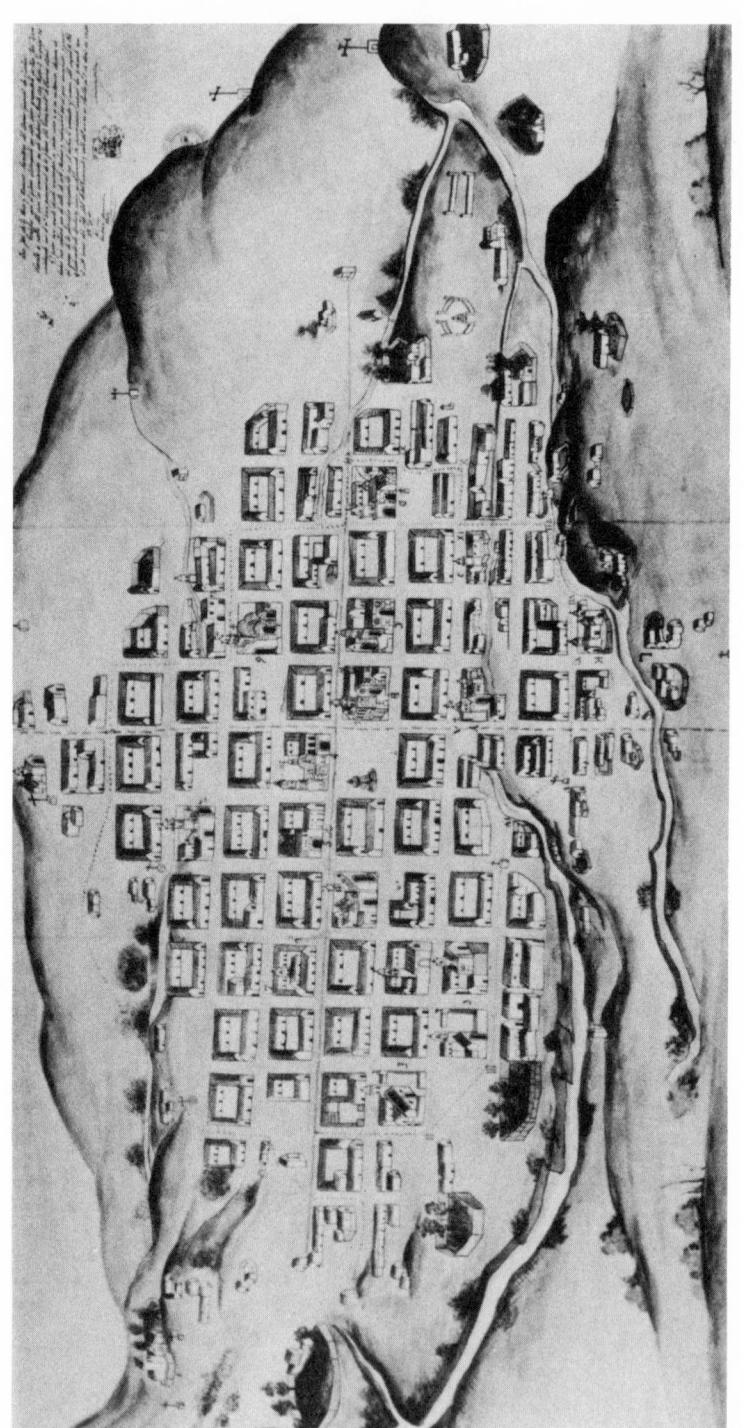

Colonial Town Planning, La Plata, *ca.* 1778

❧ 11 ❧

Concolorcorvo's Description of Travel by *Carreta* in the Argentine (1773)

———◆◆◆———

Colonial accounts of travel overland are compara-
tively rare, but the picaresque Lazarillo de Ciegos
Caminantes desde Buenos Aires hasta Lima (1773),
whose title has been translated as A Guide for Inexperienced Travelers between Buenos Aires and
Lima, *has attained the status of a literary classic of*
the period. It partakes of the nature of a "tourists'
guidebook," with often witty comments on varied
aspects of a journey through the heartland of South
America from Montevideo to the viceregal capital of
Peru. The tone of the narrative is often ironic and
jocular, as it presents sharp vignettes of the vast ter-
rain over which toiled the two-wheeled, oxen drawn
carretas, *the "covered carts" that provided the freight*
and passenger service of the Argentine Pampas. Al-
legedly written by a half-caste called Concolorcórvo,
the true author is Alonso Carrió de la Vandera
(1715– after 1778), a Spaniard commissioned to in-
spect and reorganize the postal service across the

The following selection is taken from *El Lazarillo de Ciegos*
(Buenos Aires: Ediciones Argentinas Solar, 1942), pp. 87–88. It
has been translated by the editor.

South American plains and mountains. Alternating
humor with seriousness, his realistic descriptions fre-
quently have documentary value, particularly the
passage devoted to the carreta *service.*

San Miguel de Tucumán, the capital city of this district
[of Argentina] . . . occupies the best site in the province;
it is situated on high, unobstructed terrain, surrounded by
fertile fields. . . . Its chief residents and city officials, num-
bering no more than twenty-four, are prudent men, reso-
lute in the protection of their rights. Some by frugal practices remain well-to-do, others grow richer in the mule
trade. Their main activity, however, is raising oxen for
freight service by carts to Buenos Aires and to Jujuy. With
permission of the Mendoza carting trade, I shall give a
description of the Tucumán *carretas,* or long, narrow carts.
   Their two wheels are about two and a half *varas* [*vara*
=2.8 feet] in diameter, the center of which is a thick,
heavy hub two or three *cuartas* [*cuarta* = ¼ *vara*] across;
an axle, fifteen *cuartas* long, extends under the middle of
the cart, whose floor or body rests upon it. This base consists of a beam seven and a half *varas* long called a *pértigo,*
with two parallel poles four and a half *varas* in length,
one on either side, that are connected to the main shaft
by four braces called *teleras,* or tie-beams, thus forming
the floor of the cart, whose width is a *vara* and a half.
Six studs or uprights are spiked to either side, each pair
connected by a strip of willow or pliable wood to form
an arching top or roof. Woven reeds, stronger than the
cat-tails used by Mendoza makers, compose the walls; pieces
of cowhide laced together cover the top as a protection
from sun and rain. To haul the cart oxen, usually called
pertigueros, are harnessed to a yoke two and a half *varas*
wide placed at the end of the seven and a half *vara* shaft.
   With an average load of 150 *arrobas* [*arroba* = 25 lbs.]
four oxen are always used on long trips; the forward two
are called *cuarteros.* This first pair are hitched to the main

shaft by a strap called a *tirador*, which has a thickness appropriate to its function; it is made of the hide of a bull or full grown steer folded four times. These oxen have the same kind of a yoke as the *pertigueros*, and it is held by the same strap. The two pairs of oxen are about three *varas* apart, corresponding to the length of a prodding goad called a *cuarta*; the latter is usually an exceptionally thick length of bamboo or other suitable wood. This long goad consists of several pieces that the hired men fit together, and it is decorated with multicolored feathers.

This prodding device hangs from a pole projecting forward a *vara* and a half or two *varas* from the top of the cart. It is suspended in such a fashion that, when properly balanced, the drivers can prod one pair of oxen with one hand and the second pair with the other by a shorter goad called a *picanilla*, for it is essential to jab all four animals nearly simultaneously. Every cart must have a driver, who sits on a chest containing his belongings in the fore part under the top. From this seat he alights only to adjust or repair the harness straps, or to guide the team across rivers or other bad stretches.

In addition to the 150 *arrobas*, the carts carry a large jug of water, firewood, and lumber for repairs; and so, counting the driver and his belongings, the load totals some 200 *arrobas*. There is not a bit of iron or nails in any part of the cart, for its structure is entirely of wood. Nearly every day grease is applied to the axle and bushing of the wheels to reduce wear; the axle does not revolve, only the wheels. The larger vehicles differ only in that the superstructure is all of wood like a ship's cabin. The floor level of the cart, a *vara* and a half from the ground, is reached by a set of steps; nine *cuartas* separate the floor from the roof. The flooring is made of pampa grass or cowhide which, when well stretched, is softer.

The Mendoza carts are wider than the Tucumán ones and carry 28 *arrobas* more because they encounter fewer road obstacles. Those of Tucuman have to travel from

Córdova to Jujuy through thick woods, which make the road very narrow. The Mendoza carts, on the other hand, journey across the level plains of the open pampas where the upper structure is not damaged by protruding branches of trees. Though the Tucuman carts ford many streams, they never have to be unloaded because the oxen seldom lose their footing. When this happens it is only briefly, for they are soon helped by sliding heavy square blocks underneath, on which the tough hoofs of the oxen can get a firm hold. The Mendoza teamsters unload carts only when the water is high in the deep gullies which they call *desaguaderos.* To ferry the freight, they quickly make small rafts of the yokes tightly bound together by harness straps and halters. Cowhide is also used, a practice followed by the people living along the banks of the Tercero and other rivers. This species of beasts of burden is everywhere conceded to be the most powerful. With the building of large roadways in Spain during the present reign, the number of these animals has greatly increased.

It is 407 road leagues from Buenos Aires to Jujuy, and shipping by oxcart costs eight *reales* per *arroba,* which seems incredibly cheap to those who have not tried it. The transportation of goods from Buenos Aires to Jujuy by muleback would be very difficult and exceedingly expensive because much of the way is through thick woods, where many mules would get lost and where, even though shipments were encased in leather, entangling thorny branches of trees would damage them to the great detriment of the merchandise itself. The mules would be continuously disabled, their backs strained, and their hoofs would become unshod; added to these disadvantages are the many rivers in flood that they could not cross with loads on their backs, owing to a natural timidity and an inherent tendency to travel downstream.

The only thing that bothers the oxen, on the other hand, is the sun's heat, for which reason a stop is regularly made at ten o'clock in the morning. After a check-up of the whole caravan, which depends on the number of carts, each driver quickly unhitches the four oxen, and an attendant takes them among the relay animals to eat, drink, and rest until at least four o'clock in the afternoon. In these six hours, more or less, food is prepared for the members of the caravan, each hired hand contenting himself with a poorly roasted hunk of beef. If needed, they kill a head of cattle, and they grease the hubs of the wheels, all of which is speedily accomplished. A few travelers seek the shade of high trees while others rest under the carts, whose height from the ground is considerable. The longest assured shade and the most airy is created by putting two carts side by side with space enough between for a third. Two or three of the long prodding goads are laid across the tops of the carts, over which a canvas or awning is spread to ward off the sun's rays. In this way a tent cover is formed sufficient to shelter eight people comfortably. Some passengers bring their own folding camp chairs with seats of woven reed or canvas. The latter I consider better because, even if they get wet, they readily dry without becoming stiff and they are not so apt to break as the woven reed bottoms. The hired men always store these articles under the overlap on the outside of the cart where they often get wet, or projecting branches of low trees along the way break or tear them. Consequently, a careful traveler packs them inside, and likewise his little camp table, on which it is so handy to eat, read, or write.

The trip resumes at four o'clock in the afternoon, and a second stop is made long enough to cook supper so that, if the night is clear and the road presents no difficulties, the oxen are hitched up again at eleven o'clock at night and travel until daybreak. While these beasts of burden are being changed for fresh ones, there is time for a breakfast of chocolate, yerba mate, or a bit of fried food by those who want something more substantial, whereupon the journey continues until ten o'clock. Inactive passengers remain in the carts with the windows and doors wide open, either reading or observing the condition of the road or anything else in sight. The more energetic ride horse-

back ahead or behind as suits their fancy to look at the
farms and their rustic inhabitants. These are usually
women, since the men leave for work in the fields before
dawn and do not return until the sun's heat wearies them
or hunger overtakes them. They satisfy its pangs by exactly
four pounds of rich, *descansada* [i.e., "rested"] meat, as
they term whatever they bring back from the woods and
kill on the way. As used to be true and invariably happened in the large scale slaughtering that took place near
the bigger communities like Buenos Aires, these workers
would round up a considerable herd of cattle in the afternoon and hamstring them. The miserable creatures would
lie bellowing all over the field until the next day when
their throats were slit and they were hacked into bloody
pieces. That's the kind of meat these people call *cansada*
[*sic*], but I call it baneful!

A normal day's run of a "fleet of carts," as they call a
caravan in Tucumán and elsewhere, is seven leagues although, since they ford numerous streams, I calculate
that they do not average much over five leagues. The
Mendoza teamsters cover more in a day because the terrain
they cross offers fewer obstacles in the form of rivers and
streams, and it has many *travesías,* as they call the long,
level stretches of open, waterless country. For the latter,
and especially the Corocoro section, they have relays of
trained oxen called *rocines.* The rest of the livestock moves
ahead faster, while these *rocines* haul the heavily loaded
carts, often drinking no water for forty-eight hours; even
then, if a stream is low, they do not quench their thirst
in it because they sense that its water is bitter and infected.
The untrained oxen, on the other hand, will invariably
stop to drink even though they are hurriedly urged on,
with the result that they become sick and the death rate
is sometimes high.

On the long stretches the oxen stop for rest only when
worn out by the burning sun, at which time the mess
servants make cold food ready for the night. The best procedure, however, is to move well ahead in the afternoon,
bringing along firewood and whatever is needed to prepare

a meal, keeping in mind that, morning, noon, and night, the trained oxen travel far and at a fast rate. Also it is essential to know where the teams will be changed for fresh animals so that there is ample time to set up the cooking equipment and everything else without delaying the teamsters. No great reliance should be placed on the helpers since, for the most part, they are Negroes recently arrived from Africa, who lose or ruin a lot of badly needed articles.

Some travelers have their own horses, usually bought for two pesos each. This practice is a great mistake because these beasts flee back to their former haunts or prowlers maim them. The safest arrangement is one with the owner or leader of the "fleet" who rarely loses a horse; indeed, he frequently increases the number by picking up a stray one wandering about the plains or one that the mule boys bring in—a way of evening losses.

While some people marvel at the stamina of the Mendoza *rocines,* or trained oxen, others are equally amazed on seeing the Tucumán ones cross wide flowing rivers, breasting the swiftest currents, and hauling such heavily laden carts as I have indicated; against the impact of the waves they offer extraordinary resistance. When they first step into the stream they betray some fear, but they do not draw back nor become frightened when the water covers them, even up to their eyes, provided always that their ears remain above the surface. If they are unable to haul the carts, they stand firmly and wait until other beasts are brought to their aid with which they cooperate effectively. Then, with more assurance and boldness, they plunge into the second, third, and fourth streams, encouraged by the hired men who call them by name. If they become entangled in the harness of the assisting animals, they make it known by movements of their hoofs so that the men release them. In short, this sight is one of the most intriguing that I have ever witnessed. At first I was sure that these passive oxen would inevitably drown, when I saw them under water for an hour with only their ears showing. Repeated observation, however, has made me

understand how persistent and reliable such useful creatures really are, and how much their invaluable services
should be appreciated.

When a traveler is a passenger in a cart the load is
reduced by one third to accommodate him, his bed, trunk,
and other belongings. Carts carrying solely freight have
no rear door but are open at the front so as to manage
the team, watch for water dripping in, and to carry out
other functions.

It is highly advisable and even indispensable for passengers to look into the background of the carters they
travel with, because these carriers ordinarily fall into three
classes. The first includes the most respected men in
Mendoza, San Juan de la Frontera, Santiago del Estero,
and San Miguel de Tucumán. They were the ones who
established this freight service to take surplus products
from their farms such as wines, brandies, flour, dried
peaches, and other fruits to the Buenos Aires and Córdova
markets; they sell available space in the carts at a moderate
rate to travelers and private individuals. Nearly always the
proceeds of this trade are used to purchase European goods
for their homes and private businesses. As the value of
what they fetch in twenty carts in this exchange could be
brought back in one or two of these conveyances, they
lease all the others to the first carrier who comes along
at a price that is subject to the varying amounts of freight
to be moved and to the number of excess carts.

The second kind of carter has fewer personal means, less
business acumen, and occasion more trip delays. The third
group are men of expediency. They invariably demand
freight charges in advance, and often a creditor appears
at the moment of departure to prevent it. The shippers
then find that they are not only obliged to pay off the carrier's debts but must supply their own needs and other
contingencies on the journey. It is, therefore, a whole lot
safer to pay ten pesos extra per cart to carriers in the first
category.

Everyone in Tucumán deals in freight, and the three

types indicated are also among them. The carters of Santa Fe and Corrientes convey all the yerba mate of Paraguay to Buenos Aires and its environs and as far away as Chile for distribution throughout the jurisdiction of the Audiencia of Lima. Carriers take freight from Buenos Aires to any destination because they are unable to pick up return loads to their own places of origin. In general, they are poor folks with no other resources than to bargain, which comes down to plain trickery, exposing shippers to many delays. But keeping in mind these admonitions and other precautions that wisdom suggests, journeys both ways can be [made] comfortable by taking care always to have the carts well protected against leaks in the top, and to have two little windows open on the sides, one in front of the other, to ventilate the mid part of the interior. This arrangement permits entry of gentle breezes that are so fragrant that they move one to scorn the freshness underneath the trees, and they cool the water wonderfully.

Care should be taken with lighted candles at night, for it is difficult to extinguish a fire spreading to the dry, woven reeds of the walls of the covered carts. The larger ones with walls of wood are freer from this ever-present danger; they also have the advantage that fewer ugly little birds nest in them, especially in the province of Tucumán, where it is warm and somewhat humid. Lanterns are needed at night to get in and out of both kinds of carts and, of course, to move about outside when it is dark and windy. For rainy periods it is well to bring along a V-shaped tent so that the mess cooks can conveniently prepare meals and keep their fires from going out because of carelessness with candles, sulphur matches, flint, and steel. Servants of this sort are notoriously wasteful in these and in all other matters entrusted to them; they thus create irreparable losses. And now let us leave behind the district of San Miguel de Tucumán.

Early nineteenth-century map showing routes to
South America from France and Gibraltar.

John Mawe's Journey into the Interior of Brazil (1809)

—•◦•—

*The discovery of precious metals and stones came
late in colonial Portuguese America. The year 1693
marked the beginning of a gold rush in the interior,
followed in 1728 by the uncovering of diamond
mines there. Travel, particularly of foreigners, in
these domains of Portugal, never as frequent as in
the colonies of Spain, was virtually excluded in the
eighteenth century by the Portuguese authorities,
jealous of their monopoly of the newfound wealth of
Brazil. It was not until the royal family, fleeing from
the armies of Napoleon early in the nineteenth century, had taken refuge in this transatlantic possession,
and the gold and diamond boom had greatly declined, that the ban against foreign visitors was
lifted. Practically the first beneficiary was an English
mineralogist, John Mawe (1764–1829), who received
permission in 1809 to journey into the mining and
other inland regions. The principal work of this native of Derbyshire, England, and author of numerous
technical treatises, is* Travels in the Interior of Brazil
*(London, 1812). In this narrative he recounts his visits
to the decaying communities and countryside of the*

The following excerpts are taken from *Travels in the Interior
of Brazil* (1812), published in London.

mining districts and gives interesting details concern-
ing the social, cultural, and economic life of their in-
habitants. Typical are his observations in the vicinity
of the former populous mining center, Villa Rica
(modern Ouro Preto).

A Journey to Villa Rica
(Modern Ouro Preto) and Its Region

After I had thoroughly recovered from the fatigues of my
late journey, I solicited His Royal Highness for permission to go and explore the diamond mines of Serra do
Frío. This favor had never as yet been granted to a foreigner, nor had any Portuguese been permitted to visit
the district where the works are situated, except on business
relative to them, and even then, under restrictions which
rendered it impossible to acquire the means of giving an
adequate description of them to the public. Through the
kind mediation of the Conde de Linhares, the permission
was granted, and my passports and letters of recommenda-
tion were speedily made out. Lord Strangford used his
influence to further my undertaking, and it was through
his goodness in recommending me that I obtained admission
to the archives, for the purpose of examining all the manuscript maps, and of copying from any of them whatever
might be necessary to guide me in my route. It may here
be proper to observe that the most eligible mode of traveling in the interior of Brazil, especially on such an excur-
sion as I had undertaken, is to procure orders from the
government, and an escort of soldiers, who have a right,
under such orders, to require proper relays of mules from
all persons who reside on or near the road. The Conde
de Linhares intimated to me, that I might select any two
soldiers I thought proper. . . .

Villa Rica (founded in 1711 by the Paulistas in their
search for gold) at the present day scarcely retains a shadow

of its former splendor. Its inhabitants, with the exception of the shopkeepers, are void of employment; they totally neglect the fine country around them, which, by proper cultivation, would amply compensate for the loss of the wealth which their ancestors drew from its bosom. Their education, their habits, their hereditary prejudices, alike unfit them for active life; perpetually indulging in visionary prospects of sudden wealth, they fancy themselves exempted from that universal law of nature which ordains that man shall live by the sweat of his brow. In contemplating the fortunes accumulated by their predecessors, they overlook the industry and perseverance which obtained them, and entirely lose sight of the change of circumstances which renders those qualities now doubly necessary. The successors of men who rise to opulence from small beginnings seldom follow the example set before them, even when trained to it; how then should a Creole, reared in idleness and ignorance, feel anything of the benefits of industry! His Negroes constitute his principal property, and them he manages so ill, that the profits of their labor hardly defray the expenses of their maintenance. In the regular course of nature they become old and unable to work, yet he continues in the same listless and slothful way, or sinks into a state of absolute inactivity, not knowing what to do from morning to night. This deplorable degeneracy is almost the universal characteristic of the descendants of the original settlers; every trade is occupied either by mulattoes or Negroes, both of which classes seem superior in intellect to their masters, because they make a better use of it. . . .

Having resided in Villa Rica nearly a fortnight, I expressed a desire to visit two estates, forty miles distant, known by the names of Barro and Castro, both belonging to the Conde de Linhares. Between the years 1730 and 1740 these estates produced much gold, and were then in the possession of Senhor Matthias Barbosa, a settler of great respectability, who took up these lands and drove the anthropophagi [cannibals] from them. . . .

His Excellency the Conde's steward furnished me and my worthy friend with mules, and Mr. Lucas, the judge, obligingly ordered every necessary to be provided for our journey. We rode through Mariana, and arrived at Alto de Chapada, a village, three miles distant from it, situated on an elevation in the midst of a fine plain. We soon afterward reached a very high and confined situation, between two perpendicular mountains, from whence we had a bird's eye view of the village of St. Sebastian. From this steep we descended, with great difficulty, on foot, to the Río del Carmen at its base, over which is a very high-arched and picturesque bridge. Passing this ravine, we proceeded a full league by the riverside, through a rich country abounding in fine sloping hills and fertile plains, watered by numerous streams which flow into the river in various directions, and all of which bear vestiges of having been formerly washed for gold. The road side exhibited similar remains, and seemed to have been at some period connected with the river, which, in this part, is as large as the Thames at Windsor. We passed through San Giatanha, a straggling thinly-peopled village, and proceeding about three miles further, arrived at an indifferent house, called Labras Velhas, where we halted for the night, having performed half our journey. The owner of this place found it difficult, with thirty or forty Negroes, to maintain himself decently, though the land was susceptible of every species of culture, and needed only the hand of industry to render it productive. Everything about the establishment exhibited a pitiful spectacle of neglect, indifference, and sloth. It is but justice to add that he treated us with the greatest civility, and amply supplied our necessities.

Leaving Labras Velhas at eight next morning, we passed Moro dos Arreas, the country presenting still finer valleys and excellent timber, but totally destitute of cattle. Ascending a high hill, we were immersed for about an hour in a cloud and exposed to some small rain, but not sufficient to penetrate our coats. This was the only rain we experienced on the road by day. In the night the rain sometimes fell plentifully. We observed some exceedingly large worms, stretched motionless on the road, which our guide told us were sure signs of wet weather. From this height we saw the Río Gualacha, which, with another river, joins the Río del Carmen about ten leagues below, and forms the Río San José. Proceeding in that direction through a fine country, we reached Altos de St. Michael, where the river last mentioned is of considerable width, but not deep. Its waters are extremely turbid, on account of the mud brought from the gold-washings along the banks, from its source to this place. These heights command a fine view of three windings of the river; at their base there are vestiges of one of the oldest and most extensive gold-washings, which yielded much treasure to its discoverer and proprietor, Senhor Matthias Barbosa. The country is well-wooded, but rather thinly peopled; I expressed some surprise at observing no good dwelling-houses in a district which formerly produced so much wealth, and was informed that the first miners, eager to take the cream of the gold to as large an extent as they could, seldom remained long on the same spot, and contented themselves with building sheds or ranchos to serve for their temporary residence.

Fazenda do Barro

Descending this mountain, we entered upon the estate of His Excellency, called Fazenda do Barro, and were shown the house at a distance of nearly a league, on a pleasing eminence, near the riverside. On arriving, an excellent dinner was provided for us, of which, having been eight hours on our mules, we partook very heartily.

The house, and indeed the whole establishment, were strikingly superior, in point of convenience, to the miserable places we had lately passed. Having dined, we refreshed ourselves with a walk in garden, where the coffee-trees in full blossom showed, at a distance, as if loaded with snow. This spot afforded a view of a most enchanting country, diversified with gentle eminences and large valleys well clothed with timber. From the farther margin of the river, which flows at one hundred yards distance in front of the house, rises a fine hill, well calculated for the culture of every species of produce, and connected with others of equal fertility.

On the following day I was chiefly occupied in visiting every part of the establishment. The distil-house, sugar-engine, and corn-mill, were very much out of repair; the two latter were worked by horizontal water-wheels of great power. The buildings of the fazenda form a square, the southern side being occupied by the house, and the three others consisting of dwellings for the Negroes, storehouses, carpenters' and blacksmiths' shops, and other offices equally useful. . . .

In the afternoon I rode out to see the gold-washings. On arriving I saw a great extent of ground already worked, and immense heaps of quartzose stones. On the margin of the river where they were then working, I found them cutting away the bank, to the depth of at least ten feet, to get at the *cascalhão* incumbent on the rock. The substance they had to cut through was clay, so strong that, though falls of water were let upon it, and Negroes were constantly working it with hoes of various kinds, it was with difficulty to be removed. This was not the only impediment, for, by the constant precipitation of mud, the *cascalhão* was five feet below the bed of the river; hence, when they had sunk their pits, they had to use [hydraulic] means for drawing the water from them. . . .

In the operation of getting gold, the heavy work is assigned to the male Negroes, and the lighter labor to the females. The *cascalhão*, dug from these pits by the former, is carried away by the latter in *gamellas*, or bowls, to be washed. . . . I perceived, however, that here they did not, in the first instance, attempt to separate the gold from the black oxide of iron, but emptied their *gamellas* into a larger vessel, by rinsing them in the water which it contained. The substance deposited in this vessel was delivered out, in small portions of about a pound each, to the most skillful washers, as the operation of washing, or, as it was termed, purifying it, required great niceness and dexterity. Some of the grains of gold were so fine as to float on the surface, and of course were liable to be washed away in these repeated changes of water; to prevent which the Negroes bruised a few handfuls of herbs on a stone, and mixed the juice in small proportions with the water in their *gamellas*. Whether this liquid did in reality tend to precipitate the gold, I could not positively ascertain, but the Negroes certainly used it with the greatest confidence. . . .

I rode over various parts of the estate, and more particularly along both banks of the river, which, as well as the bed, appeared to have been much washed. The bends, or parts where eddies were formed, were the places noted as being rich in gold. Wherever the margin formed a flat, or level, the *cascalhão* continued under the surface to some distance, appearing like a continuation of the bed of the river, which in all probability it was, as the river is known to have been much wider formerly. The parts that were then working, and others that had yet to be worked, bore a very unpromising appearance. . . .

Fazenda de Castro

Having resided at Barro some days, we set out for the Fazenda de Castro, distant about seven miles, where we arrived, after a pleasant ride over a mountainous and finely-wooded district, containing large tracts of rich virgin land, watered by many excellent streams. This noble mansion was erected by the first possessor of the district, Senhor Matthias Barbosa. It is very spacious and airy, having a gallery in front forty-eight yards long, to which open fourteen folding-doors, or windows, extending nearly from the top to the bottom of the rooms. It is situated near the confluence of the Riberón del Carmen and the Río Gualacha, which form the San José, a river as large as the Thames at Battersea.

We did not rest above an hour at this fazenda, it being our intention to visit the *aldea,* or village, of San José de Barra Longa, situated on the confines of the territory inhabited by the Bootocoody Indians. Crossing the river by a fine wooden bridge, built about fifty years ago, but still in tolerable repair, we proceeded along the bank, which was embellished with several gardens, and presented more frequent appearances of cultivation than we had of late been accustomed to view. The climate is much hotter than at Villa Rica, on account of the lowness of the situation; and we were informed that fruits of every kind, particularly the pine, grew in this soil to great perfection in size and fineness of flavor. The truth of these accounts we could not ascertain, as this was not the fruit season.

After traveling about four miles, we arrived at the village. It being Sunday, numbers of people had come from various parts in the neighborhood to attend divine service, and, after it was over, flocked in crowds to the place where we alighted. It appeared as if the whole population of the village, men, women, and children, were possessed with the same spirit of curiosity, so great was their eagerness to get a sight of us. We dined in a mixed company of ladies and gentlemen, at the house of the worthy vicar, who kept a very hospitable table, and paid us the most flattering attention. A military officer and a judge, who were of the party, entered into conversation with us; and it was difficult to decide who were the most inquisitive, they, respecting the motives and objects of our journey, or we, respecting the state of the country, the anthropophagi, etc. . . .

We now took leave of the vicar and his guests and, I may add, of all the villagers, who came out to salute us as we passed. Returning to Castro, I remained the whole of the next day to examine the establishment. It is built, like that at Barro, in the form of a square, the dwellings of the Negroes forming three sides, and the mansion the fourth, the entrance being in front through a pair of gates, which, when shut, secure the whole. The rooms in the mansion were like ancient halls, adorned with carvings, and fitted up and furnished after the old fashion. Here were blunder-busses, swords, and other weapons for defense, used in former days, when the house was liable to the continual attacks of the Bootocoodies.* The stairs, gallery, and floors were of fine wood, of a quality which time had not in any degree perceptibly injured. Attached to the house were the remains of a sugar-mill, distil-house, corn-mill, and a machine, worked by a strap and spindles, for spinning cotton, all in a state of neglect. The whole establishment bore marks of former opulence and grandeur, from which it appeared to have gradually declined as the gold-washings at the confluence of the rivers and in other parts had become exhausted. The Negroes were now all removed to Barro, except a few infirm and sick, who were stationed here to keep the mansion in order (this being considered as a light employment for them) until such time as their convalescence should fit them for resuming their labors along with their brethren at the other estate.

Having made a sketch of the house, and visited every part which interested me, I returned by the same road to Barro, where I employed myself in making a topographical map of the river, distinguishing by different colors the places already washed for gold, those which were then washing, and the yet unworked grounds. This sort of map might be made on a large scale, so as to include a whole district or parish, where the several mines, or gold-beds, in their different stages, might be exhibited at one view.

On this estate are employed one hundred and fifty-six Negroes, of all descriptions, who, on such excellent land, producing every necessary for food and clothing, might be expected to earn considerably more than their own maintenance; yet a former steward managed so ill for twenty successive years, that, although he had nothing to purchase but a little iron, and though the gold-mines were then more productive than at present, he ran the establishment

* Botocudos, tribe of Indians who dominated the province of Rio de Janeiro to Pôrto Seguro well into the mid-nineteenth century—*I. A. L.*

annually into debt to the shopkeepers of Villa Rica. A single circumstance may account for this mismanagement— the noble proprietor resided in Portugal. At present the estate is in a much more prosperous way, being entrusted to the care of another steward, and three overseers, all Creoles. The latter receive a salary of thirty *milreis* [about nine pounds sterling]* per annum, besides their mainte- nance; their business is to execute the orders of the steward, and to superintend the labor of the Negroes committed to their charge. They lead a life of extreme indolence, never putting their hands to any species of work.

The general diet of the country-people in this land of Canaan is somewhat similar to that of the miners in the vicinity of St. Paul's [São Paulo] already described. The master, his steward, and the overseers, sit down to a breakfast of kidney-beans of a black color, boiled, which they mix with the flour of Indian corn, and eat with a little dry pork fried or boiled. The dinner generally con- sists, also, of a bit of pork or bacon boiled, the water from which is poured upon a dish of the flour above-mentioned, thus forming a stiff pudding. A large quantity (about half a peck) of this food is poured in a heap on the table, and a great dish of boiled beans is set upon it: each person helps himself in the readiest way, there being only one knife, which is very often dispensed with. A plate or two of *colewort,* or cabbage leaves, complete the repast. The food is commonly served up in the earthen vessels used for cooking it; sometimes on pewter dishes. The general beverage is water. At supper nothing is seen but large quantities of boiled greens, with a little bit of poor bacon to flavor them. On any festive occasion, or when strangers appear, the dinner or supper is improved by the addition of a stewed fowl.

The food prepared for the Negroes is Indian corn-flour, mixed with hot water, in which a bit of pork has been boiled. This dish serves both for breakfast and supper.

---

* John Mawe inserted this parenthetical reference.

Their dinner consists of beans boiled in the same way. This unfortunate race of men are here treated with great kindness and humanity, which, indeed, their good behavior seems to deserve. They are allowed as much land as they can, at their leisure, cultivate, (Sundays and holidays being by law allotted to them for that purpose,) and are permitted to sell or dispose of their produce as they please. Their owners clothe them with shirts and trousers made of coarse cotton, which is grown and woven on the estate. Their days of labor are rather long: before sunrise a bell rings to summon them to prayers, which are recited by one of the overseers, and repeated by the congregation; after worship is over they proceed to work, at which they continue till after sunset, when prayers are said as in the morning. An hour after supper they are employed in preparing wood to burn, taking Indian corn from the husk, and in other indoor operations. Swelled necks are not uncommon among the men Negroes, but in other respects they appear healthy: I saw few or none afflicted with elephantiasis, or with any cutaneous disease. There were many very aged of both sexes; a few could even remember their old master, the first possessor, though he has been dead upwards of sixty years.

Their principal article of diet, the *farinha de mielho,* or flour of Indian corn, appeared so platable and nutritive, that, after living upon it for some time, I had the curiosity to inquire into the mode of preparing it from the grain. It is first soaked in water, and afterward pounded in its swelled and moist state, to separate the outer husk. It then appears almost granulated, and is put upon copper pans, which have a fire underneath, and in these it is kept constantly stirred until it is dry and fit for eating. This substitute for bread is as common among the inhabitants here as is the *farinha de Pão* or *mandioca* among the people of Río de Janeiro, St. Paul's, and other districts.

The grain is grown always on virgin lands, cleared by burning, after the manner already described. In good seasons, or, in other words, when the dry weather allows the felled wood to be completely reduced to ashes, the return is from one hundred and fifty to two hundred bushels for one. Weeding is only performed after the seed has been a short time in the ground; indeed, the growing crops suffer less from the neglect of that operation than from the depredations of rats, which are frequently very considerable.

On the state of society here I had little leisure to make observations. A general debility seemed to prevail among the females, which I imputed to the want of better food and more exercise: they confine themselves principally to the sedentary employments of sewing or making lace. While at St. José I saw many females from the country, dressed in gowns made of English prints; some of them had woolen mantles, edged with gold lace or Manchester velvet, thrown loosely over their shoulders. Their hair was invariably fastened with combs, and they in general wore men's hats. The men, most of whom belonged to the militia, appeared in uniforms. No two things can be more different than the deshabille and full-dress of a nominal militia officer. When at home he seldom puts on more than half his clothes, over which he throws an old great coat; and saunters about the house in this attire from morning till night, a true picture of idleness. On Sundays, or on gala-days, after some hours spent in decorating his person, he sallies forth, completely metamorphosed from a slip-shod sloven into a spruce officer, glittering in a weight of gold lace, on a horse caparisoned with equal splendor, forming as fine a sight for the gazing multitude as a general at a review. He observes no medium between these extremes, being always very shabby or very fine. . . . We now took leave of the good people at the fazenda, and returned to Villa Rica by the way we came. . . .

⋙ 13 ⋘

Travels of
Alexander von Humboldt
Among the Carib Indians
of Venezuela
(1800)

—————◆●◆—————

In the twilight years of Spanish and Portuguese rule in the New World, the greatest of scholar-travelers, Baron Alexander von Humboldt (1769–1859), a remarkable representative of German scientific culture, spent the years 1799 to 1804 exploring and studying the regions of northern South America, Mexico, and Cuba. A naturalist, geographer, and historian, his voluminous writings on those areas still remain authoritative and indispensable. Early in 1800 he and the French naturalist Aimé-Jacques Alexandre Bonplan (1773–1858) spent four months in the wild Orinoco country and the llanos, or backlands of Venezuela. There he observed the habits of the surviving Carib Indians, or Caribbees, the nomadic tribe

---

The selection on the Caribs is taken from *Personal Narrative of Travels in the Equinoctial Regions of the New Continent during the Years 1799–1804*. By Alexander von Humboldt and Aimé Bonplan . . . Written in French by Alexander von Humboldt, and translated into English by Helen Maria Williams (London, 1814–1829: 7 vols, reprinted New York: AMS Press, Inc., 1966), Vol. vi, part i, book ix, chap. xxv. The passage on Caracas is from Vol. iii, book iii, chap. xiii.

*that Columbus had encountered three centuries be-
fore in the islands of the sea that received their name.
It is of interest to conclude this collection of excerpts
of travel narratives with Humboldt's brief description
of Caracas, the capital city of Venezuela, where important events of the War of Independence were soon
to transpire.*

The Caribbees of the Venezuelan Llanos

On the 13th of July we arrived at the village of Cari,* the
first of the Caribbee missions in the *llanos* that are under
the monks (Franciscans) of the Observance of the college
of Piritu. We lodged as usual at the convent, that is with
the clergyman. We had, beside our passports from the
captain-general of the province, recommendations from the
bishops and the guardian of the missions of the Orinoco.
From the coasts of New California to Valdivia in Chile
and the mouth of the Río de la Plata, a space of two
thousand leagues, every difficulty of a long journey by land
may be surmounted, if the traveller enjoy the protection
of the American clergy. The power which this body ex-
ercises in the state is too well established to be soon shaken
by a new order of things. Our host could scarcely comprehend, "how natives of the north of Europe could arrive
at his dwelling from the frontiers of Brazil by the Río
Negro, and not by way of the coast of Cumaná [in Vene-
zuela]." He behaved to us, however, in the most affable
manner, and showed a curiosity somewhat importunate
respecting us, which the appearance of a stranger, who is
not a Spaniard, always excites in South America. The
minerals, which we had collected, must contain gold; the
plants, dried with so much care, must be medicinal. Here,
as in many parts of Europe, the sciences are thought worthy

* Nuestra Señora del Socorro del Cari, founded in 1761—
Williams.

to occupy the mind only so far as they confer some solid benefit on society.

We found more than five hundred Caribbees in the village of Cari and saw many others in the surrounding missions. It is curious to observe a nomad people, recently attached to the soil, and differing from all the other' Indians in their physical and intellectual powers. I have no where seen a taller race of men (from five feet six inches, to five feet nine inches to six feet two), and of a more colossal stature. The men, which is common in America, are more clothed than the women. The latter wear only the *guajuco,* or *perizoma,* in the form of a band. The men have the lower part of the body as far as the hips wrapped in a piece of blue cloth, so dark as to be almost black. This drapery is so ample that, when the temperature lowers toward the evening, the Caribbees throw it over their shoulders. Their bodies being tinged with *onoto* (dye from ornotto tree) their tall figures, of a reddish copper-colour, with their picturesque drapery, projecting from the horizon of the steppe against the sky as a background, resemble antique statues of bronze. The men cut their hair in a very characteristic manner, like the monks, or the children of the choir. A part of the forehead is shaved, which makes it appear extremely large. A large tuft of hair, cut in a circle, begins very near the top of the head. This resemblance of the Caribbees to the monks is not the result of living in the missions; it is not owing, as it has been erroneously asserted, to the desire of the natives to imitate their masters, the fathers of the order of Saint Francis. The tribes, that have preserved their savage independence, between the sources of the Carony and the Río Branco, are distinguished by the same *cerquillo de frailes,* which the first Spanish historians at the time of the discovery of America attributed to the nations of Caribbee origin. All the men of this race, whom we saw either during our voyage on the Lower Orinoco, or in the missions of Piritoo, differ from the other Indians not only by their tallness, but also by the regularity of their features. Their nose is not so large, and less flattened; the cheek-bones are not so high; and their physiognomy has less of the Mongul cast. Their eyes, darker than those of the other hordes of Guyana, denote intelligence—I had almost said the habit of reflexion. The Caribbees have a gravity in their manners and something of sadness in their look, which is found for the most part among the primitive inhabitants of the New World. The expression of severity in their features is singularly increased by the rage they have for dying their eyebrows with the juice of the caruto, enlarging them, and joining them together. They often mark the whole face with black spots, in order to appear more savage. The magistrates of the place, the *Governador* and the *Alcaldes,* who alone have the privilege of carrying long canes, came to visit us. Among them were some young Indians from eighteen to twenty years of age, the choice depending solely on the will of the missionary. We were struck at finding among these Caribbees painted with arnotto the same airs of importance, the stiff mien, and the cold and disdainful manners, which are sometimes met with among people in office, in the old continent. The Caribbee women are less robust and uglier than the men. On them devolves almost the whole burden of domestic labours, as well as those of the fields. They asked us with earnestness for pins; which, having no pockets, they placed under the lower lip, piercing the skin, so that the head of the pin remained within the mouth. The young girls are dyed with red; and, except the *guajuco,* are naked. Among the different nations of the two worlds the idea of nudity is altogether relative. A woman in some parts of Asia is not permitted to show the end of her fingers; while an Indian of the Caribbee race is far from considering herself as naked, when she wears a *guajuco* two inches broad. Even this band is regarded as a less essential part of dress than the pigment, which covers the skin. To go out of the hut without being painted with arnotto, is to transgress all the rules of Caribbean decency.

The Indians of the missions of Piritoo attracted still more our attention on account of their belonging to a nation, which, by its daringness, its warlike enterprises, and its mercantile spirit, has exerted a great influence on the vast country, that extends from the equator toward the northern coasts. We found traces everywhere on the Orinoco of the hostile incursions of the Caribbees, which they pushed heretofore from the sources of the Carony and the Erevato as far as the banks of the Ventuari, the Atacavi, and the Río Negro. The Caribbean language is consequently the most general in this part of the world; it has even passed to tribes which have not the same origin. . . .

The fine nation of Caribbees now inhabits but a small part of the country, which it occupied at the time of the discovery of America. The cruelties exercised by the Europeans have made them disappear entirely from the West India islands, and the coasts of Darién; while, subjected to the government of the missions, they have formed populous villages in the provinces of New Barcelona [Venezuela] and Spanish Guyana. I believe the Caribbees, who inhabit the *Llanos* of Piritoo, and the banks of the Carony and the Cuyuni, may be estimated at more than thirty-five thousand. If we add to this number the independent Caribbees, who live west of the mountains of Cayenne and Pacaraymo, between the sources of the Essequibo and the Río Branco, we shall no doubt obtain a total of forty thousand individuals of pure race, unmixed with any other race of natives. . . .

The contrast in the Caribbee nations between the dialect of the two sexes is so great, that to explain it in a satisfactory manner we must have recourse to another cause; and this may perhaps be found in the barbarous custom, practised by those nations, of killing their male prisoners, and carrying the wives of the vanquished into captivity. When the Caribbees made an irruption into the archipelago of the West India islands, they arrived there as a band of warriors, not as planters accompanied by their families. The language of the female sex was formed by degrees, as the conquerors contracted alliances with the foreign women; it was composed of new elements, words distinct from the Caribbee words which in the interior of the female organs were transmitted from generation to generation, but on which the structure, the combinations, the grammatical forms of the language of the men exerted their influence. What then took place in a small community we now find in the whole group of the nations of the New Continent. . . .

The dominion, which the Caribbees so long exercised over a great part of the continent, and the remembrance of their ancient greatness, have inspired them with a sentiment of dignity and national superiority, which displays itself in their manners and their discourse. "We alone are a nation," say they proverbially; "the rest of mankind (*oquili*) are made to serve us."

This contempt of the Caribbees for their ancient enemies is so strong, that I saw a child of ten years of age foam with rage on being called a *Cabre* or *Cavere*; though he had never in his life seen an individual of this unfortunate people, who gave their name to the town of Cabruta [Cabritu]; and who, after a long resistance, were almost entirely exterminated by the Caribbees. Thus we find among half-savage hordes, as in the most civilized part of Europe, those inveterate animosities, which have caused the names of nations that are enemies to pass into their respective languages as appellations the most opprobrious.

The missionary led us into several Indian huts, where an extreme neatness and order prevailed. We saw with pain the torments which the Caribbee mothers inflict on their infants, in order not only to enlarge the calf of the leg, but to raise the flesh in alternate stripes from the ankle to the top of the thighs. Bands of leather, or of woven cotton, are placed like narrow ligatures at two or three inches distant; and being tightened more and more, the muscles between the bands become swelled. Our infants when swaddled suffer much less than these Caribbee children, in a nation which is said to be so much nearer a state of nature. In vain the monks of the missions, without knowing the works or the name of Rousseau, attempt to oppose this ancient system of physical education. Man when just issued from the woods, and who is thought to be so simple in his manners, is far from being docile with respect to his ornaments and the ideas which he has formed of beauty and propriety. I observed however with surprise, that the manner in which these poor children are bound, and which seems to obstruct the circulation of the blood, does not weaken their muscular movements. There is no race of men more robust, and swifter in running, than the Caribbees.

If the women labor to form the legs and thighs of their children so as to produce what the painters call undulating outlines, they abstain, at least in the *Llanos,* from flattening the head, by compressing it between cushions and planks from the most tender age. This usage, so common heretofore in the islands, and among several tribes of the Caribbees of Parima and French Guyana, is not practised in the missions which we visited. The men there leave the forehead rounder than the Chaymas, the Otomacks, the Macoes, the Maravitans, and the greater part of the inhabitants of the Orinoco. A systematizer would say, that it is such as the intellectual faculties require. We were so much the more struck by this observation, as the skulls of Caribbees engraved in Europe in some works of anatomy are distinguished from all other human skulls by the most depressed forehead, and the most acute facial angle. But in osteological collections the productions of art have been confounded with the state of nature. What are shown as the skulls of Caribbees of the island of Saint Vincent, "almost destitute of forehead," are skulls shaped between planks, and belonging to Zamboes (black Caribbees), who are descended from Negroes and true Caribbees. The barbarous habit of flattening the forehead is found among several nations that are not of the same race, and has been observed recently as far as in North America; but nothing is more vague than the conclusion that some conformity of customs and manners proves an identity of origin. The traveller who observes the spirit of order and submission that prevails in the Caribbee missions can scarcely persuade himself that he is among cannibals. This American word, of a somewhat doubtful signification, is probably derived from the language of Haiti, or that of Puerto Rico; it has passed into the languages of Europe, since the end of the fifteenth century, as synonimous with that of anthropophagi. . . .

We were assured by all the missionaries of the Carony, the Lower Orinoco, and the *Llanos del Cari,* whom we had an opportunity of consulting, that the Caribbees are perhaps the least anthropophagous nations of the New Continent. They extend this assertion even to the independent hordes who wander on the east of the Esmeralda, between the sources of the Río Branco and the Essequibo. We may conceive that the fury and despair with which the unhappy Caribbees defended themselves against the Spaniards, when in 1504 a royal decree declared them slaves, may have contributed to the reputation they have acquired of ferocity. . . .

We observed with surprise, during our abode in the Caribbee missions, the facility with which young Indians of eighteen or twenty years of age, when raised to the employment of *alguacil,* or *fiscal,* harangued the municipality for whole hours. Their enunciation, the gravity of their deportment, the gestures which accompanied their speech, all denoted an intelligent people capable of a high degree of civilization. A Franciscan monk, who knew enough of the Caribbee language to preach in it occasionally, made us notice in the discourses of the Indians, how long and harmonious the periods were, without ever being confused or obscure. . . .

The whole village assembles on holidays before the church, after the celebration of mass. The young girls place at the feet of the missionary faggots of wood, bunches of plantains, and other provision of which he stands in need for his household. At the same time the *governador,* the *fiscal,* and other municipal officers, all of whom are Indians, exhort the natives to labor, proclaim the occupations of the ensuing week, reprimand the idle, and, since it must be told, severely cudgel the untractable. The strokes of the cane are received with the same insensibility with which they are given. These acts of distributive justice appear very long and frequent to travellers, who cross the *Llanos* in their way from Angostura to the coasts. It were to be wished that the priest did not dictate these corporal punishments at the instant of quitting the altar, and that he were not in his sacerdotal habits the spectator of this chastisement of men and women; but this abuse, or, if the reader prefer the term, this want of propriety, arises from the principle on which the strange government of the missions is founded. The most arbitrary civil power is strictly connected with the rights, which the priest exerts over the little community; and, although the Caribbees are not *cannibals*, and we would wish to see them treated with mildness and indulgence, it may be conceived that energetic measures are sometimes necessary to maintain tranquillity in this rising society.

The difficulty of fixing the Caribbees to the soil is so much the greater, as they have been for ages in the habit of trading on the rivers. We have described above this active people, at once commercial and warlike, occupied in the traffic of slaves, and carrying merchandize from the coasts of Dutch Guyana to the basin of the Amazon. The travelling Caribbees were the Bukharians of equinoctial America; accordingly the necessity of counting the objects of their little trade, and transmitting intelligence, had led them to extend and improve the use of the *quipus*, or, as they call them in the missions, the *cordoncillos con nudos*. . . .

The independent Caribbees, who inhabit the country so little known between the sources of the Oroonoko, and those of the rivers Essequibo, Carony, and Parima, are divided into tribes and form a political confederation. This system is the most suitable to the spirit of liberty, which prevails in those warlike hordes, who see no advantage in the ties of society but for common defence. The pride of the Caribbees leads them to withdraw themselves from every other tribe, even from those to whom from their language they have some relation.

They claim the same separation in the missions, which seldom prosper when any attempt is made to associate them with other mixed communities, that is with villages, where every hut is inhabited by a family belonging to another nation, and speaking another idiom. The chiefs of the independent Caribbees are hereditary in the male line only, the children of sisters being excluded from the succession. This is founded on a system of mistrust, which denotes no great purity of manners. . . . The young chiefs, like the youths who are desirous of marrying, are subjected to the most extraordinary fasts and penances. They are purged with the fruit of some of the euphorbiaceae; are sweated in stoves; and take medicines prepared by the *marirris* or *piaches,* which are called war-physic. The Caribbee *marirris* are the most celebrated of all: at once priests, jugglers, and physicians, they transmit to their successors their doctrine, their artifices, and the remedies they employ. The latter are accompanied with laying on of hands, and certain gestures and mysterious practices, which appear to be connected with the most anciently known processes of animal magnetism. Although I had opportunities of seeing many persons who had closely observed the confederated Caribbees, I could not learn whether the *marirris* belong to a particular cast. . . .

In order to study thoroughly the manners and customs of the great Caribbee nation, it is requisite to visit the missions of the *Llanos,* those of the Carony, and the savannahs that extend to the South of the mountains of Pacaraymo. The more we learn to know them, say the monks of Saint Francis, the more we lose the prejudices, which prevail against them in Europe, as being more savage, or as being less liberal than the other tribes of Guyana. The language of the Caribbees of the Continent is the same from the source of Río Branco to the steppes of Cumaná. . . .

On quitting the mission of Cari, we had some difficulties

to settle with our Indian muleteers. They had perceived, to our great astonishment, that we had brought skeletons with us from the cavern of Ataruipe; and they were firmly persuaded that the beasts of burden, which carried "the bodies of their old relations," would perish in the journey. Every precaution we had taken had been useless; nothing escapes the penetration and the sense of smell of a Caribbee, and it required all the authority of the missionary to forward our baggage. We had to cross the Río Cari in a boat, and the *Río de agua clara,* by fording, I might almost say by swimming. The quicksands of the bed of this river render the passage very difficult at the season when the waters are high. The strength of the currents seems surprising in so flat a country.

Caracas

I remained two months at Caracas, where Mr. Aimé Bonpland [1773–1858; French naturalist] and I lived in a large and nearly solitary house, in the highest part of the town. From a gallery we could survey at once the summit of the Silla Mountain, the serrated ridge of the Gallipano, and the charming valley of the Guayra, the rich cultivation of which formed a pleasing contrast with the gloomy curtain of the surrounding mountains. It·was the season of drought, and in order to improve the pasturage, the savannahs, and the turf that covers the steepest rocks, were set on fire. These vast conflagrations, viewed from a distance, produce the most singular effects of light. Wherever the savannahs, following the undulating slope of the rocks, have filled up the furrows hollowed out by the waters, the inflamed land appears in a dark night like currents of lava suspended over the valley. Their vivid but steady light assumes a reddish tint, when the wind, descending from the Silla, accumulates streams of vapour in the low regions. At other times, and this aspect is still more solemn, these luminous bands, enveloped in thick clouds, appear only at intervals, where it

is clear; and as the clouds ascend, their edges reflect a
splendid light. These various phenomena, so common under the tropics, become still more interesting from the form
of the mountain, the disposition of the slopes, and the
height of the savannahs covered with alpine grasses. During
the day, the wind of Petare, blowing from the east, drives
the smoke toward the town, and diminishes the transparency
of the air.

If we had reason to be satisfied with the situation of our
house, we had still greater cause of satisfaction in the reception we met with from all classes of the inhabitants. I
feel it a duty to cite the noble hospitality exercised toward
us by the chief of the government, Mr. de Guevara-Vascon-
zelos, then captain-general of the provinces of Venezuela.
Although I had the advantage, which few Spaniards have
shared with me, of having successively visited Caracas, the
Havana, Santa Fe de Bogotá, Quito, Lima, and Mexico, and
of having been connected in these six capitals of Spanish
America with men of all ranks, I shall not venture to decide on the various degrees of civilization which society has
attained in the different colonies. It is easier to indicate the
different shades of national improvement, and the point
toward which the unfolding of the intellect tends in pref-
erence, than to compare and class things that cannot be
investigated under the same point of view. It appeared to
me that a strong tendency toward the study of the sciences
prevailed at Mexico and Santa Fe de Bogotá; more taste for
literature, and whatever can charm an ardent and lively
imagination, at Quito and Lima; more accurate notions of
the political relations of countries, and more enlarged
views of the state of colonies and their mother countries,
at the Havana and Caracas. The numerous communica-
tions with commercial Europe, with that sea of the West
Indies, which we have described as a Mediterranean with
many outlets, have had a powerful influence on the progress of society in the island of Cuba, and in the five provinces of Venezuela. Civilization has in no other part of
Spanish America assumed a more European physiognomy.

Notwithstanding the increase of the black population, we seem to be nearer Cádiz and the United States at Caracas and the Havana, than in any other part of the New World.

Caracas being situate on the continent, and its population less mutable than that of the islands, the national manners have been better preserved than at the Havana. Society does not present very animated and varied pleasures; but that feeling of comfort is experienced in domestic life, which leads to uniform cheerfulness and cordiality united with politeness of manners. There exists at Caracas, as in every place where a great change in the ideas is preparing, two races of men, we might say two distinct generations; one, of which but a small number remains, preserves a strong attachment for ancient customs, simplicity of manners, and moderation in their desires. They live only in the images of the past. America appears to them a property conquered by their ancestors. Abhorring what is called the enlightened state of the age, they carefully preserve hereditary prejudices as a part of their patrimony. The other class, less occupied even by the present than by the future, have a propensity, often ill-judged, for new habits and ideas. When this tendency is allied to the love of solid instruction, restrained and guided by a strong and enlightened reason, its effects become beneficial to society. I knew at Caracas, among the second generation, several men equally distinguished by their taste for study, the mildness of their manners, and the elevation of their sentiments. I have also known men, who, disdaining all that is excellent in the character, the literature, and the arts of the Spaniards, have lost their national individuality, without having acquired from their connexions with foreigners any just ideas of the real bases of happiness and social order.

Since the reign of Charles V [1516–1556], the corporation spirit and municipal habits having passed from the mother country to the colonies, men take a pleasure at Cumana, and in other commercial towns of Tierra Firma (northern South America), in exaggerating the pretensions to nobility of the most illustrious families of Caracas, known

by the name of los Mantuanos. I am ignorant in what manner these pretensions were formerly manifested; but it appeared to me that the progress of knowledge and the change
effected in manners have gradually and pretty generally
destroyed whatever is offensive in those distinctions among
the Whites. In all the colonies there exist two kinds of
nobility. One is composed of the Creoles, whose ancestors
have very recently filled great stations in America. Their
prerogatives are partly founded on the distinction they
enjoy in the mother country; and they imagine they can
retain them beyond the sea, whatever may be the date of
their settlement in the colonies. The other nobility has
more of an American cast. It is composed of the descendants
of the *Conquistadores*, that is to say, of the Spaniards who
served in the army at the time of the first conquest. Among
the warriors who fought with Cortez, Losada, and Pizarro,
several belonged to the most distinguished families of the
peninsula; others, born in the inferior classes of the people,
have illustrated their names by that chivalrous spirit, which
prevailed at the beginning of the sixteenth century. I have
observed that in the records of those times of religious and
military enthusiasm, we find, among the followers of the
great captains, many simple, virtuous, and generous characters, who reprobated the cruelties that stained the glory
of the Spanish name, but who, confounded in the mass,
have not escaped the general proscription. The name of
Conquistadores remains the more odious, as the greater
number of them, after having outraged peaceful nations,
and lived in the midst of opulence, did not experience toward the end of their career those long misfortunes, which
appease ᷉ne hatred of mankind, and sometimes soften the
severity of the historian.

But it is not only the progress of ideas and the conflict
between two classes of different origin which have induced
the privileged casts to abandon their pretensions, or at
least to conceal them carefully. Aristocracy in the Spanish
colonies has a counterpoise of another kind, and of which
the action becomes every day more powerful. A sentiment

of equality among the whites has penetrated every bosom. Wherever men of colour are either considered as slaves, or as having been enfranchised, what constitutes nobility is hereditary liberty, is the proud boast of having never reckoned among ancestors any but freemen. In the colonies, the colour of the skin is the real badge of nobility. In Mexico, as well as Peru, at Caracas as in the island of Cuba, a barefooted fellow is often heard exclaiming: "Does that rich white man think himself whiter than I am?" The population which Europe pours into America being very considerable, it may easily be supposed, that the axiom, every white man is noble, *todo blanco es caballero,* must singularly wound the pretensions of a great number of ancient and illustrious European families. But we may observe farther, that the truth of this axiom has long since been recognized in Spain, among a people justly celebrated for probity, industry, and national spirit. Every Biscayan [Basque] calls himself noble; and there being a greater number of Biscayans in America and the Philippine Islands than in the peninsula, the whites of this race have contributed in no small degree to propagate in the colonies the system of equality among all men whose blood has not been contaminated by the African race.

Moreover, the countries of which the inhabitants, even without a representative government, or any institution of peerage, annex so much importance to genealogy, and the advantages of birth, are not always those where the aristocracy of families is the most offensive. We should seek in vain among the natives of Spanish origin that cold and assuming air, which the character of modern civilization seems to have rendered more common in the rest of Europe. Conviviality, candour, and a great simplicity of manners unite the different classes of society in the colonies, as well as in the mother country. We might even venture to say, that the expressions of vanity and self-love are less offensive when they retain something of simplicity and frankness.

I found in several families at Caracas a taste for instruction, a knowledge of the masterpieces of French and Italian literature, and a particular predilection for music, which is cultivated with success, and which, as it always happens in the pursuit of the fine arts, serves to bring the different classes of society nearer to each other. The mathematical sciences, drawing, and painting cannot here boast of any of those establishments with which royal munificence and the patriotic zeal of the inhabitants have enriched Mexico. In the midst of the marvels of Nature, so rich in productions, no person on this coast was devoted to the study of plants and minerals. In a convent of St. Francis alone I met with a respectable old gentleman who calculated the almanac for all the provinces of Venezuela, and who possessed some precise ideas on the state of modern astronomy. Our instruments interested him deeply, and one day our house was filled with all the monks of St. Francis, begging to see a dipping-needle. The curiosity that dwells on physical phenomena is augmented in countries undermined by volcanic fires, and in a climate where nature is at once so overwhelming, and so mysteriously agitated. . . .

In a country that presents such enchanting views, and at a period when, notwithstanding some symptoms of popular commotions, the greater part of the inhabitants seem only to direct their thoughts toward physical objects, the fertility of the year, the long drought, or the conflict of the two winds of Petare and Catia, I believed that I should find many persons well acquainted with the lofty surrounding mountains. My expectations, however, were not realized; we could not discover at Caracas a single person who had visited the summit of the Silla. The hunters do not climb so high on the ridges of mountains; and no journies are undertaken in these countries to gather alpine-plants, to carry a barometer to an elevated spot, or to examine the nature of rocks. Accustomed to a uniform and domestic life, they dread fatigue, and sudden changes of climate. It would seem as if they live not to enjoy life, but only to prolong its duration. . . .

Related Reading

Acosta, José de. *The Natural and Moral History of the Indies (1590)*. Edward Gimston (tr.). London: Hakluyt Society, 1604. Vols. 60, 61.

Boxer, C. R. *Four Centuries of Portuguese Expansion: A Succinct Study*. Berkeley and Los Angeles: University of California Press, 1969.

"Concolorcorvo." *El Lazarillo: A Guide for Inexperienced Travelers between Buenos Aires and Lima*. Walter D. Kline (tr.). Bloomington: Indiana University Press, 1965.

Cox, Edward G. "The New World," in *A Reference Guide to the Literature of Travel, including Voyages, Geographical Descriptions, Shipwrecks, and Expeditions*. 2 vols. Seattle: University of Washington Press, 1935. Vol. 2.

Gage, Thomas. *The English American: A New Survey of the West Indies, 1648*. London: George Routledge & Sons, 1946.

Hanson, Earl Parker (ed.). *South from the Spanish Main. South America Seen Through Eyes of Its Discoverers*. New York: Delacorte Press, 1967.

Heawood, Edward. *A History of Geographic Discovery in the Seventeenth and Eighteenth Centuries*. Cambridge, Eng.: Cambridge University Press, 1912.

Juan, Jorge, and Antonio de Ulloa. *A Voyage to South America*. Introduction by Irving A. Leonard. New York: Knopf, 1964.

Newton, Arthur P. (ed.). *The Great Age of Discovery*. London, 1932.

———. *Travel and Travellers of the Middle Ages*. Freeport, N.Y.: Books for Libraries Press, 1967. First printing 1930.

Parry, J. H. *The Age of Reconnaissance*. Cleveland: World Publishers, 1963; New York: Mentor Book, 1964.

———. *The Spanish Seaborne Empire*. New York: Knopf, 1966.

Penrose, Boise. *Travel and Discovery in the Renaissance, 1420–1620*. Cambridge, Mass.: Harvard University Press, 1952; New York: Atheneum, 1962.

Ruiz, Hipólito. *Travels of Ruiz, Pavón, and Dombey in Peru and Chile (1777–1788)*. B. E. Dahlgren (tr.). Chicago: Field Museum of Natural History, 1940.

Schurz, William Lytle. *The Manila Galleon*. New York: Dutton, 1939; paperback ed., 1959.

Glossary

aguacate: avocado, alligator pear

alcalde: justice of the peace

alguacil: constable, peace officer

almiranta: vice admiral's ship, flagship

arriero: muleteer

arroba: weight of 25 pounds, or about 11½ kilograms

auto (de fe): Inquisition ceremony of sentencing heretics

azumbre: liquid measure, about 2 liters

biao (bijao): tropical plant with large leaves like banana tree

bozal: Negro immigrant recently from Africa who has not yet been assimilated into the culture

cabre (cabra?): goat

cacao: cacao tree; chocolate

cachoretas: surmullet, perchlike saltwater fish; red mullet

cacique: chieftain

camote: sweet potato

cañafístula: cassia fístula; tropical tree with long pods

capitana: admiral's ship

Carreira da India: Portuguese fleet to the Indian Ocean and Far East

carreta: long, narrow, two-wheeled cart

Casa de contratación: House of Trade established in Seville in 1503 to administer commerce and navigation with the Spanish New World

cascalhão: gravel, slag, dross

cerquillo de frailes: friar's tonsure

chaco: hunt (Peru)

chicha: fermented beverage

chinampas: small garden tract in lakes near Mexico City

chirrión: tumbrel, creaking cart

chirrionero: driver of a *chirrión*

cordoncillos con nudos: see *quipu*

corpo sancto: corposant, a glowing ball of electrical discharge on ships' masts; also called St. Elmo's fire

corregidor: chief magistrate

cuarta: ¼ *vara,* about .7 feet; auxiliary team (horses, mules, oxen)

cuarteros: fore oxen of a team

cumbe: delicately woven fabric (Peru)

curaca: boss (Peru)

desaguadero: gully

encomendero: overlord

escudo: coin of varying value

esparto: long, coarse grass

estado: measure of length, about 1.85 yards

estrado: drawing room; low platform

fanega: grain measure, about 1.6 bushels

farinha de mielho: flour of Indian corn

fazenda: plantation

fiscal: district attorney, prosecutor

Flota: annual fleet of merchantmen with convoy

gamella: bowl

garúa: misty drizzle of rain (Peru)

golilla: ruff, collar worn by magistrates

gorgojos: weevils

gregorillo: neckcloth

guajuco: narrow loincloth worn by Indian women (Venezuela)

guanaco: a kind of *llama*

giulii: "smallest money worth anything" (i.e., "farthing")

habillas: sea chestnuts

hidalgo: member of the lesser nobility

icho: matweed (Peru)

juego de cañas: jousting with reed canes

juego de toros: jousting of bulls and steers

llama: South American animal related to camel but smaller and without hump and used as beast of burden

llano: plain, flatland

locro: stew (Peru)

maravedi: old Spanish coin of slight monetary value

milreis: former Brazilian monetary unit and silver coin

mita: system of enforced labor (Peru)

patagón (patacón): silver dollar

patata: potato

perizoma: see *guajuco*

pertigueros: oxen attached to *pértigo,* or shaft

pértigo: shaft

peso: monetary unit of varied value

prao: Asiatic canoe of hollowed log and outriggers

pulpería: food and wine shop; general store

quipu: device of colored, knotted cords to keep records (Peru)

real: silver coin of varying value

recua: packtrain of beasts of burden, usually mules

salsaparilla: sarsaparilla; aromatic roots of tropical American plants used as a tonic and for flavoring, much sought for in 16th century for alleged medicinal value

sambo (zambo): mixture of Negro and Indian

San Benito (sambenito): garment worn by penitents of the Inquisition

saya: skirt or tunic

supay: devil (Quechua)

soroche: altitude sickness (Peru)

tambo: inn

tasajo frito: fried jerked beef

teleras: braces, tie pieces

tezontle: porous building stone (Mexico)

tirador: strap

tomín: silver coin of slight value

toppile: village chief (Aztec)

travesía: level plain

vara: variable unit of length, about 2.8 feet

vicuña: cud-chewing animal of South America related to camel family

vincha: kerchief for the head or hair

vizcacha: South American rodent